One Hero's Fight on Two Fronts—Abroad and Within

TYNDALE HOUSE PUBLISHERS, INC. • CAROL STREAM, ILLINOIS

TV
WA

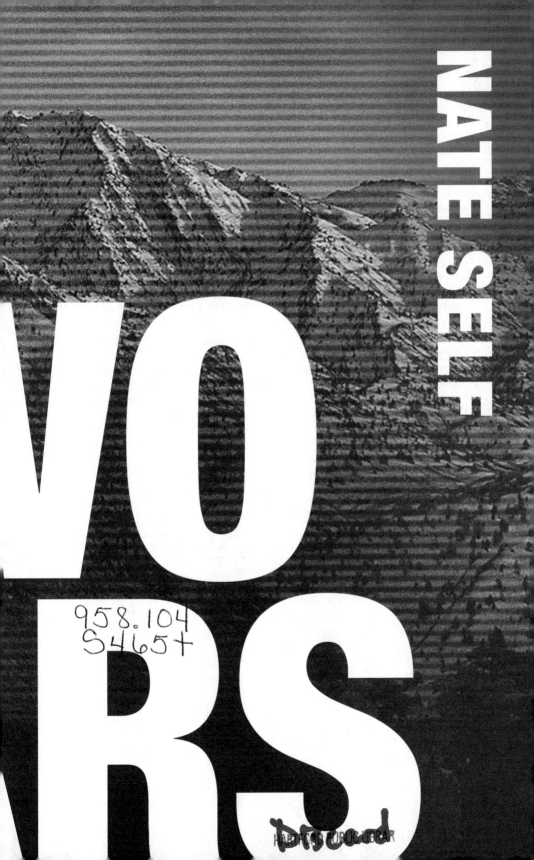

NATE SELF

VO
RS

Visit Tyndale's exciting Web site at www.tyndale.com

TYNDALE and Tyndale's quill logo are registered trademarks of Tyndale House Publishers, Inc.

Two Wars: One Hero's Fight on Two Fronts—Abroad and Within

Designed by Ron Kaufmann

Edited by Cara Peterson and Dave Lindstedt

Published in association with the literary agency of Alive Communications, Inc., 7680 Goddard Street, Suite 200, Colorado Springs, CO 80920.

Library of Congress Cataloging-in-Publication Data

Self, Nate.
   Two wars : one hero's fight on two fronts—abroad and within / Nate Self.
     p. cm.
   Includes bibliographical references.
   ISBN-13: 978-1-4143-2009-0 (hc)
   ISBN-10: 1-4143-2009-4 (hc)
   1. Self, Nate. 2. Afghan War, 2001—Veterans—United States—Biography. 3. Post-traumatic stress disorder—Patients—United States—Biography. I. Title.
   DS371.412.S45 2008
   958.104'7—dc22
   [B]   2008009521

★

To the men who fought on Takur Ghar,
to the families and friends who love them,
and to the One who stands ready to rescue us all,
no matter how high the climb.

★

CONTENTS

PUBLISHER'S NOTE

Dear Reader:

The story you are about to read is true. The events depicted include violence and vulgar language of a kind that typically doesn't appear in books we publish. But after careful consideration, we decided to include some dialogue that, though potentially offensive, is historically accurate, helps to capture in an authentic way the intensity of the events, and gives a truthful illustration of the human condition, including our brokenness and need for redemption. In this way, we believe our decision is consistent with the biblical principle of showing life as it truly is, without attempting to whitewash human nature.

When a warrior fights not for himself,

but for his brothers,

when his most passionately sought goal is neither glory

nor his own life's preservation,

but to spend his substance for them, his comrades,

not to abandon them, not to prove unworthy of them,

then his heart truly has achieved contempt for death,

and with that he transcends himself

and his actions touch the sublime.

★

STEVEN PRESSFIELD

Gates of Fire

PROLOGUE

My grandfather, the only military man in my bloodline, had served in Normandy after the initial Allied invasion of France. After the war, he turned into a gambling, abusive alcoholic, abandoning my grandmother with three children. My mother was the youngest, three years old when he left. The first time I saw him was at his funeral.

When I was a kid, my grandmother gave me a tattered black book that captured my attention. The book told of a great story, one that I read three times before I was a teenager, one that stirred me somewhere deep inside, in the space between my heart and spine. The book told of American fighting men who floated down from aircraft and stormed the beaches of Normandy from landing craft on June 6, 1944, to meet the world's enemy on D-Day, on what would become known as The Longest Day.

Before I read a word of the text, the black-and-white pictures showed me the core of the message—one I could not explain but intuitively knew. I felt somehow connected to the men in my book. I could feel the tossing of the waves as in my mind I looked down the ramp of the assault landing craft with the heights of Vierville looming ahead, just minutes before H-Hour. I gazed at the blurry H-Hour photo of an American soldier neck-deep in the surf off Omaha Beach until I could feel my pulse throbbing in my neck. I stared at the photo of American soldiers lying limp on the beach, with others moving beyond. I imagined myself walking up to the eight dead paratroopers lined up outside their crashed glider, so I could see their faces.

That tattered black book was the only war story I had ever known.

04 0612 MAR 02 (DELTA)
SOMEWHERE OVER AFGHANISTAN

I feel like I'm about to vomit.

Our helicopter careens around the snow-covered mountain, banking hard right, looking for our target. Though it's just before dawn in Afghanistan, the sky is dark, clear, and cold.

"Where's this landing zone?"

"On top of a ten-thousand-foot mountain," says a voice on the radio.

"Roger."

We're on a rescue mission, and I'm in command of a thirteen-man Quick Reaction Force (QRF). We're searching for a missing American who fell out of a helicopter in enemy territory two hours ago. He is somewhere below us in the Shah-i-Khot Valley, an area teeming with hundreds of al-Qaeda fighters. Right now, there's no place on earth more hostile to U.S. soldiers—and no place my team would rather be. We're here because we're Rangers, and we have a creed to uphold: *Never leave a fallen comrade.*

It's 6:12 a.m. The eight-man flight crew is not under my command, but they share my resolve. Every member of the flight crew is alert, scanning the terrain beneath the aircraft. They've been awake for more than thirty-six hours flying missions in their double-rotor Special Ops helicopter. These are the men of the 160th Special Operations Aviation Regiment (SOAR), the "Night Stalkers." They're the best in the world. They fly an MH-47E Chinook, which looks like a black school bus crowned with two spinning telephone poles. I watch them balance against the pilot's evasive nap-of-the-earth flight techniques—it's possibly the only nonlethal example of their experience and skill. We've flown together many times before, both here and in the States. According to their motto, the Night Stalkers Don't Quit. I've been around them enough to know that those aren't mere words.

"I don't see it. That can't be it. On top of *that*? Ask him again."

"Toolbox, this is Razor Zero-One; say again grid; over." No answer.

With no seats in the aircraft, I am sitting on the slick metal floor. I pull a wrinkled map out of my thigh pocket to check the target coordinates. Though I remember writing the digits in tidy block letters at our headquarters in Bagram, the bouncing of the aircraft reduces them to a shimmy of ink. My eyes feel like they're being tossed around inside my head. I can't decipher a single number.

"Try Razor Zero-Two." The other half of our QRF. "Maybe they got it."

"I tried. We've lost radio contact with them."

I look past the other Rangers and out the open ramp, a gaping hole in the back of the aircraft. I survey the pearling expanse for a sign of our trail bird, the landscape behind the aircraft blurred through the oily smudges of exhaust fumes. The last time I checked, the other helicopter was following us, mimicking our every movement, but now I see nothing but flour-white mountains, jagged and ominous.

Knowing what's been happening among these peaks for the last two days demands respect—we're entering the sanctum of warfare. It's our nation's freshest battlefield, where American infantrymen have been clashing with al-Qaeda fighters and struggling against the vicious terrain for the last fifty hours as part of Operation Anaconda. As I prepare to join them, two faces flash in my mind: my wife's and our four-month-old son's. I yearn to tell them I love them. They're sleeping on the other side of the world, unaware of my situation. Even if I could talk to them now, I wouldn't tell them what I'm doing. Right now my eyes are on my Rangers, these fathers of other sons, these sons of other fathers, who depend on me as their platoon leader. And I'm certain their eyes are on me.

Proud to be Rangers, we know their history—our history—by heart. Our Ranger forefathers led the way: June 6 at the cliffs of Pointe-du-Hoc and the surf of Omaha Beach; April 24 in Iran's Dasht-e Kavir desert; October 25 on the Point Salines Airfield in Grenada; December 20 at Noriega's compound in Panama; October 3 in the streets of Mogadishu. Today, it's March 4 in the Shah-i-Khot Valley, and now it's our turn. Combat is near—I can taste it.

Across from me in the cabin, now filling with the soft gray that precedes the sunrise, an Air Force pararescue jumper, or "PJ," removes the night-vision goggles mounted on his helmet and stows them in his medical aid bag. I look around to see the others removing their goggles and making final adjustments—tightening chin straps, ensuring they have rounds chambered, adjusting body armor, checking their weapons' optics.

Moral shorthand equates darkness with evil, but here in the sphere of combat, we hold the darkness sacred. We invade the blackness with our goggles, lasers, and infrared sights. As special operators, we welcome the nightfall; its shadows are our foxholes. But as we circle the mountain, the sun's arrival is imminent, and with it, a reprieve for the enemy. Whatever this mission requires of us, we'll accomplish it without the advantage of our night training and technology.

I do nothing to my equipment. I'm thinking of finding our man. Circling the mountain, I feel a tinge of anxiety thinking of the scenarios that could develop soon—but when I hold out my hand, it's steady. I'm no longer nauseated.

"Okay. We're taking it. Thirty seconds," the pilot says.

"Thirty seconds!" The crew chiefs hold up a thumb and index finger with only an inch in between.

"THIR-TY SECONDS!"

We finish our third orbit of the mountain. Glancing around at the handful of warriors inside the aircraft, I'm hit by a strange mix of confidence and humility—each of these special men is under my command. In our unit, we don't wear markings or nametags. We don't need them, anyway, in such a tight team. Despite our coverings of body armor, weapons, and gear, we recognize each other by the way we hold our rifles, by the way we dive for cover, by the way we move in the shadows.

One by one I meet their gazes, nodding in acknowledgment or encouragement. I squeeze the knotted shoulder of the man next to me. Each Ranger is a precious military asset—lethal, but fragile in the flesh. Our country has spent several hundred thousand dollars training our bodies and minds, and most of the investment lies in the latter. We can do things with our hands and weapons better than anyone—kill with any weapon from any position with either hand, or kill with *only* our hands—and yet hours before, several of us sat in Bible study, exploring and discussing the Psalms. It's such a strange reconciliation—the life of the warrior with the life of the faithful. And we *are* warriors.

The pilot's voice comes over the intercom system: "Here we go."

I squint at nothing and lose my breath as the fifty-two-foot war machine levels, the whopping of its blades indicating our descent. Every shooter on board crouches rearward, thighs burning, anticipating touchdown. It's exactly 6:14 a.m.

"Team leader off," I say. I unplug my headset's cable from the aircraft's intercom system. According to our procedure, none of us are to unhook our safety lines from the floor's D rings until the aircraft is settled on the ground, but I choose not to follow procedure. Once we hit the ground, I want nothing slowing me down.

The aircraft bucks, flaring to land in the snow. Its engines howl as the grainy snow flushes through the windows and ramp. The icy air shocks my lungs and adrenalizes my body. My vision blurs as the bird begins to vibrate. This is it: we are here to get our man out, wherever he is. I shut my eyes, waiting to feel the wheels hit the ground.

The right door gunner spots something below him: a dirty man in a ski jacket and plastic shoes has a rocket-propelled grenade launcher aimed at us.

"I've got an RPG—one o'clock! Three o'clock! Engaging!" The door gunner leans into his minigun's trigger.

The M134 Gatling gun belches, accompanied by three rounds from the aircraft's M60 machine gun in the rear. Their tandem fury jolts me. The machine guns riddle the Arab's body, pinning him against a boulder, but not before he launches the RPG. Our gunners are too late.

I hear the air tearing as the rocket-propelled grenade screams toward us. The detonating shaped charge rips into the aircraft's right engine, jolting the helicopter. A second RPG pierces the windshield glass, detonating inside and spraying hot metal throughout the cockpit. The helicopter falls with a queasy rush. In an instant, nearly fifty thousand pounds of rubber, steel, and American flesh crash to the earth.

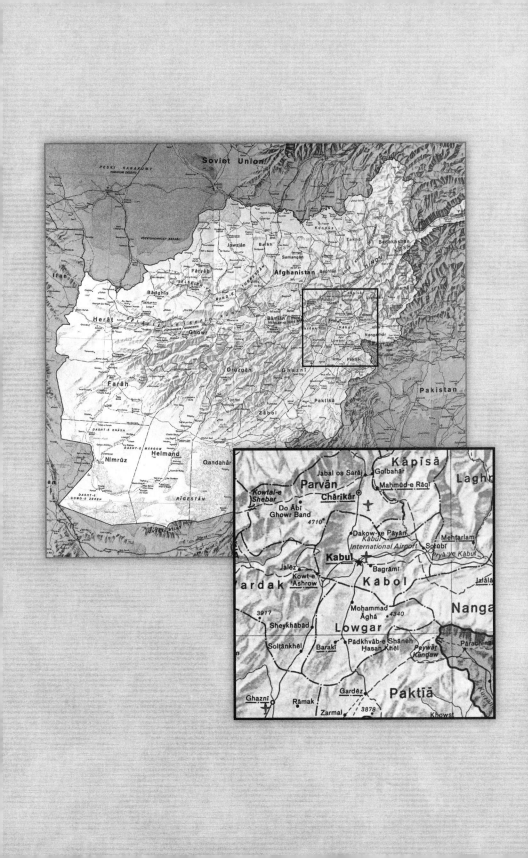

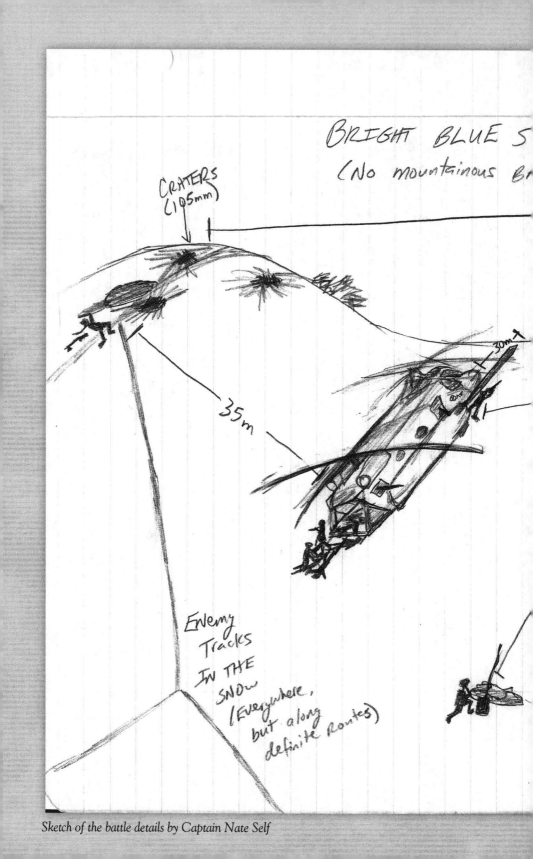

Sketch of the battle details by Captain Nate Self

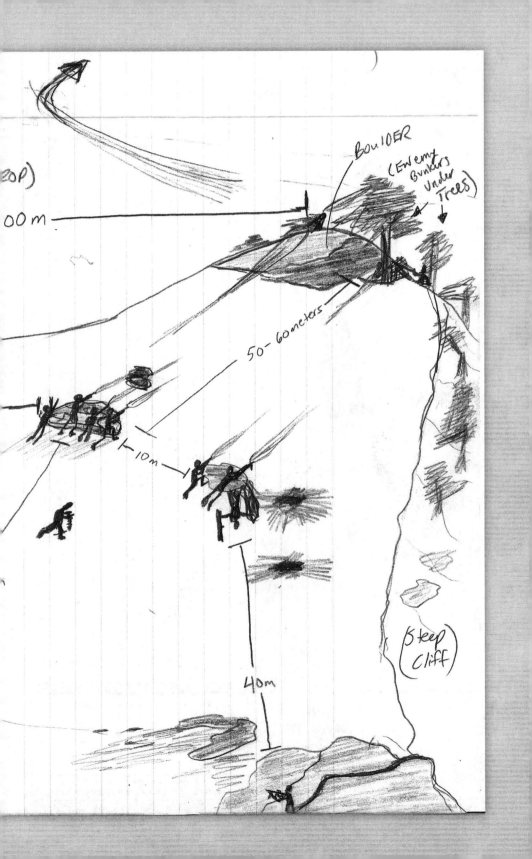

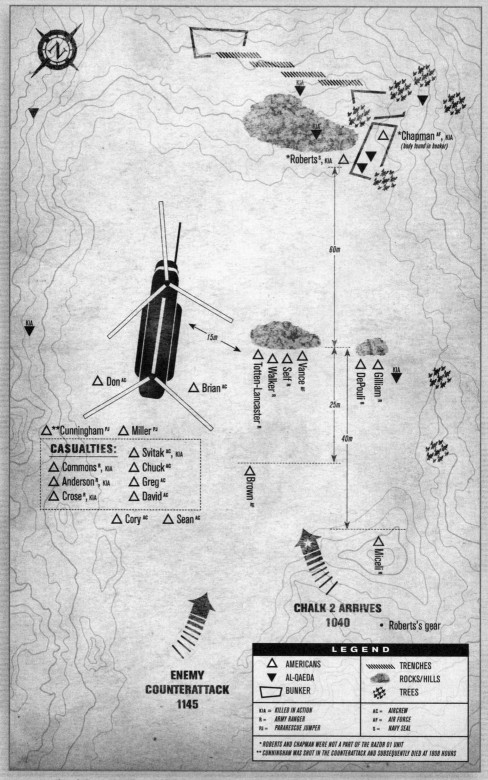

Razor 01 battle scenario approximately 0730

★ ★

PART ONE

THE CALL

1

That's what it takes to be a hero, a little gem of innocence inside you that makes you want to believe that there still exists a right and wrong, that decency will somehow triumph in the end. :: LISE HAND

FEBRUARY 14, 1993
CHINA SPRING, TEXAS

I was eager for church to conclude so I could grab lunch and run a few errands. I still needed to buy a Valentine's Day gift and card for my new girlfriend, Julie Wenzel. We had been dating for a couple of months. She was a year younger at age fifteen—a skinny blonde as tall as me, with a captivating presence and sparkling blue gray eyes as inviting as a dip in the pool. We had planned an early dinner for Valentine's, and I looked forward to seeing her as soon as I could.

The pastor closed with a benediction, and I bolted to my baby blue '65 Chevy pickup in the back of the gravel parking lot. I loved shifting through that three-speed-in-the-floor V8 305 engine with the Eagles in the tape deck, and on the way home I imagined Julie sitting next to me with the gears at her feet, holding my arm through the bends in the road to keep herself from sliding across the vinyl bench seat.

Stop signs were optional along the empty country roads to our house in China Spring, Texas—population fifteen hundred. As I pulled into our gravel driveway at home, I stopped to pick up yesterday's mail, which included the normal bevy of postcards and mailers from universities wooing high school juniors like me. A heavy, full-color catalog was wrapped around it all, a catalog that I had ordered from the most intriguing school on my list: West Point.

I went inside to the table with my sister and parents. But I had trouble paying attention to them as I thumbed through the literature.

"You seem to be into that," my mother said.

"Did you see this place?" I asked. I turned the catalog around for her to see the cover photo of massive gray granite buildings in front of an emerald parade field.

"Looks like a pretty place," she said. "Is that a school?"

"Well, yeah, it's a school, but in the military," I said. "West Point. It's the college for the Army."

"I thought you said you weren't interested in the Army."

"I said I wasn't interested in joining the Army through a recruiter. This is different."

"Whatever happened to being an eye doctor?" she asked. I didn't reply, continuing to flip through the pages.

"I'm fine with you dressing up and playing army as a kid, but not as a man."

"What's wrong with the military?" I asked.

"I just don't like it," she said. "You could get hurt."

"Being in the Army doesn't mean someone's shooting at you. They have doctors, too," I said. "Think about how much money it takes to get through medical school and set up a practice."

"Well, some things aren't worth the money," she said.

"Momma, I'm just looking into it. The Army seems like a boring life, anyway."

I left the table, went to my room, and placed the West Point catalog on my dresser. Growing up during the cold war, I really *had* seen the Army as boring. But what interested me about West Point wasn't the free education, or the free ticket to becoming a doctor, or even really the Army. West Point drew me in a romantic sort of way.

Maybe part of me wanted to try something I wasn't sure I could do. Maybe part of me wanted to be a part of that history, to walk the same path as Eisenhower and Bradley and so many others. Maybe part of me wanted to find out why I felt connected to the men in that tattered black book, why my chest got hot when I read their story.

2

FEBRUARY 26, 1993
NEW YORK, NEW YORK

Six months ago, Ramzi Yousef departed a mujahideen training camp in eastern Afghanistan en route to New York City. He had devised a plot to attack the World Trade Center in Lower Manhattan—to strike at the roots of one of the Twin Towers, to send one weakened tower crashing into the other, to kill 250,000 Americans in one day. At last, that day had come.

Airborne snowflakes drifted under the shadows of the towers as Yousef slithered away—down Church Street or Liberty Street, or maybe somewhere to the east. Perhaps he took the Holland Tunnel under the Hudson River to his New Jersey home. Perhaps he crossed the Brooklyn Bridge to the Al-Farooq Mosque two miles away, where mujahideen leaders had raised funds and recruited jihadists in cooperation with the CIA over the past decade. Perhaps he drove to the airport to leave the United States. His direction of travel was less important than where he had been and what he had left behind, parked two levels below grade of the World Trade Center in garage B2: a yellow Ryder Econoline van filled with fifteen hundred pounds of urea nitrate explosives, built and fused by men trained for war against the Soviets in Afghanistan.

Across Liberty Street from the World Trade Center, two companies of New York firefighters prepared lunch in a discreet gray brick firehouse known as Ten House. This red-doored corner garage held the men of Engine Company 10 and Ladder Company 10—men who were responsible for Lower Manhattan's Twin Towers, men whose logo emblem depicted a caricatured firefighter standing atop the Twin Towers engulfed in flames. These men came to work at Ten House knowing they were always "a ladder rung from death" as they protected the epicenter of the world's financial markets, the symbol of American economic strength.

At eighteen minutes past noon, the men at Ten House felt a rumble as the yellow Ryder van exploded in the belly of the World Trade Center. The blast jawed a crater through seven foundational layers. The firefighters rushed into the street, where thick black smoke pumped into the frigid winter air from the tower's crumpled basement garage doors.

The blast cut electrical power in the complex, leaving more than fifty thousand people in the dark, in suspended elevator cars, and in crowded stairwells as smoke billowed inside the towers, now 110-story chimneys.

The men of Ten House were the first to the scene, and they performed heroically in the basement of the complex, sawing through doors and picking through flames and rubble to reach people trapped, dead and alive, in the bomb crater. Over the next several hours, more than 45 percent of the city's firefighters joined Ten House to evacuate both towers. It was the largest incident in the department's 128-year history.

Six Americans died in the attack, and more than a thousand were injured. But despite the relatively low number of casualties—the bombers intended to kill a quarter-million people that day—all was not well. One survivor's description of the bomb blast would seem eerily prophetic eight and a half years later: "It felt like an airplane hit the building."

3

You always admire what you really don't understand. :: BLAISE PASCAL

AUGUST 1994
WEST POINT, NEW YORK

Fifty-one miles upstream from New York City, along the steep western banks of the Hudson River, stands the United States Military Academy. Once a strategic location during the Revolutionary War, always a strategic location in America's military history, West Point got its name from its defensive posture overlooking a narrow S curve of the Hudson. George Washington and Benedict Arnold had both commanded garrisons in the area, and many of America's great generals—men such as Pershing, MacArthur, Patton, and Schwartzkopf—laid their military foundations at West Point. Over the past two months as a new cadet, I had tromped the same ground as those great men. My mother's nightmare and my emerging dream—that I'd become a military man—had been my sole focus.

The rectangular barracks room that I shared with two other cadets had three white walls, one lime green, and was banded by chestnut cabinetry. A tile floor reflected the dullness of the windows in the back of the room, which trembled with each bass boom outside. There was a radiator under the windows, three sets of furniture, a rifle rack, and the aseptic smell of bleach in the air. Bunks tight, windows aligned, floor swept, trash emptied, hangers spaced and canted, mirror clean, sink dry.

I would be done with my duties as soon as I finished polishing the faucet—except for my "daily knowledge," mandatory memorization from an extensive catalog of information including West Point history, famous quotes, U.S. Army unit designations, weapon-systems data, awards and decorations, the names of the Army mules, and much more. Every week, the upperclassmen expected us to have a progressively more daunting amount of "knowledge"—and they tested our retention of such factoids at any point in time, standing and sometimes yelling two inches from our faces. It was an intimidating way to demonstrate memory.

I felt around inside the cardboard box under the sink, looking for Windex. The box contained well over one hundred dollars' worth of cleaning supplies. We had a certain tool for every job: shoe polish, Brasso, edge dressing, mink oil, alcohol, distilled water, Mop & Glo, Tilex, toothbrushes, boot brushes, Simple Green, green Brillo pads, old T-shirts, parade gloss, towels, Q-tips, Clorox, nail files, Formula 409, Nevr-Dull, cotton balls, and some Army-issue cleaning solution that would kill the stubborn stains that had endured our previous efforts. That mysterious government concoction, which we called our "blunt force option," guaranteed stain removal—and the collateral damage of stripping the varnish off the cabinets, the color off the linoleum floor, or the skin off our hands.

Even after six weeks of Cadet Basic Training at West Point, known as "Beast Barracks," our routines were never routine. The upperclassmen appended and morphed our daily duties, increasing our standards of performance. They could make the simplest tasks seem nearly impossible. The triumph of surviving each day was fleeting—and tempered with the realization that the next day would require at least one skill I did not yet possess.

On this day, I chose to care for my body rather than study the articles from the *New York Times* and other required daily knowledge I could be called upon to recite prior to breakfast formation. I was more concerned with the march ahead of me. Within the hour, I would hike with a thousand others to beautiful Lake Frederick, a mountainous fourteen miles away. We would culminate our summer training there with two weeks of military exercises. No barracks, no newspapers, just training.

"I'm done with the sports page if you need it," my roommate said. "Did you copy down the meals last night?"

"Nah," I said. "Packed my ruck three times."

The one thing I still needed to pack was a Ziploc bag of letters from home. A letter from Momma and Daddy, a note from a friend, a postcard from the women's prayer group at church. My collection of correspondence held a musty odor after absorbing the sweat and grime from my hands all summer. For the past six weeks, I had read the letters over and over. Many of them were from my girlfriend, Julie. I had broken up with her when I received my appointment in the spring, thinking I should be single minded in my pursuit of West Point. But we'd gotten back together the month before I came to Beast—I couldn't bear to be away from her during my last month of freedom, knowing that anything could happen to our relationship after I left home. She was a senior in high school and would soon head off to college; she might even find someone else. For at least that last month, I wanted to be close to her.

With a similar yearning, I took every chance to stare at the collage of photos in the one picture frame permitted to me during Beast. The snapshot of Tom King, the friend from church with Down syndrome who had saluted me at the airport in Waco as I left to come to West Point. A picture of my parents and sister: my mother, who had warmed up to the idea of West Point, and my father, who was proud of me in his usual understated way. He was always so soft spoken. I'd never heard him raise his voice in my life. Then there was the picture of Julie leaning against a white wooden fence, wearing a sleeveless blouse, blonde hair wrapped around her shoulder in the wind, her smile seemingly teasing me to lean on the fence alongside her. There was also a picture of the two of us at prom, dancing close.

During the past few weeks, I had stolen moments whenever possible to stare at those pictures. One thing I hadn't expected to learn at West Point was just how much I loved the people I had left at home in Texas.

Nor had I expected to encounter West Point's stuffy, confining environment. Of course, I'd seen West Point before in pictures and on television. I'd even visited the campus. From the outside—the monuments, Gothic architecture, crisp uniforms, lineage of heroes—all was honorable and stately, somewhat transcendental. But the world I encountered on the inside was not the public's West Point. I was in the Army's West Point, the Corps's West Point. On the inside, in the bowels of the Beast, it felt primitive and claustrophobic.

I made my final preparation before stepping into the hallway: sticking moleskin on the bottoms of my feet for protection. Though my mind and body had been systematically broken down during Beast, my boots had maintained their rigidity. As a result, I battled a burgeoning blister on my left foot. Fourteen miles was sure to be a challenge. I had learned through the pain of experience that without proper care of the feet, which depended on the boots, even the bravest of foot soldiers is useless.

The Academy has a strange affinity for leather—or maybe it's a cattle fixation. Any former cadet could cite the evidence: the insistence on outfitting us with leather equipment when much better materials were available, the cultlike following of boot care in search of the perfect "Mop & Glo" shine, the nicknaming of the juniors as "cows," the requirement that we learn cow trivia.

I got even angrier at my stubborn boots as I pondered the "cow knowledge" I'd had to memorize and repeat ad nauseam when prompted by upperclassmen.

"New Cadet, give me the definition of leather."

"Sir, if the fresh skin of an animal, cleaned and divested of all hair, fat, and other extraneous matter, be immersed in a dilute solution of tannic acid, a chemical combination ensues; the gelatinous tissue of the skin is converted into a nonputrescible substance, impervious to and insoluble in water; this, sir, is leather."

"New Cadet, how's the cow?"

"Sir, she walks, she talks, she's full of chalk; the lacteal fluid extracted from the female of the bovine species is highly prolific to the nth degree."

After a month of hating leather and cows, I decided that I disagreed with the Academy's definition. "Highly, prolifically *painful* to the nth degree" seemed far more accurate. That's how the cow was.

What I didn't know, or realize for several years to come, was that the tedium of memorizing and reciting seemingly useless details was a skill—one I would need while leading soldiers in the field. The ability to retain data such as radio call signs, frequencies, and written or verbal orders was at the heart of managing information on the battlefield. Still, in Beast Barracks, it was a simple, clever tool used to transform stress and frustration into humility.

I threw on my rucksack and Kevlar helmet, took a deep breath, and stepped into the soda-straw hallway. Within a few steps, someone was yelling at me.

"You—get on that wall!"

I obeyed. It would've been foolish to pretend I didn't hear. The upperclassman moved in and stood inches from me, inspecting me up and down. He stared into my eyes and then grinned, apparently satisfied with my appearance.

"New Cadet, what's for breakfast?" It was an easy question, a final check. But one I didn't know the answer to.

"Sir," I said, "I do not know." I braced myself for his reply.

With this start and fourteen miles ahead of me, it was sure to be a long day.

4

I've never learned anything of value outside of suffering. :: DAVID WILKERSON

Several miles into the foot march, I realized just how thirsty I was. After all I'd learned in six weeks at West Point, I still couldn't properly drink from my canteens. That is, not while walking in the woods with a rucksack on my back and a rifle in my hands. The simple function of drinking water had become the most fatiguing of tasks. Canteens snapped inside canvas pouches, clipped behind me on a web belt, wedged between my rump and the rucksack, all tangled in a nylon lanyard—I was pathetic. I usually preferred thirst to the struggle. With such demonstrated incompetence, how would I ever lead soldiers?

The blister on my left foot ruptured. It flooded my sock with pus as I stepped off the paved road onto a rocky trail. We trudged along in two files, one on each side of a drab, crushed-stone trail. As I ratcheted down the shoulder straps on my rucksack in order to reposition my load, the heat rash on my back sent a million needle pricks shooting through my skin. The camouflage field pack, scorned by cadets as "the green tick," was living up to its moniker. It was full of junk along for the ride—things I knew I wouldn't use but had to carry anyway. The pack had no frame for support. The formless, bulging leech was latched to my body, sucking the energy out of me.

Resting on my skull, my helmet's leather headband was a size too large and stiff from newness—another leather accessory that I had failed to break in. The excess cowhide had impressed its rough contours into the center of my forehead, bearing down on me in some sort of subtle torture. Climbing uphill, I felt as if every nerve ending in my body were suffering under the abrasions of those worthless leather boots and that worthless leather headband. It reinforced my hatred of the cows.

As I shuffled along, discomfort occupied my thoughts until I noticed my fellow new cadets. They were strung out ahead of and behind me, some limping, some slouching, many apparently day-dreaming. Maybe they, too, thought of how their lives had changed forever, how distant they were from their former selves. Maybe they were thinking that even if they quit now and went back home, they would find that the people they used to be no longer existed.

The previous six weeks of Beast had revealed to us our youth, and by this revelation had somehow managed to diminish it. It was as if the choice that had always been somewhere in our future—the choice between who we were and who we might become—was no longer in some distant potential but had arrived as a tangible and unavoidable fact. I felt as if I'd lost something, without quite under-standing what it was I'd had.

The transition from gravel to paved road signaled our arrival at Camp Buckner, which was a nearby outpost where the sophomore cadets conducted their summer military training. Camp Buckner was our ten-mile mark and the last flat stretch of the trail before we trudged up formidable Bull Hill, which was the Mount Everest of West Point. Camp Buckner was not what I had envisioned. It prob-ably wasn't what the camp's namesake, General Buckner, would have had in mind, either.

The sights, sounds, and smells were those of a beach party. Bar-becue smoke swirled as the sophomores, or "yearlings," played vol-leyball or stretched out on the sand. Beck's "Loser" echoed across a glassy elliptical lake, the water broken only by a few canoes and the sheer rock banks of the far side. The small beach was packed with cadets and was guarded on all sides by red wooden beach houses, screened-in bungalows, and bookend boulders.

We walked on, one hundred meters past a slight rise, where the scene shifted. Here were cadets, their heads shaved, uniforms caked with mud, eyes gaunt but sparkling, seated in circles scrubbing their weapons. Rising above the dirty cadets were echeloned rows of battleship gray living bays, tucked into the forest. Glancing across the road, I saw cadets shooting baskets and playing tennis within fifty meters of those cleaning weapons. Others were fishing and smoking cigarettes. In the center of it all, a lone cadet played his guitar and sang about something unintelligible. The strange juxtaposition of activities and postures was like flipping television channels from MTV to the History Channel to ESPN to Outdoor Living Network to a Vietnam War movie.

I couldn't comprehend the yearlings' apparent fusion of a patently military lifestyle with recreational normalcy. What I saw jarred my expectations of the future, the notion that life at the Academy—and indeed, in the Army—was purely military.

I thought back to the dreary images of West Point I'd seen in the high school guidance counselor's office: cadets in starched military uniforms building miniature wooden truss bridges, some mixing chemicals in a laboratory, many wearing bulky, horn-rimmed "birth control" glasses (so called because wearing them would guarantee repulsion of the opposite sex). From those images, I had come to accept that my social life was over—that upon taking the oath, serving in uniform required a single-minded pursuit of all things military. And until then, West Point seemed to be aligned with my perceptions: Beast was a vector focused on becoming a cadet, a soldier, and an officer.

Suddenly it occurred to me that life would go on in so many of the same ways, that maybe I wouldn't have to leave behind the Academy in order to have what I thought had been lost. It was then I realized my psychological metamorphosis had just begun.

I regained focus as the road curved to reveal Bull Hill. The mountain seemed to shoot out of the earth. The upperclassmen had told us stories about Bull Hill, that it was the physical and figurative pinnacle of Beast.

"Beast ain't halfway over until you see the back side of Bull Hill," they said, even though it was literally three-quarters complete from a temporal perspective. Once we reached the top of the mountain, it would be, quite literally, all downhill from there.

The group of new cadets ahead were piling up at the base of the mountain after embarking on their climb and then slowing to a crawl. Rather than feed the bottleneck, our cadre instructed us to take a knee, which proved to be much more painful than standing. Squinting upward, I found it difficult to determine where Bull Hill ended and the sun began.

The surge of new cadets against the base of the mountain began to ease, and the upperclassmen gestured at us to start moving again. We labored to our feet, stretching out muscles that had become rigid and sore. Taken as a whole, our long line of new cadets was as recalcitrant and balky as a mule or an ox or any other dumb animal forced to work against its will. Our bodies were more stubborn than usual, with our momentum from the earlier march a distant memory. And the exertion promised by the steep mountain ahead was not a particularly inspiring prospect.

What was I doing this time last year? I thought. Probably driving steel T-posts into the burned Texas ground, with the nearest shade miles away. I had worked the last three summers on a ranch in Crawford, Texas, just west of my house. At that point, I knew Crawford only for its mesquite trees and the stubborn limestone rock squatting two feet beneath the topsoil. Little did I know that a few years later some of the land I worked would become part of George W. Bush's "Western White House." Had I known, perhaps I would've labored more vigorously for my future commander in chief. But at the time,

I was just about as far away from West Point as Bush was from the presidency, and I doubted that even the president could make life any better for me in Beast Barracks, anyway. My world had been reduced to the sagging pack of the new cadet in front of me, and beyond him, the mountain.

I peered up at the path above. The trail switched back every few meters, forming a zigzag of new cadets as far up the mountain as I could see. Most were stopped, waiting on someone above them to take another step. Some of the stronger new cadets were carrying two rucks, one in the back and one in the front, helping their squadmates who were weak, hobbled, or downtrodden, striving as a team to negotiate the slope. We started moving again. Within twenty minutes, I carried two rifles, and minutes later, two rucks. One of our squad members had made it ten miles on a badly sprained ankle and couldn't bear the weight anymore—the climb was too much.

My calves and shins smoldered after five minutes of walking uphill with the extra equipment. The burn reminded me of football practice back home. Two-a-days in 105-degree swelter. Here in Beast they forced us to drink two quarts of water just before bed at night and a quart per hour on the march. My high school football coaches hadn't let us drink anything, thinking we'd get "waterlogged" and vomit. That was a different army, and much more fun.

Desperate for a rest, I hoped that the group in front would bunch up so I could stop for a few seconds to relax. We weren't even halfway up the hill. My thighs were cramping from the heat and dehydration. Something inside me told me it wasn't worth it—all the pressure, all the angst—and somewhere in the back of my mind, the temptation to walk away from it all was quietly rallying support.

I can just go home to Julie, I thought. Life would be easier at a normal college.

Closing my eyes, I resisted the thought and said a prayer. *Give me the strength to make this, God.*

Just then I heard singing. A man's voice boomed through the forest—a deep, baritone voice that wobbled with intensity.

"On a hill like this. On a hill like this. On a hill like thisss."

Chaplain Camp, the Academy's head pastor, stood on a boulder above wearing green fatigues and leaning on a thick, smooth staff. His silver hair streamed from under a floppy patrol cap, framing his gentle face. He was such an oddity against the backdrop of a thousand straining eighteen-year-olds with buzz cuts.

"I need—the Lord—to help me," he sang. "On a day like this. On a day like this . . ."

I respected his effort, but at the moment his singing just made things worse, intruding on my pain in an infuriating sensory overload. The heat in my thighs collected in my chest, gathered pressure, and shot up to my head. I didn't need a song. I needed a lift ticket, someone to carry me to the top of Bull Hill—or else push me down it.

Then God stepped in.

"I lift up my eyes to the hills! Where does my help come from?" the chaplain said. "My help comes from the Lord! Maker of heaven and earth!"

It was a psalm—Psalm 121.

I stopped and looked at him. The Scripture calmed me. I became somewhat glad he was there, amid the circumstances. My thighs were still aflame; the load was still heavy; the footing, still uncertain. But I felt strong. I felt confident.

I looked to the top of Bull Hill. It was still a long way off, but I imagined there would be a view.

The rest of the climb seemed to dissolve. The encouragement I received on the south face of Bull Hill eased my worries about the challenges of Beast and West Point. God had spoken to me, softly, through an old man singing out of tune. When I lifted my eyes to the hills, I found God there, ready to carry me. I decided it didn't matter what sort of innocence I had lost at Beast—I had found something valuable to replace it.

5

The basic difference between an ordinary man and a warrior is that a warrior takes everything as a challenge while an ordinary man takes everything either as a blessing or a curse.
:: CARLOS CASTANEDA

AUGUST 15, 1994
THE PLAIN, WEST POINT, NEW YORK

I stood with four thousand other cadets on the last day of Beast Barracks, on the parade field known as "The Plain," when a storm blustered in from the north and dumped its payload. It was an embarrassing kind of wet, the kind that erodes and exposes. I had nothing to hide, for after six weeks of Beast, any falsities I had were far removed. I had been stripped to the core.

I could see through everyone's shirts. Some wore undershirts, some did not. Some were physically fit, some were not. I stood with them, just as transparent. Being wet was nothing new, as the summer had kept me in a constant state of perspiration. Sweating had become my most proficient task. Now as an official member of the Corps of Cadets, I tasted the water on my lip. It was salty, but cool.

Back in the barracks, my roommates and I stripped off our starched cross belts and brass buckles, preparing for our first night of privileges outside the Academy—hamburgers and phone calls home. We disassembled our M14 carbines, wiped them dry, and arranged them on our bunks. An upperclassman bolted into the room, still dripping from his nose and ears.

"Good job, smackers. Look what I do for you. This shirt's ruined."

His leather rifle sling had bled a brown streak onto his shoulder, just like the rest of us.

"No excuse, sir."

"That's right," he said. "Anyway, congratulations."

"Thank you, sir."

"And by the way, you know what rain on your Acceptance Day Parade means?"

"No, sir."

"It means your class is going to war. Welcome to the Corps."

Warriorship is not for everyone. In past martial cultures the warrior caste was occupied by an elite few, usually chosen from birth. They were admired and respected by the rest of society because of their noble birth. Gone now are the days of inherited status. To achieve admiration and respect today, the warrior must set himself apart from the rest of society by his personal excellence. Where warriorship was once a birthright, it is now a calling. :: FORREST MORGAN, *Living the Martial Way*

MARCH 1998
WEST POINT, NEW YORK

I had taken my fours years at West Point a step at a time. I learned throughout my time at the Academy that every time I tried to plan for the future, I had been grossly inaccurate. For example, I came to West Point wanting to be an eye doctor. After two semesters, I decided against that, not wanting to sacrifice the time required to be a premed student—especially as I was gaining interest in more things military, like shooting and maneuvers. I also thought for a long time that I wanted to become an engineer officer, to leverage my academic major and to build things in the Army. But when it came time to choose my branch of the Army, I chose the Infantry out of pure love for the foot soldier. In the same way, every other major decision I made at West Point was last-minute, unplanned instinct, just trusting God with the lead. Whenever I actually had a plan, it always fell through. Maybe God knew that if he gave me a road map, I'd likely never ask him for directions again.

Two months before graduation, I had one last major decision to make: *where* I wanted my initial post to be. On this decision night, known as "post night," we had a grand dinner in the mess hall—a "super supper"—where the government lavished us with steak, lobster, and Boston cream pie in what I could only conclude was a rebate meal—maybe from the mess staff collecting UPCs from the thousands of milk cartons we disposed of daily.

After I stuffed myself on surf and turf, I climbed five flights of stairs directly above the mess hall to a dank auditorium, where we would gather to select our duty stations. The collection of aromas from feeding four thousand cadets the extravagant meal had pooled in the room in a revolting sort of apartment-hallway smell.

After nearly four years of analyzing all that the Army could offer, I had narrowed my future to a pair of options: Hawaii or Germany. I inched into the lecture hall looking for a friendly face. Still undecided, I just needed to ask for one more opinion before I settled the matter.

As a newly engaged man, I was wise to take into account Julie's preferences first. But she—perhaps also wisely—told me to do what

I thought was best; all she wanted was to be together. In a couple of months, I would graduate as part of the rare 2 percent club—that group of cadets who had kept the same girlfriend throughout the four years at West Point.

Julie and I had dated for six and a half years but had to wait until after graduation to get married. By regulation, cadets were forbidden from having dependents of any kind while at the Academy, but brand-new lieutenants were free to acquire as many as possible, as quickly as they pleased. Soon-to-be lieutenants considered graduation from West Point as a sort of opening day for the spouse-hunting season, evidenced by the many that married within hours of receiving diplomas. Julie and I were set to marry two weeks after graduation. I was more proud and happy that we had stayed together than I was to be graduating from the Academy.

I wanted to serve overseas first, to increase the likelihood that we'd be in the States whenever we finally had children, but I also knew that Hawaii would be fun for Julie, who really loves the beach. And I figured serving in the Army was the only way we'd ever afford living there. Germany offered a launching point for travel across Europe. But I had another reason to go to Germany, a hidden one. What I didn't tell Julie was that I had a desire to operate at the tip of the spear, to be out front, to be involved in the action. Serving in Germany would nearly guarantee a real-world deployment to Bosnia, and I felt drawn to that.

The room hummed with conversation. I saw Dave Blank, an old roommate, sitting near the front, so I slid into the chair next to him. Dave's demeanor made him easy to underestimate. He carried all the soft-spoken pleasantries of a politician's son, with a blushed complexion that belied his aggressive ambition. He was deeply engaging and insightful, and he had a balanced perspective of military service in light of his overall life. We had enjoyed rooming together, playing our guitars and writing music at all hours of the night. But we had even more fun working up risky stunts and practical jokes—the crown jewel of which was when we sneaked one of Dave's high school buddies into the barracks. He was just a normal college guy with a short haircut, but when we put him in uniform and taught him how to salute and where to stand, he managed to successfully impersonate a cadet for three days.

Dave slapped his knee. "Well?" he asked me. "Where are you going?"

"Either Hawaii or Germany."

"You haven't *decided?*"

A tall Army officer brought the meeting to order, sending my classmates rustling to their seats. An accomplished Infantry officer, he was the physical embodiment of what I aspired to be. Physically fit, visibly striking, silently commanding a presence, deeply knowledgeable of the history of warfare, tactically wise, strategically shrewd, and—most exciting to me—a load of wrath, cocked and ready, awaiting the fall of the hammer.

He was a veteran of the Gulf War, as were many of our instructors at West Point. And, like most of the others, he displayed some of the attendant decorations: there were combat patches from Army divisions, valor awards, parachute wings, combat infantryman badges. I studied the various badges, tabs, and accoutrements, which, when presented as a whole, retold an officer's experiences—but vaguely, mystically. They were trail markings hinting at the path each had taken—a path I had yet to begin.

I felt embarrassed that I still hadn't made up my mind about where I wanted to serve. This night was called "post night" because the entire senior class would pick their first duty locations, or posts, based on class rank. This last major decision at West Point would launch us on approximately 850 separate trajectories throughout the world in obedience to our nation's bidding. This decision would determine my future choices for the next twenty years, the location of my bride's first home away from home, the names and faces of the soldiers I would lead, the patch I would wear on my sleeve.

I leaned over to Dave.

"So, where do *you* want to go?" I asked.

"Germany," he said.

Although I would make my own decision, his carried some weight, as did the opinions of all those in the room. We were classmates. Four years ago, each of us had flowed in through the gates of the Academy at his own time, with his own hairstyle, with his own flavor of clothing, with his own expectation of the West Point experience, and bearing the unique pride of his hometown. West Point combined it all; it smelted all of our talents, reputations, and designs on the future in the crucible of shared hardship until we possessed a refined piece of each other, a piece of the whole.

Somewhere in the process we were imbued with the collective personality of the class, the Class of '98, with the motto Duty Will Not Wait. In this room, we were classmates, we were peers, we were brothers at arms, and we would soon be fellow infantrymen. In a few short months, every cadet in the room would reconvene at Fort Benning, Georgia, to complete our forging into a distinct brand of officer—Lieutenants of Infantry.

With that, I reflected on why I had chosen the Infantry as my branch. Many of the officers I respected most at West Point were infantrymen. West Point's commandant of cadets, Brigadier General John Abizaid, was chief among them. He came to the Academy from a tour in Bosnia and emphasized combat-focused, real-world leader development over the archaic Academy-peculiar traditions. Nicknamed the "Mad Arab," Abizaid was an old Ranger Regiment veteran. He had led a Ranger company in the Grenada parachute assault of 1983, jumped from a helicopter onto the landing strip, and ordered one of his Rangers to drive a hot-wired bulldozer toward the Cubans as he advanced behind it—a scene reenacted in Clint Eastwood's 1986 film *Heartbreak Ridge*.

Aside from Abizaid's legend, I had chosen the Infantry for a modest and fundamental reason. I had fallen in love with the infantrymen who had trained me in the summers—their discipline and sense of practicality—and because, in my somewhat romanticized view of war, I thought the best leaders were needed "in the trenches" with the foot soldiers. In such a talented class, I did not consider myself one of the best leaders, but I was going to do everything I could to become one.

"Cadet Self, Nathan E.," the major said. "Your selection."

I stood up and thought of Julie.

"Germany."

I was the first in the Infantry branch to choose Germany, though I felt I'd somehow stolen Dave's idea. By our tradition, the first man to pick a certain duty location would receive a bevy of mementos and playful gifts harkening to his destination. I stepped to the front of the lecture hall to receive a German newspaper and a warm can of imported beer. As I sat down, I gave the beer to Dave.

7

JUNE 13, 1998
WACO, TEXAS

We knelt on the polished, jet-black granite, hand in hand, praying over a white Bible. I wore the blank dress blue uniform of a new Infantry officer; she, the white dress of a June bride. Tears fell from my face onto her veil and onto the stone floor, cut from the same quarry as the Vietnam Memorial. Same stone, different purpose—yet still consecrated. Julie heard me crying. Her other hand covered mine; her touch told me that she would hold me as long as she was alive to do so. That caveat was the source of my grief: our joyous wedding ceremony was but an interlude to an absentee romance, to hints and plans and dreams never realized. I gathered myself and wiped my tears before the minister concluded. At least we belonged to each other, if only in eternity. After the prayer, we rose to meet a new world as one.

"Welcome to the Army, Mrs. Self."

With that greeting and a gentle swat on the behind with a cavalry saber, Julie marched out of the church as a married woman. She was on my arm, and I was the proudest and happiest I'd been in my life. We had both won the prize—each other—by enduring years of separation. But instead of finally enjoying the culmination of our courting, we merely put off the beginning of another long-term divide, this time as husband and wife.

The summer dissolved in one full blink. Jamaica, golf, sleeping in, other weddings, and a few glimpses of our future. The summer drew to a close, and I was geographically single again as quickly as I had graduated and gotten married. Julie stayed in Waco to finish her senior year at Baylor while I departed to begin my training pipeline, which consisted of at least ten months of school at Fort Benning, Georgia. According to plan, we would reunite near our one-year anniversary and head overseas to Germany—that is, if I could make it straight through the infamous Ranger School without recycling a phase.

8

At 9:45 a.m., "Azzam" and his friend Mohamed Rashed Daoud Al-Owhali fired up the engine on the truck, adjusted the seats for the first time, and eased into the sparse traffic. Al-Owhali slid a cassette of chants into the tape deck for motivation. It was a holy day for them.

They followed a white pickup through the veins of the capital, the traffic thickening as they neared the heart of the city. The truck rode low, with the ballast of heavy wooden boxes behind the cab seeming to steady their course. Their destination was a five-story building at the intersection of Moi and Haile Selassie avenues—the U.S. Embassy.

Their fellow jihadists had departed Kenya under strict orders in the last few days: some to Pakistan, some to unknown places, most to Afghanistan, their base of operations, their training ground.

Al-Owhali was ready. He and Azzam had trained at Khalden, at Al Farooq, at Sadeek, at the jihad war camp. He had asked for this opportunity for years, long before the fatwahs against America were handed down. His video was complete. He had a handgun in his jacket and four homemade flashbang grenades tucked in the belt of his jeans. He remembered his walk around the embassy just two days before, envisioning his actions and his imminence in paradise.

"Brother, take off that jacket," Azzam said. "You'll not be able to get to the grenades."

Their escort diverged at a traffic circle, indicating the short and final leg of the route, the portion they would navigate alone. They reached the main traffic circle in front of the embassy, a perpetual cog of vehicles that gave life to the downtown area. Al-Owhali beheld the prize, the building with which he would soon die. Inside, some two hundred Americans and Kenyans—U.S. foreign service officers, longtime Kenyan employees, high school and college summer hires and interns, and those whose random business had brought them there that day—paced through the motions of their daily routine.

Azzam veered the truck from the circle and boxed around the building to the rear gate. He stopped the truck at the drop bar blocking the driveway. The pedestrian flow broke around the truck, as the law of fluids would have it. Al-Owhali spotted the guard and got out of the truck. He realized he'd left his gun in his jacket, which was lying on the seat in the truck. He reached to his belt and brandished a grenade to threaten the guard to open the gate. The guard hesitated. Al-Owhali set off the grenade, and the bystanders scattered. Curious people inside the embassy and the adjacent buildings moved to the windows to investigate as Azzam backed the truck close to the embassy wall. He pulled Al-Owhali's pistol from his friend's jacket and started shooting at the building, eager to contribute to the attack.

Al-Owhali stood detached, watching the unfolding action. He saw the truck parked against the wall. He turned and ran away from the embassy, away from his friend.

Azzam did not run. He sat in the truck and triggered an electrical jolt that detonated five hundred kilograms of TNT, aluminum nitrate, and aluminum powder.

The clocks in the embassy stopped at 10:35. There was no sound. Al-Owhali hit the ground without knowing it, washed over by a blast of heat, glass, and concrete. Somewhere in his distant subconscious, he heard echoes rumbling through the city and back again to where they began, where he lay. He was still alive. He choked in the thick cloud of dust and smoke and stumbled over the twisted metal, glass, and shattered humanity. In all, 213 people died, and more than four thousand were injured in the blast. Four minutes later and 450 miles away, another jihadist detonated himself on a truckload of explosives at the U.S. Embassy in Dar es Salaam, Tanzania.

The telephone rang in London, in the offices of the pan-Arab newspaper known as Al-Quds Al-Arabi, or "Arab Jerusalem." The facsimile machine answered the call and printed a message transmitted from an office in Baku, Egypt—an office shared by the Egyptian Islamic Jihad and an Afghani veterans organization called al-Qaeda—announcing the formation of the Islamic Army for the Liberation of the Holy Places.

As Al-Owhali limped to a hospital in Nairobi for treatment of his wounds, the leaders of al-Qaeda huddled in caves in eastern Afghanistan—caves they had carved for the mujahideen nearly twenty years before—caves safe enough to hold a leadership summit in the days following the impressive simultaneous attack on the most powerful nation in history.

Two weeks later, the dark decks of U.S. Navy cruisers pumped Tomahawk cruise missiles into the night somewhere over the Red Sea. At 10:00 p.m., seventy-five warheads ripped into the solid rock hideout of Zhawar Kili in Afghanistan, where the U.S. government believed top al-Qaeda operatives were meeting. The attack was meant to disrupt the Islamic militant and terrorist groups linked to Usama bin Laden, al-Qaeda's leader. The attacks were meant to kill bin Laden.

Zhawar Kili was the site of Usama bin Laden's fatwah six months earlier, in which he had declared war on "Crusaders and Jews," and where he had conceived his plans to challenge the world's foremost superpower. The cavernous stronghold where the mujahideen had twice repelled the Soviets had become a womb of warfare. The Tomahawks killed thirty-four people, but bin Laden had escaped a few hours before the strike.

9

The purpose of the eight-nighter is to drive the individuals of the division, and the unit itself, beyond the point of humor. It is when the jokes stop, they say, that the real lessons are learned and each man, and the *mora* as a whole, make those incremental advances which pay off in the ultimate crucible. The hardship of the exercises is intended less to strengthen the back than to toughen the mind. The Spartans say that any army may win while it still has its legs under it; the real test comes when all strength is fled and the men must produce victory on will alone. :: STEVEN PRESSFIELD, *Gates of Fire*

MARCH 24, 1999
CAMP DARBY, GEORGIA

Just after midnight on day fifteen of Ranger School, I realized the moon was out. I couldn't recall seeing it in the previous two weeks, as the cold, driving rain had dominated my life. I was lying prone behind a machine gun, resting on an inch of pasty red Georgia clay and scanning for an enemy counterattack. We had seized a fictitious enemy objective, but we were late. A white-light search of the enemy pierced the night and confirmed our fears: the high-value target (HVT) had escaped.

"Dry hole," the patrol leader said. "All right. Let's get our casualties packaged."

"Litter bearers," the medic said, "on me."

I heard a familiar voice volunteering to carry the Ranger students who were designated as casualties. It was Dave Blank. He and I were together again, assigned to the same platoon for Ranger School.

We knew not to show up in Germany without our Ranger tabs. It was expected of Infantry lieutenants to have graduated from the nine-week Ranger School. They were expected to have earned the certificate, the thirty-cent black-and-gold patch, and—most importantly—the respect of the platoons assigned to them. Officers viewed Ranger School as a leadership school first, and as such, it was a high priority for lieutenants. It tested and refined future combat leaders in near-combat conditions—at least, as near to combat as possible without the shooting, the civilians on the battlefield, and the potential strategic ramifications of every action. Little food, less sleep, and long foot movements claimed many candidates before the tactical field exercises accounted for the remainder of those that would fail to graduate: 50 percent, on average.

Ranger School was created to breed throughout the Army the ethos and excellence displayed by the elite Ranger units that dated back to the Revolutionary War. Throughout their history, Ranger units have specialized in conducting swift raids and ambushes, stealthy reconnaissance, and piercing infantry attacks. The modern Ranger units—the ones that had fought in Grenada, Panama, and Somalia—were highly selective, accounting for less than a half percent of the Army. Earning a Ranger tab was merely a prerequisite for the units, not a rite of passage. The Rangers took on only a handful of the Army's experienced and proven officers to serve there. I assumed leading a Ranger platoon would be a challenge. It was the mind-set: the airborne, quick-strike, superfit, kill-with-your-hands, pick-a-fight-with-anyone-who-glances-in-your-direction mind-set that was trademark Ranger. These were modern-day gladiators, the best infantry in the world, and they expected good leadership. I possessed a growing desire to serve there, but the first step was to earn my tab.

We had been on the objective too long, even for the first phase of Ranger School. This poorly executed mission put the patrol leader in jeopardy of recycling the phase. Before we even hit the objective, we had spooked the HVT. Our casualties were everywhere, and we were going to miss our next hit time. At least we had gotten the "enemy" computers, loaded with valuable data.

"Just lost our medevac bird due to weather. We'll hump the wounded out."

Bad weather was scarcely plausible. I looked up at the brilliant stars. You could've started an IV by the light of the moon. But in Ranger School, whatever the instructors said was the law. We weren't getting aircraft for our casualties, no matter the reason. Whether the instructors were condemning our performance, testing our will, or just following the script, we were about to drag three guys and all their gear to our linkup point with the trucks.

"Everybody on a knee."

That command was an indication that we were about to move out. I hoisted the thirty-pound machine gun, rested it on my thigh, and lashed the sling across the back of my sore neck.

"We're headed five clicks along a 225," the patrol leader said.

"Spread it out. We've got good illume tonight."

Our intended azimuth was the shortest route to the linkup point, but not the easiest. Within ten minutes I felt cold, damp air rising to my face, which told me we were heading down into another swollen creek bed. Soon the patrol struggled through a thicket of briars and "wait a minute" vines. The poor casualties had it worst, being dragged through the vegetation, wrapped like taquitos in thick green sheets of plastic known as Skedco litters.

I heard an instructor's voice from the front erupt in anger. Our patrol leader had just failed his second patrol of the course and would recycle to day one, which would be like restarting a marathon after six miles. "Everybody drink water while I get this hair ball sorted out."

"Thank you, God," I whispered. It had been a long day, made even longer by the poor leadership. We waited for a change of command and prayed for a change of route—something more navigable.

"All right, Rangers, bring it in," the instructor said. "Hurry up, bring it in."

I moved quickly, hoping that a shake-up in leadership would allow me to do something besides lug a machine gun—something like walk "on point." I loved being the point man, with the whole patrol trusting me to plan the route and lead the movement. I came alive with that responsibility. Earlier in the day, I had successfully navigated on point to recover a downed pilot. Dave was in charge of that mission. His mission order was a surprise (as I'm sure most downed-pilot recoveries are), and he was given an unrealistically tight timeline to reach the pilot ahead of the enemy. During that frantic movement through the woods, I imagined I was going in to rescue Scott O'Grady, who had been shot down over Bosnia in '95 and survived. Now, after such a long day, I was ready to give up the machine gun, point man or not.

Nearing the front of the formation, I broke through the brush and found the patrol gathered in a clearing, helmets outlined by moonlight and glowing green underneath from night vision goggles. I joined the group.

The instructor stepped to the center of the group and lowered the radio from his ear.

"I got something to tell you, and it ain't part of the scenario," he said. He looked back and forth at us.

"The United States is at war. We just bombed the f— out of Kosovo."

10

The innocent and the beautiful have no enemy but time. :: WILLIAM BUTLER YEATS

MAY 15, 1999
BAYLOR UNIVERSITY, WACO, TEXAS

After a year of marriage, Julie and I were finally together. We had driven all night from my Ranger School graduation to the campus of Baylor University, where I watched Julie graduate with honors. I was so proud of her. She had demonstrated the discipline to finish college when many speculated she would quit and run to my side in Georgia. I was even more excited that we were finally free of life's preparatory encumbrances that had separated us.

Julie and I were so accustomed to being apart that we had learned to love in the present, when we were together, cherishing every moment. We shared rare weekends together and then used those snapshot memories to cover our gaps in togetherness, even trying to keep our past in the present. Occasionally, we'd dream of the future and our plans to be a normal couple.

But life in the Army meant that all of life's preparations would be replaced with life's real-world contingencies. As eager as I was to experience newlywed life in Germany, I knew that a deployment to Kosovo loomed ahead. My time in Germany would be fleeting, yet another period in which Julie and I said "until then," in hopes that life would someday settle down.

We flew in to Frankfurt's Rhein-Main Air Force Base in the middle of a misty Friday afternoon and learned that it was the beginning of a three-day holiday for the whole U.S. military in Europe. There were no buses to shuttle us to the *kasernes*, or barracks, around Germany. We were stuck on the base all weekend. Defeated and embarrassed, I dragged my bride through the cold rain to the

Air Force transient barracks, where we checked in with a sergeant at the desk. He handed us a stack of off-white linens, a room key, and a smudged strip map of the base.

"Base Exchange closes at 1700 if you're needing something to eat," he said. "Or, there's the chow hall." I looked at my watch. It showed 1645.

For the next three days, Julie and I snuggled together on a plastic-sheathed twin bed, trying to adjust to the time change, laboring to sleep under the droning of the Air Force jets. I was afraid our first weekend in Europe had left as bad an impression on Julie as it had on me. But every time I looked at her, she smiled back. We were together, which was more than we usually had.

The bus ride from Frankfurt to Vilseck, the place of our first home, took five hours. I fell in love with the terrain. The contrast was abrupt between the wide, flowing autobahns and the tight, rural roads. The land looked clean and cultivated, the villages wholesome, every building like a postcard in my mind. The magnificent countryside seemed to be flaunting its beauty—I sensed inherent wealth in the land. It was difficult to envision the madness that had ignited world wars being birthed from such a beautiful place. We were half a century into the occupation of Germany—and almost ten years removed from the fall of the Berlin Wall. Was there still a need for our presence? The history of two world wars cautioned that there was.

Julie and I arrived at a sun-splashed, rainbow-wrapped Bavaria the evening before I was to report. I had been assigned to 2nd Battalion, 2nd Infantry Regiment, otherwise known as 2-2 Infantry. The unit had received orders to assume the peace-support mission in Kosovo within a few months, and I jumped into an aggressive training plan, ramping up for the deployment. Time in the field, time on the ranges, time in the motor pool—though we now lived together, I seemed to have no time with my wife.

Dave Blank had arrived a month before us but was still searching for the perfect bachelor's crib on the German economy. He moved in with us, sleeping on the couch, because he had yet to find the right pad and he, too, had a long deployment coming. Dave and I had lived together longer than Julie and I had: at the Academy, at Fort Benning, and in the woods at Ranger School. Julie and I shared our precious newlywed time with him for the next few months as we learned how to live with each other—and anticipated parting again soon.

As my time with Julie waned, time with my platoon increased. I learned as much as I could about my new bride, but I also felt drawn to learn more about my new platoon. I had been taught to care for them, to understand them; to track their vitals, their uniform sizes, and their qualifications in a tidy leader's book. This mechanical approach to leadership or management—trying to learn about them because it was my job—never seemed to work.

They were all unique, with accents and mannerisms that were not indicative of their hometowns but of them as individuals. To me, Owens didn't talk like an Irishman; he talked like Owens. Bates wasn't a New Yorker; he was just Bates. What became a genuine interest of mine was learning about them first as men—men with whom I spent much of my time, men with whom I would live for most of the next year, men whom I would soon ask to do dangerous things.

One evening my company commander and I visited the local German hospital where one of my soldiers' wives had just given birth to their first child. Away from the military maneuvers and formations, my soldier's new fatherhood enlightened me to the human depth of my responsibility as a leader. The word *care* took on a new meaning for me.

As I rode away from the hospital in the company commander's

Volvo station wagon, he and I discussed the burden of leading soldiers and how that burden shaped our preparatory tasks for the upcoming deployment to Kosovo. Before we reached my apartment,
he abruptly changed the subject.

"Do you ever think about the Rangers?"

A flash of heat washed my face. He had struck something deep
inside me. I didn't understand my reaction. Maybe I had developed a
deep connection to the Rangers I'd met. Suddenly I was embarrassed,
like the time I was caught at a cattle auction mimicking the bidders:
The auctioneer stopped everything, drop-dead silent, with everyone
looking at me stink eyed, even the castrated bull, staring like I was
holding up his appointment with the butcher. The auctioneer asked
me a simple question, yet one I couldn't answer. "You biddin'? You
there—you biddin'?" I just slumped into my chair with a sheepish
shake of the head. Here in the Volvo, I tried to hide my interest in
the Rangers.

"Rangers? Sure. What do you mean?"

"I mean, did you ever think of applying for the Ranger Regiment? I think you'd be a good fit."

I had to be careful. Every Infantry lieutenant dreamed of serving
in the Ranger Regiment, but a lieutenant declaring plans to leave
the unit as soon as possible to move to the next best thing was like
walking into the church and asking for directions to the juice and
crackers. I'd been in the unit only three months. My interest in the
Rangers could be considered a statement of disloyalty.

"Well, sir, I think every platoon leader thinks about it, but I
know I have to prove my—"

"I'm gonna talk to Colonel Snow about it . . . tell him you're
interested."

I didn't want to say no, but I feared the backlash of the propo-
sition.

Two days later, I sat on a butternut leather couch in the battalion commander's office, studying the rows of souvenir Army unit coins adorning an end table. On the far left was our coin—2nd Battalion, 2nd Infantry Regiment—displaying the arched motto *Noli me Tangere*, "Don't touch me." I waited for Lieutenant Colonel Snow to send an e-mail and begin initial counseling with me.

"Well, Nate, you got to the unit at the perfect time—a good ramp-up. You did well at gunnery and the live fires, and with this rotation to the training center next month—it's a good ramp-up. You ready for this deployment?"

I nodded. "Roger, sir."

"We had a commanders' conference last week with the new division commander—General Abizaid. He's refitting the training center to look and feel like the Balkans. Role players from Hungary, scenarios straight from Kosovo, continuous peace-support operations. Should be a good test."

He gave me the standard preformatted counseling form: an overview of his command philosophy, some rules of thumb for decision making, tips for executing vigorously. The last item on his list was professional reading. Here, he scribbled with his pen and deviated from his standard pitch to new lieutenants.

"What are you reading right now—specifically for professional development?"

"Nothing, sir."

"It's time to start. Set some goals. Focus first on recent accounts of real combat—have you heard of *We Were Soldiers Once . . . and Young?*"

"Yes, sir; great read. Hal Moore gave us a lecture at West Point with pictures of the battle."

"Read it again; look over the tactics and lessons of their helicopter assaults—we may be flying a lot in Kosovo."

He looked over the counseling sheet, dated it, and signed his initials. I closed my notebook.

"Your CO says you want to put in a packet with the Rangers. That true?"

I hesitated, wishing my commanding officer hadn't said anything. "Well, sir, I'm focused on this deployment. We've got a job to do; I've got a platoon to lead."

"That's right. Kosovo's first. There'll be time to think about the Rangers later. You've got plenty of time."

"Yes, sir."

"But I'd be open to that. I'm not going to stand in the way of a guy's dreams. If it fits, then we'll see," he said. After a pause, he seemed to have an idea. "Speaking of Rangers . . ."

He leaned back in his chair to his bookcase, running his fingers across the spines. He pulled a black book with red and gold letters.

"I tell you what—why don't you take this," he said. "This will give you an idea of what you're asking for."

It was a clean, first-edition copy of *Black Hawk Down*, personalized and autographed by the author. I thanked him, saluted, and left his office. As I sat in my car, not having a hint of what the book was about, I flipped to the end of the book to see the point of it all, and here's what I read: "Their fight was neither triumph nor defeat; it just didn't matter. It's as though their firefight was a bizarre two-day adventure, like some extreme Outward Bound experience where things got out of hand and some of the guys got killed. I wrote this book for them."

The words *it just didn't matter* echoed in my mind. I did not know the story of their fight, or even who they were, but I resolved that day to discover something that *did* matter in their fight, and—for myself—to always make it matter.

11

It is a pity that, as one gradually gains experience, one loses one's youth. :: VINCENT VAN GOGH

NOVEMBER 27, 1999
ROSE BARRACKS, VILSECK, GERMANY

We made our third attempt to deploy to Kosovo with two feet of snow on the ground. We had been weathered out before and had twice said good-bye and hello again to our families. We held formation at midnight, and after four hours of loading bags, checking serial numbers, and saying good-bye to loved ones, we boarded buses bound for Frankfurt.

I took my time telling Julie good-bye. Leaving was hard. After all our separation, I had grown accustomed to living with her over the last few months, and I didn't want to let go. When I finally released her and stepped onto the bus, the platoon started ribbing me for being soft.

"Aw, the Ranger's got tears in his eyes."

"All right, all right," I said.

"How you 'sposed to lead us if you cryin'?"

"Knock it off," my platoon sergeant said. "Get some sleep."

I was embarrassed. But I knew these guys saw it as their jobs to tease me a little; without it, I'd begin to worry that something was wrong. I also thought that there were certain things we would all cry over—but I hoped none of those happened while we were in Kosovo.

As the bus rolled, "Tequila Sunrise" played on the radio. I nestled in and chuckled to myself at the irony of it: none of the soldiers would be drinking for the next seven months because of General Order No. 1—the prohibition of alcohol during deployment—and the sun was a long way from rising.

I reached into my backpack and slipped out the colonel's copy of *Black Hawk Down*. The book had become my addiction. I carried it with me everywhere. Every night at home in bed, I had read the book with Julie resting next to me in a pillow of her own hair. At those times, my head entertained devils—the savage scent to kill, the raw fear of the war story—even as Julie's paced breathing and empty, cherubic expression offered me a periodic escape from the Rangers. I would sometimes break from the book and stare at her, wondering if by my obsession I had invited demons to invade our home and her dreams. I would force the book down and labor to sleep, envisioning the eye-widening combat stories the Rangers in Somalia had endured. I wondered how men could stand up to such extreme conditions. My desire to join them was growing, and with it, the recognition of my own inadequacies.

Here on the bus, partway through my third reading, I dozed off somewhere around the Rangers' second rescue attempt.

12

The first condition of understanding a foreign country is to smell it. :: RUDYARD KIPLING

DECEMBER 7, 1999
PASJANE, KOSOVO

We occupied and operated from a large unfinished house on the edge of Pasjane, where rival Albanian villages encircled the Serb town like a noose.

Violence had escalated between the Albanian insurgency and Serbian police for the past several years, as the Albanians used guerrilla and terrorist tactics to force greater autonomy in the province of Kosovo. The past several months, however, had gotten the world's attention. The international media clamored at reports of grisly genocide, atrocious killings of Albanian civilians, burned towns, and mass graves.

The United Nations wanted to halt the crimes against humanity and douse the incendiary Balkans, but in March, Serbian president Slobodan Milosevic refused to sign peace agreements. Ensuing NATO air strikes, led by the United States, forced the "peace" by bombing Serb forces out of Kosovo. Within hours, KFOR, a NATO-led Kosovo Force occupied the province of Kosovo to perform peacekeeping duties and assist the return of refugees. I was now part of that force and lived in a town of Serbs, whose army and secret police we had bombed into submission.

I took my squad leaders on a reconnaissance patrol on the road leading from our compound to Serbia. As we neared the border area, the zigzag potholes startled me, those diagonals in the road that had once been antitank mines. At that sobering moment, I realized that despite the current cease-fire, we were in a war zone, a land riddled with mines and other remnants of centuries of conflict. We were there to keep people from killing each other.

Two days after we had established our presence, an elderly, half-conscious man limped to the gate of our compound. He was missing a chunk of his right calf, and his foot was a mangled mass. The right side of his face was burned smooth, and shrapnel peppered the area around his eye. He had stepped on a mine. Our medic began giving aid to the man as we vectored in a medevac helicopter to fly him to the nearest NATO surgical facility. We learned through the interpreter that the old man had been gathering wood near the border. We had patrolled that same stretch of border two days earlier. A chill ripped through members of the platoon who had walked the same ground.

Early conversation with the locals was just as sobering. People seemed filled with sorrow and malice at the same time. Men whose cattle had been stolen, children with stump extremities from the minefields, women who said their husbands had been kidnapped, men who had witnessed their brothers being murdered. The years of violence had spun a cycle of perpetual vengeance. The blood feud was alive.

I first put a human face on the problem of so-called ethnic cleansing in Vlastica, a nearby Albanian village. We drove into the town just before dusk. Charred building carcasses stood against the lavender sky. The acrid smell of burning trash lingered somewhere behind my nose, the same smell from every town, but deceiving me here to believe these buildings were still smoldering. Graffiti on a bullet-pocked wall said, "MR Klinton king OF tHe WorlD." I stopped and walked a dirt street, the wrinkled lines of erosion leading to piles of garbage, those deposits of once-meaningful possessions. I met an old man wearing a round white skullcap, the signature Albanian male headgear.

The old man told me how the U.S. Marines had come to his village that summer and found thirteen bodies in the rubble of a home, broken and burned. The Marines had found four more bodies in a shallow grave outside of town, but two more people were missing. After searching the mountainside above the village, they found one of them tied to a tree, with no head.

The man pointed to a line of mounds where they had buried all the victims.

While I listened to him, a girl crept up and nestled in behind him. A shawl covered her head, but I noticed a long scar running up her left cheek. He told me that the girl's parents, brother, and grandfather were all killed; she was the only one left. I felt compassion for her.

"Tell her that she is a miracle," I said to my interpreter.

The man attempted to smile.

I gave the man a hug, and then the girl. I agreed to have tea with him the next time I came to the village. We loaded up the Humvees and drove away.

The next morning, we visited the school in Pasjane, where we would place guards to protect the students. Upon entering the building, I was surprised at how normal the school looked, how happy the kids seemed, their jovial banter warming the hallways with a soothing hum. It reminded me of the States. There were crayon drawings taped to the walls, just like I'd seen in American schools, like I'd drawn as a kid. Except that these pictures reflected the lives of children living in a war zone: colorful caricatures of planes dropping bombs on patchwork landscapes, green blob tanks shooting red blob bullets, and buildings aflame with streaks of red, orange, and yellow.

I wondered what the children thought of me, standing in their hallway, a burly rifle- and pistol-wearing soldier with a backward American flag sewn to my shoulder. Disturbed, I turned to look at them, to see how they looked at me. The eyes I saw glancing at me reminded me of the girl I met in Vlastica. I wondered, if she were here, whether these children would hate her or play with her. I took off my helmet and slung my rifle across my back. *I'm here for these children.*

I found the superintendent's meager second-floor office, where he was having tea with two other men. He wore a black sport coat over a black ribbed sweater, his silver-white hair slicked rearward atop a weathered forehead. His deep onyx eyes hinted of a dimension far darker than that of an elementary school, like the wind on a winter night. He seemed oddly pleased by our presence and fired up a pipe, immediately engaging my interpreter in an extended dialogue. They soon began raising their voices in argument.

"What's he talking about?" I finally asked my interpreter. "What's wrong with you? *I'm* supposed to talk, remember?"

The interpreter explained that the superintendent was talking about Serbian nationalism.

"But he is wrong," the interpreter said. "This is always the problem."

"Tell him to talk to me, not you. You just translate and stop arguing."

Flanked on the walls by a Mercator projection and a portrait of Milosevic, the superintendent told me that he was once the town's mayor, that he had served in the Serbian army, and that the United States was wrong to invade and occupy Kosovo, a province of sovereign Serbia. I told him we were in Kosovo to keep the peace, to protect his village, to enforce the U.N. resolution. I was surprised by his brazen confrontation of my presence, how his haughty attitude filled the room like his sweet pipe smoke. I thought I could appeal to his duty as superintendent.

"I saw the children's drawings on the walls. They are good artists," I said. "You must be proud."

I paused for my interpreter to convey the message.

He relit his pipe. "They don't want you here either," the superintendent said, speaking in clear English. "You are wrong to be here. They say you are wrong too."

I made no progress with him. I left his office angry that such a man molded the minds of Pasjane's next generation. When I reached the foot of the stairs, I found a short, unkempt man waiting for me. He raised his hand as if to hail me, and he introduced himself to our group as the physical education teacher. I noticed a gentleness about him; I saw it in the way he looked at the passing kids and how they looked at me in his presence. He invited me to visit his house in two days to meet his family and have fish for dinner.

In that man, I met the hope of Pasjane's children.

13

What a cruel thing is war: to separate and destroy families and friends, and mar the purest joys and happiness God has granted us in this world; to fill our hearts with hatred instead of love for our neighbors, and to devastate the fair face of this beautiful world. :: ROBERT E. LEE

DECEMBER 12, 1999
PASJANE, KOSOVO

I came down the curved concrete stairway to the sound of dominoes and the smell of bacon and eggs. The logistics patrol had already made it to our compound with breakfast, and I was hungry. I stopped at the radio table to check the guard shift. The colonel's copy of *Black Hawk Down* sat on the table looking like an accordion file, now bloated to twice its original thickness, with dark greasy smudges all over the cover. As with the rest of my books, I had offered it to the platoon. It made for good night-shift reading.

The main room in our platoon's building served as our dining room, our game room, our equipment room, our TV room, and our orders-briefing room. The platoon shared meals around a large picnic table, which created a family atmosphere. I loved breaking bread with the boys. Just as I poured a syrup packet over a plate of greenish eggs and sausage links, the radio guard called for me.

"Lieutenant Self! Two guys at the gate want to see you." My food was already cold, anyway.

I stopped at our interpreters' room to take one outside with me. Only Farooq, one of our two Muslim Albanian interpreters, was available; the other was on vacation, and our Christian Macedonian interpreter was taking a much-needed shower at Camp Monteith, our battalion's forward operating base (FOB). Farooq and I went outside to decipher what was going on.

The men looked scared. The younger man had dirt stains on his shoulder. They said they had been ambushed in the hills while bird hunting.

"Some men started shooting at them," the interpreter said. "This man jumped on the ground so he would not be killed."

I felt angry at the two Serbian men, who had ventured outside the umbrella of security we provided. Hunting in the hills was not an activity we could protect. The Serbs explained something else to us.

"They say two men are missing," the interpreter said.

"Take us there," I said.

I ran inside to alert the platoon. We loaded a squad of soldiers onto two Bradley Fighting Vehicles (BFV), heavily armed personnel carriers with tracks. We followed the men through the narrow streets and up a grooved mountainside overlooking the town.

After fifteen minutes of weaving up the mountain, we came to a group of huddled men. The two men from the gate joined several others in a clearing atop the mountain. I slipped out of the turret and onto the ground near the group. Down in a ditch, I saw a man lying faceup.

I picked up my pace and hopped over to the man in the ditch. He was looking straight up to the sky with his mouth wide open. His expression was one of struggle. He was dead, and I recognized him.

The victim was the local school's physical education teacher, the first one to extend hospitality to me when so many in the village looked at us with hateful eyes. I was to have dinner with him that evening.

The young man with the dirt stain on his shoulder stormed away, putting his hands on top of his head and looking upward in one anxious, hurried motion. The Serbs started yelling at each other. They tried to grab him.

I was watching the teacher's son, the man with the dirt stain on his shirt, react to seeing his father dead. He looked as if he were about to explode. They all began scurried little circular pacing motions, looking at the horizon and then at the ground.

The Serbs around the scene were getting angry. They leaned in to peek at the body, redirecting and throwing their hands up, gesturing in the direction of a quaint town off in the valley. It was an Albanian town later identified as Ugljare. My interpreter, an eighteen-year-old Albanian student, was getting nervous.

"They say the killers are from that village," my interpreter said. "The mujahideen."

"Mujahideen? Like in Afghanistan? That's ridiculous."

"This is what they say, sir."

The men picked up 7.62-mm shell casings and shoved them in my face to show me proof that this man was murdered. I put a few in my thigh pocket, somehow wanting to hold on to them, feeling that the person who loaded the bullet had taken not only the life from this old man but also something from me.

We called for military police reinforcements to investigate the crime scene and the body. Two soldiers and I took a Humvee down the mountain through the woods toward the town of Ugljare, determined to find the killers. My company commander brought the other two platoons from Camp Monteith to clear homes and shops. For the next twelve hours, we raided several houses in Ugljare, looking for evidence of the murderers. I grew more frustrated with every building we cleared, as we found nothing but simple Albanian families with frightened children and humble accommodations.

That evening, an angry mob awaited our return to Pasjane. Villagers who had offered us food or drink the day before were now rioting, spitting at us, and brandishing farm tools. They crowded the gate to our compound, singing mournful songs and hurling insults at our soldiers. Most of their anger was directed toward Albanians, but much of it was toward us for letting it happen.

I listened to the Serbs' forceful persuasion about this being a religious fight, how the Muslims were there to kill the Christian Serbs, how I should be able to see the religious conflict there.

"Why are you helping them? Protecting them so they can kill us?" an English-speaking Serb said. "We are Christians, like you. You must agree with us. They will take our homes, like they took our brothers. They will take our land. What will you do?"

In the days that followed, we visited the family and attended the funeral. We shut down the road through Pasjane as the funeral procession carried the teacher's body on a mule cart through the town to the cemetery. I disobeyed General Order No. 1 and drank a shot of plum brandy with the teacher's family in his honor, sprinkling half the shot over his fresh grave. We kept the town locked down and increased our security in Pasjane to prevent acts of vengeance on Albanians driving through the village, as well as violence against the Serbs crowding the road.

Nothing else happened. We decided to leave the Serbs alone to grieve. I felt a sense of loss, for having failed to protect the people as much as for the meal I had missed with that kind old man. If only he hadn't gone hunting. If only we had responded sooner, maybe we could have captured or killed the murderers.

I went back to the compound and went to my one-man room, which was probably a closet in the house's intended configuration. My platoon was responsible for security here: I was responsible. I loosened my bootlaces, turned on my space heater, and rocked back on my cot. I looked at the row of books on my homemade shelf. I saw my Bible and wondered how the world could be so cruel. *Where is God in this place?*

The first few days in Kosovo had been rough. I was a man specially trained for war, yet I found myself wondering how people could hate each other so much. I lay on my cot that night, staring at the multicolored bricks that lined my unfinished bedroom wall, sympathizing with the mortar squeezed in between—and I wondered whose side I was on.

14

It's not enough that we do our best; sometimes we have to do what's required.
:: SIR WINSTON CHURCHILL

FEBRUARY 2000
PASJANE, KOSOVO

Little of the West Point curriculum seemed to apply now. The Academy had taught me how to think critically and make decisions—but nothing comparable to the overwhelming logistical and political situation in Kosovo. There were half a million troops in our army, some of them more qualified, most of them more experienced than I was. At twenty-three years old, I didn't know what I didn't know. Only time in the crucible would make me into what I needed to be.

I had not expected Kosovo to be such a complex and ambiguous environment, one in which it seemed almost impossible to distinguish between Serbs and Albanians. Sometimes I could identify the two ethnic groups by their language and their occasional ethnic headgear. Most times I relied on my interpreter to tell me who was who.

The nature of our mission was similarly confounding. The lack of substantial involvement by either the U.N. and its police force or nongovernmental organizations (NGOs) forced my platoon to shoulder the spectrum of responsibilities for Pasjane and its survival.

I made decisions daily that affected thousands of people in Pasjane, those who lived in neighboring villages, and those who passed through on the busy route south to Serbia. My platoon firebase became the military base, police station, logistical node, diplomatic center, and humanitarian aid clearinghouse for all the townspeople. This resulted in a daily barrage of requests: for food, lumber, water, seed, clothes, security, justice, money, newspapers, fuel, communications, and explanation of NATO's actions.

The emotional volatility and cultural uncertainty made day-to-day operations difficult to endure. One strained soldier's question reflected our disillusionment and exhaustion: "If I kill somebody here, will I get to go home?" One visitor to the firebase would express gratitude for giving him some clothes, while the next would curse NATO and the United States for ruining his farmland (which we were standing on). One minute, my soldiers would enjoy a game of cards while eating bread a local woman had provided. The next minute, my soldiers would react to a drive-by grenade attack that severely wounded the same woman. As a leader and a man, the personal highs and lows I experienced caused an oscillation between fits of anger and episodes of depression. Every day taxed me mentally and emotionally. And when I lay down to rest, there was no guarantee I would not be awakened by the sound of an explosion rubbling the mayor's house, killing the whole family.

Sometimes, my subordinate leaders deferred the pressure of the experience and chose not to make decisions involving the sticky nuances of civil governance and infrastructure. They would defer some decisions to me, decisions such as mediating property disputes, distributing humanitarian aid, sorting out politics. This relieved them of the added responsibility, and I accepted my duty to make those decisions, not only for the overall good of the village, but also for the well-being of my soldiers.

A visit from a couple of generals helped me gain perspective. Lieutenant General Dan Christman, West Point's superintendent, visited my platoon as he checked on recent graduates deployed to Kosovo. He exuded a familiar and motivating presence, as did his escort, General Abizaid. It was as if two surrogate dads had stopped by to say hello. They talked with the soldiers and inspected the compound. They discussed the operating environment. They asked tough questions. They were eager to hear what the Academy could do to better prepare graduates for such a mission. Christman offered his take on Kosovo.

"What strikes me is the significance of this mission at not only the tactical level but the operational and strategic levels as well," he said. "The politics, the diplomatic ambiguity, the responsibility of it all."

"Yes, sir," I said. "I feel like I don't know who to trust. I'm amazed at the complexity of this region."

"Yes, but this is not Bosnia," Abizaid said. "This is much more like Somalia. You have to be ready to switch to high-intensity conflict in a second's time."

"I've been talking about that with the NCOs in the platoon— what if the enemy thinks they can get us to leave Kosovo by killing some of us?" I asked. "It happened in Somalia."

"Well, that situation was a little different. We wouldn't respond like that here," Abizaid said. "But you still have to be ready."

"We're ready, sir."

"Well, Nate, we need to stay on schedule," Christman said. "We're headed on patrol with Dave Blank next. Do you know him well?"

"I know him real well, sir. We were roommates at school."

"Well, keep it up, Nate. We're proud of what you're doing," Christman said, giving me a rap on the back.

"Stay ready," Abizaid said.

I called the compound to attention as the generals departed. Their words had validated my difficulties with the situation—its importance, its complexity, and its danger. Making tactical decisions involving my soldiers' application of force was always a natural and effortless thing—that's what I was trained to do. Making decisions that affected the lives of a few thousand civilians was neither natural nor effortless, particularly under the mental and emotional stress I was experiencing.

I didn't realize it at the time, but making decisions under those circumstances developed in me an overall feeling of control in all situations, a sense of calm that would one day contribute to a cool head when I needed it most in the Army: when my own soldiers' lives were in question.

15

Reveal not every secret you have to a friend, for how can you tell but that friend may hereafter become an enemy. And bring not all mischief you are able to upon an enemy, for he may one day become your friend. :: SAADI, Persian poet

MARCH 2000
PASJANE, KOSOVO

We traded a squad with the Russians, who patrolled a sector to our north. The multinational nature of NATO required building relationships with foreign troops, but none was more involved or intriguing to me and to my soldiers than the Russians. Our previous Russian/American squad swap produced stories of the Russians' reckless patrolling, vile living conditions, and rampant drunkenness and drug use. I'd grown up scared that the Russians would overtake the world. Now they scared me in a much different way. Now they were apathetic, poorly equipped, and battle weary.

The Russian platoon leader told me through an interpreter that many of his soldiers had rotated straight from combat in Chechnya, where they were fighting jihadist rebels—and that many of his soldiers would rotate straight back to combat in Chechnya following their tours in Kosovo. After watching them in action, I was surprised any of them had survived combat.

We attempted to train the Russians in room-clearing and patrolling techniques; we traded weapons at the range, and we conducted joint patrols through Pasjane, where the Serbs welcomed them more than they did us because the Russians shared their Slavic ethnicity. At the end of the week, we were given a capstone mission to conduct with the Russians: a joint heliborne demonstration.

Two days later, UH-60 Blackhawks flew the Russians and us along the border with Serbia, hugging the mountains and shooting through the valleys. Watching the wind beat the Russians around me, I was struck by the irony of flying in a helicopter with them— the same men we grew up hating, the same men we studied to fight, the same men we helped shoot down over Afghanistan by supplying Stinger missiles to the mujahideen.

We landed right on the road, three helicopters blocking traffic in a dangerous show of force. After the birds lifted off, we began patrolling to Camp Monteith through the Albanian city of Gnjilane, establishing hasty traffic-control points with the Russians along the way. The Albanians on the streets looked at the Russians with disgust. And when the Russians stopped cars in this city, I noticed a difference in how they handled the Albanians. The Russians were rude, forceful, and intimidating.

These Russian soldiers saw no difference between the Muslim

mujahideen they were fighting in Chechnya and these Muslim Albanians on the streets in Kosovo. But I was starting to sympathize with the Russians' war in Chechnya against the mujahideen, and after seeing a disproportionate amount of violence against the Serbs here, I was also beginning to dislike the Albanians.

As we marched on, I studied the Russians' ruddy faces, their jaded mannerisms, their afflicted dispositions. I was beginning to look on them as I did my own soldiers. I pitied them, knowing that their looming departure from Kosovo meant a return to war in Chechnya, a war in which some would face the enemy, some would face death, and all would surely face themselves.

16

MARCH 2000
CAMP MONTEITH, KOSOVO

After three weeks without a shower, I walked onto the camp smelling like bloated prey. I usually enjoyed a shower once a week, sometimes every two weeks—whenever I had a chance to rotate back to Camp Monteith, our base camp. Our predecessors had named it after First Lieutenant Jimmie Monteith, who earned the Medal of Honor when he gave his life in Normandy on D-Day. He was a platoon leader in the 1st Infantry Division, just like me. We routinely sent groups to Monteith to clean up, work out, refit, and call home. I went there when I sensed things in Pasjane were calm enough for me to do so.

Julie and I hadn't talked for nearly a month, so I skipped the showers and went straight to the phone banks. I stood in line for forty-five minutes. We had a fifteen-minute limit on phone calls, and sometimes it took nearly that long to make a good connection all the way back to the States, where Julie was. This required a military phone call to an operator in Germany, who forwarded me to a military post in Maryland, where an operator dialed a call to Julie—collect. Because of the time difference, the phone often woke her up in the middle of the night—which I really liked. There was something about hearing her sleepy voice. It made me feel closer to her, as if I were lying next to her again.

I normally tried to keep the calls focused on Julie's life, what she had going on back in the States, and what we were going to do when I got home. I didn't want her to know what I was doing in Kosovo. I figured I'd tell her eventually, but I wouldn't tell her everything. Why defile her mind with all the violence and hatred and suffering? I would just tell her about the humanitarian aid and the school children and the beautiful mountains.

After my fifteen minutes expired, I went to Dave Blank's room to grab him for lunch. Dave lived there on the camp but spent most of his waking hours walking the streets of a dense urban area, unraveling organized-crime rings, enforcing curfews, and working the politicians. He used music to escape his dark world. I came to his to escape mine.

Dave was sitting on his footlocker playing my guitar. He had the CD cover to Pearl Jam's *Ten* album taped to his wall.

"You dog," I said. "When do I get my guitar back? That thing hasn't left your room since it got here."

"When I finish this song. I can't get the chorus right."

Dave and I enjoyed a short-order meal and a conversation about our respective sectors. After ten minutes of the same, I struggled to maintain interest. He was a first-rate friend, but I felt distracted; I missed my wife. My phone call with Julie was still on my mind.

"Is this what you want for your life?" I asked. "I don't want to do this stuff for the next twenty years. Watching people die, people hating each other. You're busting up kidnappings and sex-slave rings. This is just crazy."

"Nate, the whole world is like this, man. You go home and start looking around, it'll be the same stuff. It's everywhere."

"Yeah, well, how am I supposed to raise a family like this—always gone? I'm missing Julie pretty bad. I'm writing poems, drawing pictures of her—stuff I never do."

"Yeah, that is bad."

"I just can't see being gone like this with teenage kids who hate me for never being there."

"What would you do the rest of your life?" he asked.

"I don't know. Something good."

"You're doing something good here."

"I don't know. Sometimes I don't see any good in this place. I mean, the stuff you're seeing, the stuff I'm seeing. I'm getting tired of picking up bodies."

Dave just looked at me. I thought he agreed with me.

"Maybe I'm just tired of carrying all this stuff on my own," I said. "I see these people killing each other and I can't stop it, and I just sit alone when I have a chance and think about it. And I think, 'Where's God in this place?' I don't see him, man. I probably think too much. Am I making any sense here?"

"Are you saying God doesn't know this stuff's going on?"

"I don't know. I try to pray about it, and it doesn't seem to matter. And then I ask the chaplain to come out to the compound, but nobody wants to come to his service. I'm just out there alone."

"It's too bad you don't live here on Monteith," Dave said.

"Yeah, but if we weren't out there, then those people would kill more of each other."

"Maybe so. But *you* might be better. At least you and I could hang out."

I looked at my watch. I was late for counseling with the battalion commander.

Lieutenant Colonel Snow was still in his weekly meeting with all the company commanders when I got to his office. After ten more minutes, we began our counseling session.

"Nate, thanks for making it in for this. I know you've got plenty going on, so let's get moving. How do you think things have gone in Pasjane?"

"Okay, sir. We're doing some good things out there. But I just wish I were stopping some of the violence."

"It *has* been a hot spot," he agreed. "Nate, you've learned a lot in a short time."

"Yes, sir."

He paused and looked as if he were reserving some bad news for me.

"Here's your evaluation," he said. He slid the paper across the desk to me. I couldn't look at it.

"You know I've got to make some changes," he said. "You all can't stay in the same jobs forever. We have other lieutenants who are waiting for platoons."

"Roger, sir."

"So, I've decided to give you the Scout Platoon."

The Scout Platoon was the most desirable platoon in the battalion. I was being promoted.

"But you need to understand that you're probably not the best one for the job," he said. "A lot goes into these decisions. Lieutenant Blank was our first choice."

I was happy about the new job—but now my ego had taken a blow.

"Dave's company commander wants to keep him in the company. He can't lose him. So, it's you."

I wondered if Dave already knew. I looked down at my evaluation. The line reading "one of the top four lieutenants in the battalion" meant I was his fourth pick.

"You still thinking about a packet to the Rangers?"

"Yes, sir," I said. "I'd like to do that, sir."

"Well, we can revisit that when we get back home. For now, focus on your changeover to that Scout Platoon."

I left the office marveling at his notion to send me—only the fourth-best in the battalion—to serve with the best in the world.

17

For it is not much to be able to do violence when you have simply been preparing for it for years and when violence is more natural to you than thinking. It is a great deal, on the other hand, to face torture and death when you know that they are empty things in themselves. It is a great deal to fight while despising war, to accept losing everything while still preferring happiness, to face destruction while cherishing the idea of a higher civilization. :: ALBERT CAMUS

MARCH 2000
PASJANE, KOSOVO

Intelligence analysts detected indicators that Albanians were attempting to build an insurgent force to extort, ethnically cleanse, and otherwise intimidate all remaining Serbs out of Kosovo. The majority of activity was occurring in an area known as the "chicken leg," a triangular-shaped region where mountain passes served as natural corridors for movement between Kosovo, Serbia proper, and Macedonia.

Brigadier General Ricardo Sanchez, whom General Abizaid had given command over forces in Kosovo, decided to use SEAL Team 2 in an alpine reconnaissance and surveillance role in order to confirm or deny these insurgent actions. The plan included my platoon as the SEALs' insertion force, extraction force, and reinforcing Quick Reaction Force (QRF) should they need help.

After weeks of preparation, we were ready to insert the SEALs into their reconnaissance positions. My stomach was fluttering on mission night. We drove three Humvees forty-five minutes along a winding, pitted road to a spot where the road and a gurgling creek intersected in a valley of gravel, then followed a narrow, muddy trail along the bank of the creek into the mountains. As we slithered up the snowy mountain, the creek diminished into an intermittent ribbon of silver reflecting the moonlight as it fell farther below us down a steep drop-off. I was tense, taking shallow breaths.

We made it to the insertion point, a spot just flat enough to turn the vehicles around to head back down the trail. As we reversed the vehicles' direction, the SEALs slipped out and moved up the powdery slopes, four men who moved as one.

That night, the SEALs found what we were looking for: an insurgent hideout. They reported Muslim Albanian insurgents in an abandoned mountain village—firing weapons, digging trenches, and building bunkers. The SEALs beamed back digital photos of men in full combat gear patrolling the mountainsides, armed with automatic rifles and machine guns. We had found the bad guys.

Now that we finally had identified clearly intended aggressors, I was ready to fight. I realized that I had developed a hatred for all those in Kosovo who desired to kill, whether they were Serbs or Albanians. After five months of finding Serb bodies, I felt like we had been duped into coming to Kosovo, that the Albanians had forced us here, and now they were taking an opportunity to exploit the conditions we provided. After the blood I'd seen, I had started to hate the aggressors—the Muslim Albanian aggressors.

Within two days of finding the insurgent camp, I was again driving into the chicken leg for an insertion—only this time it was with the entire company, and we weren't hiding. We were there to raid the insurgent outpost.

We had planned to achieve a proper escalation of force through careful synchronization of assets, thereby reducing the risk of a gunfight. First, we were to surround the target and then call out the insurgents using bullhorns while another platoon inserted by helicopter on an adjacent ridge; then we would fire tear gas into the buildings and have Apache helicopters fire warning shots nearby. If all else failed, we would kick in the doors and clear the buildings as infantrymen—as we were trained to do.

I was frustrated. By announcing our presence, we were forfeiting the element of surprise, allowing the enemy time to barricade in preparation for our entry. Our graduated response plan created a paradox whereby attempting to reduce the chances of shooting would likely increase the brutality of the fight, if it came to that.

If we had to go in, Sergeant Kevin Owens's squad would be the first ones in. Across from me in the bed of a five-ton truck, Owens expressed his angst. He was my best squad leader, a former Irish special forces soldier, as well as a freelance bodyguard in Mogadishu from '92 to '93. The contentious former mercenary brewed his thoughts as boldly as his tea, and offered them just as freely.

"We should be kickin' the doors down, gons at deh ready," he said. "They're gonna get somebody killed with dees games."

I didn't say a word. I agreed with him. I pulled the map from my pants-leg pocket and studied it. My soldiers lined two bench seats in the bed of the truck. The rows of helmets recalled to me our history—First Lieutenant Jimmie Monteith and his platoon aboard a landing craft off Omaha Beach—and how they must have felt then. The scene before me was not war. Half of my soldiers were asleep.

The trucks came to a stop along the same familiar creek. We unloaded at the base of the mountains, about ten kilometers from the target objective. My platoon was charged with forging the route to the insurgents—on point again. Sergeant Owens's squad would lead the way.

"All right, Paddy, you're on," I said.

We moved for a couple of hours, stopping to check our course and to allow the 150-man company to regroup. We found deeper snowdrifts along our route as we ascended. Moisture seeped into my socks, and I pondered anew the inadequacy of my boots. My feet were wet and starting to ache. The government spent millions of dollars a year on transportation and improvements for high-tech vehicles, some of which sat in our compound in Pasjane. On this mission, I had a cheap wrapping of leather covering the only vehicle I had: my own two feet. Here again, I thought of my old enemy, the cow.

Before reaching the objective, we gathered our forces for one last check. Equipment ready, plan disseminated, radios on, cocked to go. We waited for the overwatching SEAL team's final report before we crept into the assault position. My company commander knelt next to me.

"Nate, we're waiting on the update," he said. "I'll give you the—"

"Sir, the SEALs are confirming enemy presence on the objective," the radio operator said. "Vicinity the church."

"How many?" my commander asked.

"At least two."

"Let's move out," he said.

I called ahead to Sergeant Owens and passed him the update. We then crawled through dense evergreens up a sharp face just below the church. I could smell the trees. We were getting close, less than fifty meters from the edge of the wood line. I could see the bell tower. My radio came to life in my ear.

"Red One, stop! I say again: stop!"

It was my commander. I tried to get Sergeant Owens's attention using a whisper whistle.

"Hweet! Hweet!"

Owens turned around. I held up a fist, signaling him to freeze.

"Red One. Do not proceed; over," my commander said.

I turned around to see him moving toward me. He grabbed my shoulder and pulled me close.

"The SEALs say the enemy is armed—at the church—automatic rifles and grenades. We're calling in the Apaches."

I looked to the front to see Owens's frustration. I held up my fist again. I imagined a grenade rolling down toward us. We were too close together.

I saw the teacher's dead face in my mind.

I heard the dull throbbing of helicopters pumping up the valley. Two UH-60 Blackhawks popped over the trees and darted to the mountain across the valley. The other platoon was early. Nothing was synchronized. We were fully exposed, just below the church.

"Red One, go. Red One, go."

I turned in search of my commander, looking to confirm his latest order. This was all wrong.

"Assault!" he said.

Sergeant Owens heard the command and leapt from the woods,

pistol drawn, with a fire team of soldiers. They collapsed into a tight line at the church door and then disappeared. I followed with another squad and entered the church.

It was beautiful inside. The morning sunlight filtered through the stained glass, illuminating the crucifix in the back of the sanctuary. We glided through the aisles and pews. There was no one inside.

Being in a church felt foreign to me just then, yet something within me resonated with its emptiness. I felt the pulsing message that my faith had somehow, gradually, grown as empty as this church I had seized with force, that I had allowed the mental and emotional toil of the work to eclipse my awareness of God. But I pushed those thoughts aside, turning my attention back to the mission. There would be time later to analyze my spiritual state.

The armed insurgents had fled the church when the helicopters arrived, and another group from our company detained them as they tried to escape in their SUV.

We found the insurgents' command center. Radios, weapons, uniforms, stores of food, and a hidden trapdoor to a basement, which contained gas masks and ammunition. By sundown, we had captured four more Muslim insurgents, one in the act of emplacing a minefield near another platoon.

We declared the objective secure after a full day of clearing the network of trenches, bunkers, and small buildings. My platoon spent the night on the objective to continue exploiting the target the next day. We huddled around crackling potbellied stoves in the church— staring into the flames, recounting the day's action, wondering what disasters we had averted, analyzing how easily we could've seen a firefight. Lying half asleep on a front-row pew, I thanked God that we'd made it through the day—and felt guilty for being somewhat disappointed that we hadn't killed anyone.

18

It is a mistake to try to look too far ahead. The chain of destiny can only be grasped one link at a time. :: SIR WINSTON CHURCHILL

SEPTEMBER 11, 2000
VILSECK, GERMANY

Sometimes what's printed on a sheet of paper can make it the most valued possession in your life. Three months after returning from Kosovo, I stood in the hallway of the in-and-out processing center in Vilseck holding the most coveted piece of paper in my Army career: orders assigning me to the 75th Ranger Regiment.

The timing had been improbable, yet many factors combined to make the move a reality: my growth as a platoon leader in Kosovo, the influx of extra replacement lieutenants, the graciousness of Colonel Snow, and the urgent need for platoon leaders in the Rangers.

Julie and I were in shock over the prospect of leaving Germany to pursue my dream of serving with the best infantrymen in the world. Privately, I was in shock over having been called to that stage. In the Rangers, I would be tested like never before, in ways that would expose my true abilities and weaknesses. Uncertainties aside, we were thrilled to be heading back to the States and closer to family and friends. After a year in Germany, we were ready for shopping malls and Wal-Mart, for wider streets and warmer weather, for TV and for free ketchup at McDonald's.

I ran some errands that afternoon. In between stops, I sat in my car, flipping through the Bible to random passages, looking for some reassurance in my Ranger selection. Although I was as happy as a five-year-old on Christmas morning, I wasn't sure I could meet the Rangers' expectations of me. *What have I signed up for? What if I wash out? What if I get fired?* Needing answers, I abandoned my random flip-

and-point Bible study for a method equally desperate: I read Psalm 75 to see if there was any kind of connection with the 75th Ranger Regiment. Maybe the Regiment had adopted the psalm as its own, as a number gimmick. After a few verses, I zeroed in on a passage of Scripture that made my palms sweat: "Exaltation comes neither from the east nor from the west nor from the south. But God is the Judge: He puts down one, and exalts another" (Psalm 75:6-7).

At that moment, I realized that my selection to the Rangers had little to do with my own ability, but God had purposed for me to go to Hunter Army Airfield in Savannah. The muscles between my neck and shoulder blades relaxed. I looked at my orders to the Rangers in the passenger seat and back to my Bible. I grabbed a pen from the glove box, underlined the Scripture, and dog-eared the page.

19

The long, gray line has never failed us. Were you to do so, a million gray ghosts in olive drab, in brown khaki, in blue and gray, would rise from their white crosses, thundering those magic words: Duty, honor, country. :: DOUGLAS MacARTHUR, To Cadets, May 12, 1962

SEPTEMBER 2000
NORMANDY, FRANCE

If God alone qualifies ground as sacred, why do we interpret so many places to be so? Jerusalem, Mecca, Sinai, even places like Arlington National Cemetery—do mere men assign holiness to these sites? I pondered the question as the last few feet of English Channel crashed into my calves, the undertow sucking sand from under my feet.

More than a half century ago, on D-Day, the waves at my feet carried many Americans ashore to their ultimate sacrifice, carried their blood back out to sea, and rocked their dead bodies to eternal sleep. A man not worthy of the distinction, I considered the loose beach under my feet—and the water—to be sacred.

Dave Blank was there too. He and I walked Omaha Beach with the other officers in the battalion. We started at the Rangers' breakthrough point at the "Dog One" draw, portrayed in the opening scene of *Saving Private Ryan*, then moved east to the place where our division—the 1st Infantry Division—had fought.

A granite spire monument stood there, overlooking the beach atop a terraced, thicketed crest. The monument was inscribed on all sides with names of men who gave their lives during the invasion, men like First Lieutenant Jimmie Monteith, platoon leader, whose name was highlighted with gold letters as a Medal of Honor awardee. *He was a platoon leader in the 1st Infantry Division, just like me.* I rubbed his name with my fingers and looked down to the beach.

We loaded the bus at the nearby village of Colleville-sur-Mer and drove west several miles down the beach to the knife-edge peninsula of cliffs known as Pointe-du-Hoc. This historically invincible strongpoint boasted bunkers so thick that Allied bombers had little effect on them. Rangers scaled these cliffs on D-Day with Germans firing down on them. The Rangers seized the labyrinth of defenses after several hours of fighting and against all improbabilities.

I followed the trenches to gun emplacements and cold, cave-like bunkers. Walking through the craters was like navigating the dimpled surface of a giant golf ball, with divots in the earth fifteen feet deep. I walked to the edge of the cliffs and looked down at the surf slamming into the rocks below, my legs weak in awe of what the Rangers did there—and at the realization that I would soon join these same fabled Ranger units.

We drove back to Colleville, where nearly ten thousand white grave markers populate the American Cemetery. I walked through the rows of crosses and stars until I found the grave of Jimmie Monteith. His cross faces west, as they all do, toward the setting sun and the nation for which he died. I pondered again the question of whether God considered this ground sacred.

The somber whining of a bugle somewhere in the cemetery broke the silence, calling "Retreat" to signify the end of the day. Standing alone, I faced the two United States flags flying high above the grounds. Then the bugle sounded "Taps," and I saluted the flags as they crawled into the sinking sun. Tears filled my eyes.

20

OCTOBER 12, 2000
THE RED SEA

In the black of night, the drab crimson keel of a guided-missile destroyer parted the warm waters of the Red Sea, en route to the strategic fuel-storage depot in Aden Harbor, Yemen. The ship was commissioned as the USS Cole in memory of a U.S. Marine sergeant awarded the Medal of Honor for gallantry in the battle to seize the volcanic heights of Iwo Jima, where he assaulted enemy machine-gun bunkers with grenades.

By the time the Cole moored six hundred meters offshore to take on fuel from underwater pipes, the late-morning sun had driven temperatures into the upper nineties. Jagged, bare brown peaks crowded the green harbor, threatening to push the ancient city into the water. The smell of fajitas wafted through the chambers belowdecks as the crew formed a long line for lunch.

In the harbor, a small fiberglass boat puttered low in the water, its bow bobbing, hinting in the direction of the Cole. The two men piloting the boat sat atop several hundred pounds of C-4 explosives. Their greatest concern was to keep the excessive weight from sinking their boat.

Several Cole crew members topside noticed the small boat approaching but saw it as commonplace; aside from the boats involved in the mooring efforts, normal operations in the region saw frequent visitors assisting with garbage removal.

The two men sidled their boat portside of the Cole, just opposite the hull from the full galley of sailors eating lunch. The men hailed the crew on the deck and labored to stand at attention against the jostling of the boat. They saluted the Americans in silence as their meager watercraft erupted, shredding a gash forty feet in diameter in the Cole's hull, through the half-inch steel, an engine room, and the mess deck. The Cole swallowed a gulp of seawater and lurched sideways.

Belowdecks, water rushed through the pierced chambers. The blast knocked out electricity, communications, and light, creating a blind cauldron of confusion. Some sailors died immediately from the blast; others struggled for life, trapped underwater in the black confines of rooms where they had been eating or working moments before.

Crew members on the topdeck suspected an accidental explosion during the refueling operation. They shouted and motioned to the local fuel laborers, commanding them to cease the flow of fuel to the ship. But because the fuel was not the original source of danger, stopping the flow of fuel merely prevented further damage. Seventeen sailors were dead, and the Cole lay wounded, listing several degrees to port under a billow of smoke.

In Afghanistan, Usama bin Laden again anticipated an American retaliatory strike, and again evacuated from Kandahar to the desert. The U.S. government, however, showed restraint. President Clinton and his aides suspected al-Qaeda's responsibility for the attack on the USS Cole but had not yet built a case for action. The president was reluctant to act unless the FBI and CIA were prepared to stand in front of the American public and claim bin Laden's culpability. They were not. The president and his advisers discussed issuing a last-chance ultimatum to Afghanistan's ruling group, the Taliban, to extradite bin Laden, close terrorist bases in Afghanistan, and expel all terrorists from Afghanistan within ninety days.

Such an ultimatum was never issued.

21

The Ranger battalion is to be an elite, light, and most proficient infantry battalion in the world; a battalion that can do things with its hands and weapons better than anyone. The battalion will not contain any "Hoodlums" or "Brigands" and if the battalion is formed of such persons, it will be disbanded. Wherever the battalion goes, it will be apparent that it is the best.

:: GENERAL CREIGHTON ABRAMS, Activation of 1st Ranger Battalion

OCTOBER 2000
HUNTER ARMY AIRFIELD
SAVANNAH, GEORGIA

"How does it look?" I said, looking at Julie in the hotel mirror.

"Is it supposed to be covering your ear?" she asked.

"I think so," I said. "The lower, the better."

It was the first time I'd worn a black beret, the coveted headgear of the Rangers. I was wetting, shaving, and shaping the black felt hat to a sleek, formfitting finish. Tomorrow, I would wear it in front of a platoon of forty men of the 1st Battalion of the 75th Ranger Regiment. They would know right away if I'd ever worn a beret.

I was back in Georgia, a year and a half after I graduated from Ranger School. Since then, I had lived in Germany, traveled Europe, and gained valuable experience leading two platoons in Kosovo. Tomorrow, I would begin leading some of the same "Bat Boys" that I had come to admire in Ranger School.

The next morning I kissed a sleeping Julie good-bye and drove my rental car onto Hunter Army Airfield with butterflies in my stomach. The smell of brackish water filled the air. A canopy of Spanish moss hung on the giant oak trees as if it were holding the atmosphere in place.

I reported to the battalion headquarters wearing a starched uniform, mirror-shine boots, and the black beret. The headquarters' tiny offices looked as if they'd been laid under siege by a war museum—with weapon-filled trophy cases, captured enemy flags, and combat photos encircling the workings of one of the most lethal military organizations ever assembled. Black-and-white photos of past commanders presided over the entrance, as if to approve every Ranger that darkened the halls.

The battalion adjutant greeted me and drove me not to the company area but to the airfield, where my new platoon was training. Five minutes later, a staff sergeant whipped the beret off my head and crumpled it into my pocket. At the base of a thirty-foot tower, he scrambled to outfit me in body armor, a Kevlar helmet, goggles, and gloves. His helmet's headband read *Canon*.

"Where you coming from, sir?" he said.

"Germany." I felt like a mannequin as he dressed me.

"We've been without a platoon leader for a couple of months," he said. "Hold this, sir. Have you fast-roped before?"

"Yeah, last week, in the course."

"Just remember to rotate away from the tower and keep the rope pushed away from your body. Any questions, sir? Top of the tower."

I rushed up the stairs. The wooden platform seemed like an oversize tree stand high in the pines. I leaned over the edge, grasped the three-inch rope with hands and feet, and slid down fireman-style. I hit the ground like a sock full of marbles. I strained to my feet as the Rangers tried to hide their amusement. So much for the beret being my first impression.

"All right, that's everyone. Let's get to the birds."

Thirty minutes later, I zipped down ropes under hovering helicopters, only this time when I fell on the ground, I had another Ranger barreling down the rope on top of me. I became party to at least three multiple-Ranger pileups at the bottom of the rope, each time silently pleading with fate that I not eat a twenty-eight-pound M240 machine gun falling with a 250-pound combat-equipped Ranger attached. After I roped from all types of helicopters on the airfield, I moved to the platoon and sat next to Sergeant Canon.

"How was it, sir?" he asked.

I grimaced at him and rubbed my elbow.

"Anybody who tells you fast-roping is cool hasn't fast-roped much," he said.

I chuckled to myself. I had thought fast-roping was cool just a few hours earlier.

During the next several days, I spent most of my time participating in intense mission-planning sessions that mirrored real-world scenarios—scenarios like rescuing medical students or capturing a ruthless dictator. We were locked in planning at Saber Hall, on the remote end of Hunter Army Airfield, where Rangers had planned and outloaded on MC-130 Combat Talon aircraft en route to parachute assaults on Panama and Grenada during the 1980s.

I was smoked. I had thought several times during the week that I'd made a mistake in joining the Rangers. The hundreds of new faces and names, four hours of sleep in the last three days, the new types of equipment and radios, the soldiers in my platoon who could run two miles in less than ten minutes, the airfield seizures and air assault operations. My head was hurting from thinking so hard. I was intimidated by briefing the battalion's officers gathered around a terrain model, officers who looked too young to carry so much rank, wearing the subdued Ranger combat patches on their right sleeves and gold stars on their jump wings indicating they'd parachuted in combat. And I was overwhelmed.

I was once again following the Army's simple design: placing me in a position for which I was ill prepared. This required me to teach myself—to survive, then succeed, then excel. Just when I reached that final level of performance, I was off to a new place and a new job. When the Rangers seemed to be too much to handle, I would take a moment to remind myself of Psalm 75. *God puts down one, and exalts another.* I wondered, however, how long the Scripture would carry me without some tangible reinforcement from its source.

22

Friends, acquaintances, even family often think warriors are obsessed or compulsive, but that isn't true. Obsessive and compulsive behavior are, by definition, traits of individuals unable to control themselves. The warrior is just the opposite; he is the model of control. The warrior doesn't seek pain, fear, fatigue, and the other unpleasant byproducts of constant training because he likes them. But he knows they are obstacles between him and his objectives. His goal is to overcome them, and he knows that to defeat an enemy, he must attack. It isn't that the warrior is driven. He is the driver.
:: FORREST MORGAN, *Living the Martial Way*

NOVEMBER 2000
FORT STEWART, GEORGIA

Staying awake in the back of a five-ton troop truck was never easy, but the fatiguing machinations of the past few days had made it nearly impossible. More than twenty Rangers droned and slept in the open bed of the truck that was designed to hold twelve comfortably—but that boasted the maximum troop capacity of "one more."

Our truck whined through the red dust cloud created by the convoy's weaving through the tank trails of Fort Stewart, Georgia. The sleeping Rangers' heads bowed downward as if in prayer and bobbled with every bump in the trail. Their hands seemed awake and on guard, clutching their weapons in expert ways. They had the look of men who lived in their gear; it was just another layer of skin. One Ranger near me did not sleep. I saw him studying me.

"Are you new here?" he asked.

I noticed his captain's bars. "Yes, sir."

"Well, welcome to Savannah," he said. "Can I ask you something? Do you know Jesus?"

It was an odd question, given the flavor of conversation I'd overheard since I arrived. I then saw that he was a chaplain. I nodded.

"You do? Well, praise God. I'm about to do a devotional at our next stop. They told me this test-fire range would be the only chance I'd have for a field service. You're welcome to come."

"I'll come if I can," I said. "I could use a little boost."

"My name is Randy. Kirby. I'm the battalion's chaplain."

He had long features, a slender face, and a natural expression that hinted of a smile. I trusted him immediately.

"You single?" he asked.

"No, I'm married," I said, rolling my wrist to reveal my watchband looped through my wedding band. A story I'd heard from Sergeant Owens about an Irish bloke who'd lost a finger had stuck with me.

"I'm single," Randy said. "But I'm working on that, Lord willing. Your wife's name?"

"Julie."

"Julie," he said. "Julie doing all right?"

"Yes, sir; she's fine," I said. "I've just been gone a lot."

"This place is pretty fast paced. It'll slow down, though. You came at a peak time."

I didn't reveal to him that Julie and I had seen each other an average of ten minutes a day for the last three weeks. If I came home at all, I'd creep into our apartment after midnight and slide in next to her on a borrowed air mattress on the living-room floor. She spent her days alone or substitute teaching. We had been in a one-bedroom apartment, but Julie decided to move our few bags into a two-bedroom apartment before our shipment of belongings arrived from Germany. And even when it did, our entire collection of furniture consisted of a thirty-two-inch TV, Julie's childhood daybed, and a cedar chest my parents had given us as a wedding gift. Because the chaplain was single, I wasn't sure he could relate to my situation.

The truck eased to a stop at a twenty-five-meter "flat" range, where ten other trucks had snaked into a cramped turnaround surrounded by tall dirt berms. The air crackled and snapped with the acoustics of a hundred shooters, sounding like a giant bag of popcorn. The Rangers in the truck came to life at the sounds of rifles and the absence of motion. We had an hour to test fire our weapons and confirm that our gunsights were zeroed in. After that, we would face our test.

I rehearsed the upcoming mission plan in my head. This would be my first live-fire exercise in more than a year. Within the hour, we would be firing real bullets just in front of assaulting Rangers, which would be tricky in the dense forest. Our 170-man company planned to insert on Blackhawks and Chinooks to seize an "enemy outpost" in the tall Georgia pines. We would also have our battalion's mortars firing on the target objective and attack helicopters circling overhead with rockets and heavy machine guns.

After confirming our zeroes, reviewing the plan with the squad leaders, and attending the devotional with Chaplain Kirby, we lined up on the sides of the road and marched to the helicopter pick-up zone. The helicopters, MH-47 Chinooks and MH-60 Blackhawks, came in low over the trees to pick us up, their noses filled with protruding wartlike avionics and radars, flaunting slender twenty-foot-long refueling probes that made the helicopters appear as if they were looking for a joust. These were some of the same pilots who had flown us two nights ago, some of the same pilots who had sent us down fast ropes several days ago, some of the same pilots who had flown Rangers in Somalia. Some had been shot down there. Some had died there.

I jogged in a line of Rangers to the closest Chinook, crouched low, goggles on, the debris stinging my face, my balance thrown forward and back by gusts of rotor wash. We crammed more than fifty Rangers inside the tube of metal and lifted off. Ten minutes later, the Chinook settled down in an open field right on time—plus or minus thirty seconds of H-Hour, the target-hitting standard for the Night Stalkers, the 160th Special Operations Aviation Regiment.

The platoon poured from the helicopter and moved straight into the woods, morphing its shape and pace without commands. The fifty-man unit seemed to have one mind, as if it had no use for external direction. Leading such a group would appear to be easy, but the platoon's proficiency level only elevated my responsibilities to a higher plane. The basics of movement and communication required no attention, and beyond that—I had trouble even imagining what else the job would require of me.

"Sir, close air support is two minutes out," my radio operator said.

Checking my watch, I realized that we needed to hurry, or our machine guns would not be in place to suppress the objective by the time the close air support (CAS) got there. My platoon's only task for the mission was to align parallel to the objective and provide overwhelming gunfire to support the company's perpendicular assault of the compound. Side by side, every man would suppress the bunkers, buildings, trenches, and tents—and shift their fires to the right, just ahead of advancing Rangers. The purpose of gaining superiority of firepower over the objective was to allow assaulting troops to advance unhindered by the enemy. This was the essence of my platoon's support-by-fire position.

We were one hundred meters from our position, hurdling fallen pines and underbrush, when I heard the Little Birds. The two-man black miniature attack helicopters sounded like a swarm of weed eaters moving closer. As we began to fan out to our support-by-fire position in a ditch, I heard the air ripping above me, then felt the ground thump beneath my feet. The lead Little Bird had fired rockets into the first bunker. I looked up to see the trail helo bumping up as if on the crest of a roller-coaster cliff-hanger; then it turned its nose downward and ripped off two more rockets to our front. The Little Birds looked like flying tadpoles spitting trails of smoke and fire.

The platoon began hitting the objective with loads of firepower as the Little Birds circled behind us for another run at the target. White smoke billowed in the woods near the objective, then purple and green smoke. Another platoon was preparing its assault by the standard practice of obscuring its position with smoke. Soon we would need to shift our fires to allow the other platoon to move across the objective.

I heard the sound of a subway train approaching as mortar rounds began suppressing the objective. The ground erupted with the incoming mortars, sending a splash of dirt in the air. The mortar platoon was firing from somewhere to our right-rear, but I wasn't sure exactly where. We had achieved the full synchronization of direct and indirect ordnance on the objective.

I felt a sharp sting on my neck, just under my collar, burning. Reaching inside my collar, I pulled out a brass shell casing as hundreds more rained down around me. The Little Birds were making another run on the target, firing their M134 Gatling guns, known as "miniguns," and showering us with spent 7.62-mm casings.

Two Ranger captains stood behind me and laughed. They were there to evaluate my performance but instead seemed entertained by my inexperience. One of them approached me and yelled over the roaring miniguns, which sounded more like supercharged alarm-clock buzzers than high-capacity weapons.

"Where's your sister platoon?" he asked. "Have they asked you to shift fires?"

"No, sir! Not yet!"

"What's your machine guns' rate of fire? Rapid or sustained?"

"I'm not sure, sir."

"Haven't you planned it out? Come on, this is graduate-level stuff here. You gotta think things through. Get out your stubby pencil and get your head into this."

The captain had me worried that I would run out of ammo. I moved to my machine-gun teams and ordered them to slow their rates of fire. I moved along the line of Rangers, monitoring their directions of fire, their rates, their ammo levels. In my previous training, I had learned to take charge, to be up front, in the action.

I felt a short tug on the back of my equipment, followed by a powerful yank. I was pulled rearward, nearly falling down, backpedaling as fast as I could to stay on my feet. Now fifteen yards behind the platoon, I turned to see the placid, camouflaged face of my most senior squad leader.

"Stay here," he said. He grabbed the hand mic from the radio dangling uselessly across my chest and held it to my face. "And use this."

He walked back to his squad's position and knelt behind his Rangers.

An amazing transformation of perspective took place. I could see the whole platoon in front of me. I could see the paths of attack helicopters as they approached. I could see the entire objective. For the first time since the firing began, I could hear my radio.

"Alpha One-Six, this is Alpha Six." It was my commander, calling me on the radio.

"Six, this is One-Six," I replied. I wondered how long he had been trying to reach me.

"Roger, shift your fires to phase line *coconut*. I say again, shift to coconut."

"Roger," I said.

I radioed the command to my squad leaders, also well positioned behind their men where they could see, hear, and talk. As the remainder of the assault played out in front of me, I saw how easy it was to synchronize the platoon when I removed myself from the action. Images from my previous training flashed in my mind as contradictions to what I was experiencing. All that I had learned at West Point, at Benning, in Germany—even in Kosovo—was different from this. Up to that point, I had always moved with the lead squad, always out front, always embodying the Infantry's motto, "Follow me!" Now I saw that my position as a platoon leader wasn't up front, but where I could best control the fight—which could be a different place for every mission.

The pace of the attack increased with two platoons assaulting on the objective. I heard another volley of mortar rounds incoming as we again shifted fire to the right, then the air tearing behind me again like the Little Birds were back for more runs. The Little Birds were not in the air. The ripping sound I heard was mortar rounds detonating in the trees above us, spraying shrapnel into the platoon. As the mock battle raged on, the next sounds were more chilling than any explosion.

"Medic!"

They were real cries for help. I turned over my shoulder to see if the captains behind me were going to halt the exercise. They leaned over to listen to their radio handsets, and then one of them pointed intently for me to get back to the business of supporting my company's assault.

Even in the midst of real casualties, the fight must go on.

23

By force of will and against his inner disposition, he created himself in the image to which he aspired.
:: MARTIN BLUMENSON, *The Patton Papers*

DECEMBER 2000
SAVANNAH, GEORGIA

My initial counseling session with my Ranger battalion commander began with a five-mile run at dawn. His name was Tony Thomas, and he was the epitome, even as an officer, of what every young Ranger aspired to be. He had woven his way in and out of Special Operations units, from the Rangers to supersecret units that people only whispered about, units into which we all wished to one day disappear.

Colonel Thomas hadn't served in a conventional army unit since he was a lieutenant. He had parachuted into the fights in Grenada and Panama as a Ranger platoon leader and Ranger company commander respectively, sporting the rare two combat stars known as "headlights" on his airborne wings. He was a no-frills operator, a former track star with strawberry-blond hair, piercing eyes, complex thoughts, and plain words. He seemed to have no temper, just varying levels of intensity. I wondered how officers of such caliber evolved. Where did leaders like him begin? After the workout and some simple guidance in his office, he told me to read two books: *Gates of Fire* and *Spec Ops*. As I left his office, I saw the miniature battalion flag of 2-2 Infantry framed on his wall—the same unit I had left in Germany. Colonel Thomas had served as a lieutenant in the same battalion I had, but nearly twenty years earlier.

I arrived to the company area, where Rangers finished their morning physical training, or "PT." There were squads climbing thick ropes high in the trees, returning from long runs wearing gas masks, or negotiating the red and black obstacle course across the street, while wearing body armor. Physical fitness built the foundation for everything we did and planned to do. I remembered an instructor of mine who had aptly described the culture of the Rangers with two numbers and one letter: 23M.

"That's all you gotta know," he had said. "Twenty-three mike. Those Rangers are an average of twenty-three years old, and they're all male. All they judge you on is how hard you are and whether you can hang in PT. They don't care how smart you are or how savvy you are—remember, twenty-three mike." After my run with Colonel Thomas, I realized why the "23M" Rangers had such respect for him.

I walked into the first-floor barracks hallway, which was painted camouflage. A faded and torn Panamanian flag hung in a homemade frame on the wall across from a bulletin board displaying several rows of nametags—green canvas strips embroidered with black names—remembering those who had left the platoon.

The first door on the left was my squad leaders' command post

(CP). It was a converted barracks room crammed with desks and duffel bags. The room served as a meeting place, equipment locker, lunchroom, and TV newsroom for the platoon's leadership. Sergeant Canon was there. "Hey, what's up, sir," he said. "You give yourself that haircut?"

"Yeah," I said. "Don't we all?"

"Some better than others, sir," he said. "Well, you can try again next week."

Sergeant Canon organized his squad's counseling forms in folders atop his desk, which had a neat display of rosters, weapons diagrams, and news clippings under a Plexiglas sheet. In the center of it all, he had a color picture of a bearded man in a turban. The words "Public Enemy #1" titled the photo, and sniper's crosshairs centered on the man's forehead.

"Who's that?" I asked.

"It's UBL—Usama bin Laden. He's the punk-ass terrorist who tried to bomb the World Trade Center."

"Oh," I said.

"Among other things," he said. "So. How'd it go with the colonel? Did he smoke you?"

"No, he took it easy on me."

"Good," Canon said. "That would've been a bad impression." He handed me a military-gear magazine, folded in half and dog-eared.

"Hey, sir, check out these boots," he said. "Those in the middle, the Wellcos. They've got running-shoe soles made from Goodyear rubber. I'm gonna give them a shot. Want me to order you a pair?"

"I'll wait and see how you like them."

"Worthless Army-issue boots," he said. "Rangers humping thirty miles on thirty-year-old technology. It's about time we put some thought into the fighting man's footgear."

A young man in civilian clothes knocked on the door.

"Come in," Canon said. The young man limped into the room.

"Oh, hey, Sar'nt, I'm just looking for Sar'nt Michaud."

"He's still at PT. What do you need?"

"He told me to check in with him before I went to class."

"I'll tell him," Canon said. "Sir, this is Specialist Crose. He's laid up sorry. Just had a hernia operation."

"Nice to meet you," I said.

Crose nodded. "Yes, sir."

"Crose is good s—," Canon said. "He just needs to heal up."

"Roger, Sar'nt," Crose said. "'Rangers lead the way,' sir."

"Rangers lead the way," I replied.

Crose left the room, and Canon and I parted ways. I walked to my own office to check e-mail and found Pete Marques there. He and I had been classmates at West Point and were now in the same Ranger company.

"Dude, what are you doing for the Army/Navy game?" he asked.

"Nothing yet, man," I said. "Julie's got teachers' in-service or something."

"Let's do it. We'll get pizza or something," he said. "I'll fly, you buy."

"You can come to my house, and we can sit on the floor to watch it," I said. "I've got no furniture."

"Fine by me, dude," Pete said. "You doing breakfast?"

"Might as well."

Pete and I threw on civilian sweatshirts and left the office. Just outside the office door in a dark corner of the company's orderly room, I noticed a yellowed sheet of paper framed on the wall. It was the manifest, or roster, of the company's parachute jump on October 25, 1983. The operation was listed as "Urgent Fury"—the invasion of Grenada—and the company commander was listed first on the manifest: CPT Abizaid, John P.

Wow. What a legacy.

24

Recognizing that I volunteered as a Ranger, fully knowing the hazards of my chosen profession, I will always endeavor to uphold the prestige, honor, and high "esprit de corps" of my Ranger Regiment.

:: RANGER CREED, First Stanza

JULY 2001
FORT BENNING, GEORGIA

I was ready to jump into fresh air.

I'd been in a parachute harness for four hours, the last two crammed in a C-130 Hercules aircraft with sixty-three other Rangers. The airplane's metallic petroleum odor could not mask the subtle mix of musty canvas, turboprop exhaust, and farts—all of which were familiar but far from pleasant.

We were minutes from parachuting onto Fryar Drop Zone at Fort Benning. Fryar was a vast, open, sandy area near the banks of the Chattahoochee River that had been used as an airborne drop zone for decades and was the primary drop zone for the U.S. Army's Airborne School.

Here we were jumping along with the other two Ranger battalions, to begin a weeklong "Ranger Rendezvous" that took place every two years. During the rendezvous, we'd see old friends, pummel each other in intramural grudge matches, and hold conferences to share lessons learned and to plan for the future. The jam-packed week would culminate with the Ranger Regiment's commander relinquishing command to a new colonel—who would follow in the lineage of men like Buck Kernan, David Grange, and Wayne Downing, each of whom had commanded the Ranger Regiment and were living legends in United States' Special Operations history.

This jump was less complicated than our usual airborne assaults.

We normally sat on the aircraft's metal floor, under and around Land Rovers, Little Birds, Humvees, and dirt bikes loaded inside the aircraft. We normally jumped at night, carrying almost one hundred pounds of equipment. None of those aspects was present here. What made today's jump complicated was the two thousand Rangers that would soon blanket the airspace, falling from planes en masse, as dense as the jumpmasters and pilots could drop us.

Following a series of time warnings and jump commands, I stood in line with my Rangers, faced the rear of the aircraft, hooked my static line to a metal cable above me, and held my left arm high in an L shape. The C-130 slowed and lowered to jump altitude. I always loved jumping, but I hated this part of it—the waiting, the anxiety, the nausea.

Staff Sergeant Ray DePouli stood in front of me. I had a cross-eyed, close-up view of the back of his neck and helmet. He had been with us for a couple of months, coming over from Bravo Company on an administrative reassignment. This was his last chance in the battalion. He had replaced Sergeant Canon as the 1st Squad Leader, and Canon moved to become the Weapons Squad Leader, the most senior squad leader in the platoon. DePouli had performed well in 1st Platoon so far, and as long as he kept everything in order, he would stay in the battalion.

"Thirty seconds!" The jumpmasters held up a thumb and index finger with only an inch in between.

"THIR-TY SECONDS!"

I felt a burning between my heart and stomach; any hint of nausea I had before was wiped away by excitement.

"Stand by!"

The red light behind the door turned off as the green light switched on.

"Go!"

I waddled in line with my left arm held high and in front—faster, now stop, walk steady, now faster. Like a fuse burning toward me, the line of Rangers disappeared at the door. I inched closer to detonation. Three, two, one, me.

I pushed my static line into the jumpmaster's hand, rotated to the door, and vaulted into the turboprop slipstream. Body in an L shape, chin tucked, hands on my reserve chute. I counted to four and then—*jolt*—the opening shock of my parachute. The chute felt good, holding me up in every spot it had just been pulling me down. Full canopy. The sound of wind at 1,200 feet.

A minute later, the patchwork fields and forests rushed toward me at an alarming speed. It always surprised me just how fast I fell in a parachute. I reached up to my right set of risers, pulled those thick canvas bands to my sternum, and braced for impact. *Feet-calf-thigh-butt-lat*, I reminded myself, rolling over on my shoulder in a side somersault. The plowed sand at Fryar made for a nice landing, unlike the tarmac we normally jumped onto while training to seize airfields. As with fast-roping, anybody who says seizing an airfield is cool hasn't done it much.

I packed my chute and trotted to our rally point, where a handful of Rangers had gathered just inside the wood line. Consolidation should have been easy, given that it was a daytime jump with no equipment and no tactical objectives. However, we had one problem: one of my Rangers was injured on the drop zone.

"Sir, I just saw Big A on the DZ; he's pretty messed up."

"Anderson? How's that?" I asked.

"It's his leg. He thinks it's broken," he said. "Medic's on his way."

"Of all the jumps," I said.

At thirty, Marc Anderson was bigger and older than everyone else in the platoon. He had been behind a machine gun since he joined the unit. Before becoming a Ranger, he was a shot put–throwing All-American at Florida State University, and then a junior high math teacher. Many Rangers saw Anderson as a father figure, omnipresent and all-knowing. His mental ability was rivaled only by his physical stature. He was huge and had earned himself the simple nickname of "Big A." In the end, his leg wasn't broken. It was deeply bruised when he landed on his canteen. He was still a costly loss for the battalion, as he was to have been the anchor for its tug-of-war team at the end of the week.

The platoon spent the next day in a hangar-turned-sports complex, where Rangers faced off in jiujitsu matches, boxing bouts, and other warriorcentric athletic events. Afterward, we moved as a platoon to dinner in the next hangar. There we were joined by old Rangers—some former, some current, but all seasoned in places like Vietnam, Somalia, Grenada, and Panama. They were our family, even though we hadn't met any of them before. We listened to their war stories and told some of our own about what it was like to be a Ranger in 1st Platoon, Alpha Company, 1st Battalion.

We remembered our summer deployment to Fort Bragg, where the platoon smoked the trench live-fire exercise, despite several guys nearly falling out due to the heat. We sang karaoke together on the weekends there, where we'd always end with our platoon's song—"Sweet Caroline."

Some Rangers in the platoon made fun of Big A's crutches and joked that because he was now injured, it would be the only time they wouldn't need at least two full squads of Rangers to make him "tap out" in a wrestling match. Big A appreciated the compliment.

One of the Rangers called out Jonas Polson, the strapping specialist who had challenged me to a combatives match on the range and had me completely balled up, except that I saw his foot dangling in front of my face and nearly twisted it off his leg to make him tap out. Blind luck, but it had prevented the men from challenging me again.

I remembered attending a wedding in Savannah where one of my squad leaders got married on his Harley. His bride was on her Harley too. Canon had laughed at the memory of the time my dad visited us on the firing range in Savannah and pretended he was the Land Rover salesman so we wouldn't get in trouble when he rode along on live fires. My dad and I had a Humvee all to ourselves. I drove him close behind the assaulting Rangers, explaining to him the finer intricacies of massing and synchronizing fires. It was the first time he'd seen me operating in my job.

The guys ribbed Specialist Anthony Miceli, who was a total klutz. They couldn't believe he was still alive after his dive from a speeding boat. He had ruptured his spleen and nearly died in the hospital a few days later. But he had made a full recovery, after which the platoon adopted the maxim "Nobody can kill Miceli but Miceli."

After dinner, most of the platoon headed to Victory Drive outside Fort Benning in an attempt to create more memories. Julie and I went to grab ice cream with the other lieutenants and their wives. We were finally feeling comfortable being in the Rangers. I had proven myself as a platoon leader, we were settling in as a couple, and we had found a church in Savannah that we really loved. And to put a cherry on top of it all, in three months, Julie and I were due to have a baby boy.

God was good.

25

We often give our enemies the means for our own destruction. :: AESOP

SEPTEMBER 11, 2001
SAVANNAH, GEORGIA

The traffic on Abercorn Street was not cooperating. I had departed our bare apartment a few hours later than usual and had enjoyed the extra time with Julie, but I'd not taken rush hour into account.

My commander, Joe Ryan, told the company to report late in order to compensate for the next few nights we'd spend training in the woods. I rolled through the gate of Hunter Army Airfield at a quarter of nine when I heard the radio reports of an airplane crashing into the World Trade Center in New York.

I felt sad about yet another airline tragedy, and I said a quick prayer for the families of those aboard the plane and any others who may have been hurt. As I reached the company area, Rangers operated on schedule, drawing weapons from the arms room, preparing our dull black Land Rovers for movement, and loading up targetry—all according to routine. The squad leaders, however, were noticeably absent.

I found them all in the squad leaders' CP. Arin Canon, the weapons squad leader and senior staff sergeant, was adjusting the cable connection on the back of the garage-sale television while the other squad leaders peered at a smoldering tower in New York.

I greeted them and sat on a footlocker to get an update on the platoon, as well as the events unfolding on the screen. Within seconds, we watched another airliner pierce the second tower of the World Trade Center. I was aghast.

Before I even took a breath, Canon turned from the TV.

"Sir, that was no accident," he said. "No way."

"Maybe. But who would do that?"

"Who? That's who," Canon said. He pointed to the crosshaired Usama bin Laden picture on his desk.

"What are we gonna do, sir?" Sergeant Lopez asked. "Should we tell the boys to stand by?"

I considered the question.

"Let me go ask the CO," I said.

I went to the commander's office. He was bending over his equipment, gathering his body armor, M4 rifle, and rucksack.

"Should I have the guys stand by, sir?" I asked. "You think maybe we should watch this thing for a while?"

Major Ryan stood and looked at me with a smile.

"No, we're going to the shoot house," he said. "Load up. We're gonna train."

We spent the next two days clearing rooms, blowing doors off hinges, and shooting at moving targets inside the shoot house. We got word-of-mouth updates on the developments in New York from the supply sergeant who brought us hot chow at breakfast and dinner. There were rumors of war.

Our battalion was a week away from rotating onto the highest alert cycle in the Ranger Regiment, as 3rd Ranger Battalion was rotating off. I wondered if in the next few weeks, my beeper would go off in the middle of the night and I'd be on a plane to combat within eighteen hours of kissing Julie good-bye.

26

Once we have a war there is only one thing to do. It must be won. For defeat brings worse things than any that can ever happen in war. :: ERNEST HEMINGWAY

OCTOBER 2001
SAVANNAH, GEORGIA

I usually got a daily dose of Sergeant Canon dropping by to chat just before PT formation. At a few minutes after six, he came into my office, shut the door behind him, and stood in the middle of the room. This time he appeared ready to make an official announcement of some kind, though he looked clownish in his skimpy, sheer black running shorts known as "Ranger panties."

"Listen to this, sir," he said. "This is bull—. My buddy from 3rd Battalion calls me up last night. I haven't heard from him since Rendezvous. He says to me, 'Hey dude, check it out. Last night I was disconnecting the battery cables on my truck.' Then he stops and says to me, 'Then I cleaned out my fridge so stuff wouldn't spoil.' He waits for some sort of response. I'm like, 'Yeah, man, what's the point?' and he says, 'So I was cleaning out my fridge, and I spilled mustard on my jump wings.'"

He was referring to the combat star on the Airborne wings, awarded for making a parachute assault in combat. I didn't make the connection.

"Yeah," I said. "I don't get it, Sergeant Canon."

"They're jumping into combat—soon—like real soon."

"Are you sure?"

"Positive, sir."

It didn't make sense to any of us. According to our rotation in the Regiment, we thought we had been the ones at the highest alert state and therefore most ready to deploy. A talk with my CO confirmed it: we were staying home. Some of 3rd Battalion had already departed for war.

Less than a week later, I sat with Julie in our apartment, watching the twenty-four-hour news channels loop grainy green images of American soldiers—Rangers from 3rd Battalion—pour from the belly of aircraft and float to the desert floor in Afghanistan like a line of dandelions adrift. They were going after bin Laden or Omar or somebody. They were awesome. It could have been me. It should have been me.

With no war to fight that weekend, I decided to attend a men's retreat with the church. It was important to me to get to know the men whom I'd seen every few weeks when I made it to church services. The retreat was exactly that—no televisions, no cell-phone service—just pancake breakfasts, Bibles, and bunk beds. We had a large group of more than fifty. The men accepted me as their own, something I had missed during my time in Germany and deployment to Kosovo. My weekend with the guys was cut short, though. One of the men pulled me out of a roundtable discussion just as I was getting involved.

"Nate, I just got a message on the landline from my wife," he said. "I think you'd better get home."

My heart pumped hard a couple of times. All I could think about was a car wreck.

"Nothing bad," he said. "Your wife thinks she might be in labor."

I rushed home and found Julie squatting in the same stretching positions she used daily. I was excited to see this day and determined to help Julie finish the early stages of labor; I took her outside and paced her laps around our apartment building, recording her contractions with the same stubby pencil and notebook I used for ammo calculations during live fires. Only after we had returned to our apartment did I notice the coincidence and irony of my note taking. So tightly entwined were my personal and professional lives that I used the same pencil and paper both to pace out the birth pangs of imminent life—and to divvy up ammunition to kill.

Julie and I were certain the baby was coming soon. We made two trips to the Army hospital on Fort Stewart, and after a full night of pain, Julie gave birth to Caleb, a skinny baby boy who looked more like an old man than an infant. The nurses cleaned him up and left us alone with him.

After the initial bewilderment of holding our own child, Julie and I realized that we had just ushered our firstborn into a world of fear and war, just a month after the worst terrorist act in history. The instinctive cries of an infant and the joyful tears of us as parents were bittersweet against the backdrop of 9/11 and the war that had just begun. I felt overjoyed to hold him, but part of me wished I could put him back in his mother's protective womb. Why did I bring such a precious soul into a world as evil as this? Julie rested, and all I could do was hold Caleb tight in my arms, snuggle into the recliner, and drift to sleep with my son.

Just before I faded away, I thought again of the green images of parachuting Rangers, how I had been so jealous that those black blobs in the murky picture hadn't been me. Here with my son, I thanked God that it wasn't me, that I wasn't in some hostile place on the other side of the world. My whole world was at Fort Stewart, Georgia, sleeping in that room with me.

27

Julie and I decided to forego Christmas gifts in order to focus on spending time together, as my deployment to war was only two days away. We were both quiet and detached—already mourning the lost time together and contemplating the danger involved in such a place as Afghanistan.

My mind was half deployed. I couldn't stop checking things in my head. *Have I packed everything? Are my Rangers ready? Am I ready? Is Julie ready? What if I don't come back?*

Despite our decision to omit gifts this year, I started feeling guilty about having no gifts for Julie. I ran to Wal-Mart on Christmas Eve to buy her a few things. I bought Caleb a few books and baby toys, but at two months old, he had more use for a pack of diapers. Still, as a daddy, I wanted to give him something.

When I checked my packing list one last time, I noticed my two pairs of Army-issue cold-weather boots occupied more space than they were worth. I thought of my aching feet in Kosovo, how my feet were never warm or dry. I decided to buy some new boots to wear in Afghanistan. *As a professional soldier I deserve world-class equipment. I'm an infantryman, after all. I'm a Ranger.*

I jumped on the Internet, searched for the Danner boots site, and put a rush order on a pair of new winter boots—the top of the line. I received the boots just in time. They were a little snug, but very light and flexible. I could leave behind my two pairs of Army-issue boots. I dumped them, feeling the switch as a good symbol of my progress in the Army. I had finally matured beyond the system, risen above the crowd. I was experienced as a platoon leader; I had been deployed before; I had trained with these world-class Rangers for more than a year. We were sharp, and we were ready.

Now in my duffel bags was everything I would need for the next several months. Yet, in accepting the life of a soldier, I would also leave everything behind: in that apartment was everything I would need for the rest of my life. I didn't want to leave Julie again. I didn't want to leave my new son.

I woke up earlier than normal on the day I left for war. Somehow I awoke one minute before my alarm was set to buzz, an uncanny knack I had shown at West Point and Ranger School when I needed to wake up for something important. I got dressed and leaned over to hug Julie in bed for a minute or two. I left the bedroom and crept through our apartment, careful to walk around our new dinner table. I went to the pantry and left Julie's note there. Down the short hallway, past the blue Indiglo night-light in the wall socket next to Caleb's door. I crept inside to his crib. He shifted at my presence, took in a deep breath, and let his breaths go in short segments. He was only two months old.

I knelt on the floor by his crib and slipped my hand through the wooden rail onto his tiny hand. A gentle touch, careful not to wake him.

God, you are amazing. Thank you, thank you for such a precious piece of you. God, keep them safe. Let me see his face again, let me hear him talk, let me see him run. He's in your hands.

I reached into my pocket and pulled out a 1st Ranger Battalion cloth patch in the shape of a scroll, the same one I wore on my shoulder. I also pulled out a set of polished silver captain's bars. I laid the items next to him in the crib, along with my note for him.

25 Dec 01

Caleb,
I'm sure you can't read this today, so you'll have to
believe your mom when she reads it to you. I'm sure
she'll do it justice. I just wanted to tell my little man how
much I love him (that's you). You've changed my life
in a much different way, but with the same magnitude
your mom changed it 3 ½ years ago. I can see it in your
eyes—I understand you. You are as real a person as
you'll ever be right now; don't think we don't know it.
Together, y'all are my best friends.
   You've always existed in our hearts, and you always
will be—forever. Your mom and me had this song we
liked; well, this phrase really. It's "'Til Eternity." We've
always meant that to each other and we always will—and
it applies to you as much as it does us. We'll always be
together, forever, so don't you ever worry about a thing.
Just remember, if you don't see me around, even if I step
out of the room for a minute, it's your job to keep your
mommy laughing. So throw a smile in there—she'll love
it. Never forget that wherever we are, when we lay down
to sleep, it's me and your mom, with you tucked right in
the middle. I love you, son.

Daddy

Now awake, Julie met me in the living room. We held hands, walk-ing to the door. It would be the last time I saw her, at least in the flesh, until . . . I didn't know when. We stepped outside the door, and I kissed Julie good-bye. She wouldn't let go of my neck.

"Don't go," she said. "Don't go." She began to cry.

I walked down the flight of stairs from our apartment, apartment 806, to my car just below. I slid behind the steering wheel, started the car, and rolled down the window. I looked up to the balcony above, where Julie stood, and waved good-bye.

★ ★

WHOM SHALL I FEAR?

★ ★

28

DECEMBER 31, 2001
MASIRAH ISLAND, OMAN

The tiny desert island of Masirah, fifteen miles off the eastern coast of Oman, looks like an hourglass from the air. Visiting the sandy, barren island made me feel like I was actually inside the hourglass, as the landscape and structures seem drained of every color but pale tan. I stood with my platoon on Masirah's blustery and desolate airstrip and waited to board an MC-130 bound for Afghanistan. Two years ago that day I had patrolled at the turn of the millennium under splashes of colorful fireworks and tracer fire across the Kosovar sky. This time I was deploying not for peace but for war.

The staging base on Masirah Island held a special historical significance for Rangers. In 1979 it was the launching point for a rescue mission bound for Tehran, where U.S. commandos planned to rescue fifty-three Americans held hostage by Muslim student revolutionaries at the U.S. Embassy. Twenty-two years prior, MC-130 Hercules transport aircraft had departed this runway just before dusk en route to an aborted and tragic mission. Eight U.S. servicemen died in a helicopter collision with a parked MC-130 on a makeshift airstrip named Desert One. Here as a twenty-five-year-old Ranger platoon leader, I counted my fifty-five men aboard an MC-130 on the same airstrip, with the sun slipping off the horizon.

Three and a half hours after leaving Masirah's scorching lunar landscape, we walked off the MC-130 at a former Soviet air base in Bagram, Afghanistan, an air base littered with jet aircraft and helicopter hulks and surrounded by snowcapped peaks. The valley was a chilling reminder of the war that was lost here, where the mujahideen had defeated a superpower. Yet, looking up to the surrounding mountains again stirred something deep inside me. I had operated with the Soviets in Kosovo. We were much better. Now this valley of death had become a Spartan terrorist-hunting outpost bristling with U.S. Infantry units. At the far end of the runway, a small, nondescript group of tents and bullet-pocked buildings housed the most lethal unit in Afghanistan: Task Force 11.

Members of 3rd Ranger Battalion led us to our compound. The unit we were replacing was the same unit that had parachuted into southern Afghanistan the weekend that Caleb was born. With our arrival, 3rd Battalion was returning home after two months in the desert. I entered the dilapidated headquarters building that served as our joint operations center (JOC).

The building stood as a symbol of the years of war that had ravaged the region of tribal areas known collectively throughout the world as Afghanistan. Inside, huge maps and clear plastic sheets hung over plaster walls. A crust of dried mud covered cheap Persian-style rugs that insulated the cracked and cold concrete floor. Clean handprints on gray metal folding chairs betrayed the heavy film of dust that coated everything in the room. Wires and cables snaked through boarded windows, supplying data and power to several big-screen TVs, stacks of green radios, and a one-hundred-cup coffeepot.

The first person I saw was Colonel Thomas, my battalion commander. He was engaged in an intense exchange with some bearded men in civilian clothes. I assumed they were special operators.

"Nate, come in and listen to this," he said. "You got your stuff off-loaded?"

"Not yet, sir; they're waiting on the pallet to get to the compound."

"Tell your platoon to get what they need," he said. "You may be flying soon. We have guys under fire."

Twenty minutes later, Colonel Thomas ordered us to stand down. A separate, more ready group of operators had met the requirement. That missed opportunity gained our attention. We were in Afghanistan to be a Quick Reaction Force. As part of Task Force 11, we had the mission to kill or capture the "who's who" of al-Qaeda and Taliban leadership remaining in Afghanistan, as well as fulfill any time-sensitive mission the commanders deemed necessary. The wake-up call was clear: we needed to be ready to pounce on any contingency with no notice.

Four days later, we were fast-roping from British Chinooks on the Bagram airfield when we got our second urgent call: a secret American reconnaissance unit had been ambushed. They had two bleeding casualties, one of them with a sucking chest wound.

Within thirty minutes, members of my platoon were flying on two Chinooks southward, intending to reinforce the team and provide medical evacuation for the severely wounded soldier, a Special Forces soldier assigned to a small, forward-deployed reconnaissance unit. Our target was the town of Khost, in a mountainous area near the Pakistani border where mujahideen fighters had developed an impregnable array of defenses and cave complexes during the war with the Soviets. The ambushed team had been in the area to assess bombing runs on the cave complexes. Our flight to them would take at least an hour.

The Chinooks flew low over the rugged landscape just before sunset. The jagged mountains seemed brashly offensive to me, as if they were goading men to venture closer to them. The terrain was treacherous. As radio messages came across the intercom system, I shouted in earnest to Rangers around me in an attempt to communicate our evolving plan. I turned to Sergeant DePouli, who sat next to me on the metal floor.

"We're either gonna conduct a medevac, or we're gonna reinforce their safe house!"

"What?"

"Either medevac or reinforcement!"

The radio calls confused me. I realized I had much to learn about the organizations with which we could be working on a moment's notice.

The condition of one of the wounded Americans deteriorated rapidly in Khost. *What if we pick him up? Will I see an American die in front of me on this aircraft?*

Word came over the net that another group had reached Khost before us and secured the casualty, but they needed us to loiter nearby, ready to reinforce the safe house if needed. Then, the last bit of daylight in the cabin receded as another report rang in my ears.

"Be advised, the WIA has just become KIA."

This is real. Forty-five minutes ago we were playing army in a British helicopter. This is not a game. They called us to rescue a warrior, and he has just died.

29

JANUARY 14, 2002
BAGRAM, AFGHANISTAN

Keeping track of local times could become overwhelming, especially since we could pass through multiple time zones on any particular mission. I was thankful for Task Force 11's adherence to "Zulu time"—Greenwich mean time, or GMT—which made mission planning and execution much easier than timing phone calls and e-mails home. The local time in Bagram was half an hour ahead of Masirah, 3.5 hours ahead of Zulu, 8.5 hours ahead of our base in Savannah, and 9.5 hours ahead of Julie and Caleb, who were staying with my in-laws in Texas.

We Rangers were nocturnal creatures by nature and by choice. We preferred to pounce on high-value targets (HVTs) at night, when we could maximize surprise and the advantage provided by our night-vision capabilities. To support this preference, we adopted a sleep cycle that had us sleeping throughout the day, rising just before dusk, operating all night, and bedding down just a few hours after sunrise.

We always had to be ready as Task Force 11's QRF. We slept in our clothes, with boots on, equipment stacked and clean and protected from dust, batteries charged, and radios configured. We rehearsed our actions inside Chinooks, recovering downed helicopters and pilots, killing or capturing HVTs, and getting from our rickety cots to the aircraft as quickly as possible with the right people and the right gear.

At rest, we crowded more than fifty Rangers into a pair of tan oblong tents heated by overworked heating/air-conditioning units and potbellied stoves. Within a few days, the typical elements of barracks life had sprouted everywhere. Rangers took up card games, perpetrated practical jokes, and played video games on the sixteen-inch television we had carried with us. The artists in the platoon started hanging caricatures throughout the tents, including one above Big A's cot that made him look like the bear he was and displayed the warning "Don't Feed the Anderson."

I was excited and growing impatient to do something substantial, as we were already two weeks into the deployment, which would probably last 90 to 120 days. We had all come to Afghanistan for a clear reason: to bring justice to those responsible for the 9/11 attacks. The hunt for bin Laden in the Tora Bora region had stalled in the previous few weeks, and the next potential battlefield lurked somewhere in the fog of the future. Nevertheless, I was excited on this day for another reason: more Rangers would be arriving to Bagram, flown up from Kandahar. The group included three people I longed to see: my company commander, my buddy Pete Marques, and the chaplain, Randy Kirby. Once they landed, I waited to greet them at our compound's gate. I saw Pete first. He was wearing his trademark wry grin.

"What's up, brah?" Pete said in one of his many comical accents.

I gave Pete a hug and a couple of hard raps on his back.

"Get in here, man," I said. "It's great to see you."

I showed him around the compound and took him to his tent and cot as we bantered in our usual sarcastic mix of movie quotes, anecdotal code words, and inside jokes. Within a few minutes, Pete broke out a log of summer sausage sent by his dad, along with crackers and Kraft Easy Cheese.

Randy Kirby peeked into the tent.

"This meeting private?" he asked.

I jumped up and gave him a high five and a hug.

"Listen, I gotta run to see the colonel," he said. "I just wanted to say hi. I'll check in later. Oh, yeah, do you guys have a chapel here yet?"

"No, we don't," I said.

"Okay. Catch up for prayer later? Maybe tomorrow?"

"Definitely," I said.

"Hey, how are the SEALs?" Randy asked. He knew we'd be working with a SEAL team, which we'd never done in the eighteen months I had been in the Rangers.

"Great, man," I said. "Different, though."

"All right, hang in there."

Previous Task Force 11 operators in Bagram had segregated our dusty camp—SEALs on one end and Rangers on the other. A gravel road running between SEALs' and Rangers' tents provided a physical demarcation line and served as the entry and exit route for vehicles parked in the rear of the compound. The SEALs occupied the compound's quieter side, the side nearer to the JOC. The Navy SEALs had a flair about them. We Rangers grew up watching the movies and reading the Dick Marcinko books. The SEALs in Task Force 11 were barrel-chested hulks wearing baseball caps and Patagonia sleep shirts over desert camouflage pants and assorted civilian hiking boots. In contrast, we Rangers were short haired, standardized, and young. We affectionately referred to the SEALs as the "football team with guns."

The SEALs, despite their mystique, accepted us. When we rehearsed with the SEALs, they were open to our suggestions and willing to mix us with their teams. Planning sessions with them focused on building consensus. Back at the tents, Ranger noncommissioned officers (NCOs) and SEALs in small numbers conversed and joked and played cards. And at times we invited them to witness some of our childish Ranger games.

That night, our fifty-five-man Ranger platoon crammed into my tent for a fun evening of "food challenges." It was a cold night, and Rangers were tired of eating the prepackaged MREs—"Meals Ready to Eat." Some of the Ranger NCOs went to procure some hot food at the end of the airfield occupied by the Army's 10th Mountain Division. They returned with thermostabilized rations, or "T-rats," which were sealed aluminum trays full of preservative-packed family-size portions. The Ranger sergeants began issuing challenges to the Ranger privates involving the excess pans of meatballs.

"Who thinks he can eat that whole tray of meatballs in thirty minutes?"

No answer.

"What about an hour?" a sergeant said. "For a hundred bucks?"

Some poor Ranger volunteered.

"Who can eat these two MRE crackers in two minutes with no water?"

Another private came forward.

"Okay, what about this gallon of fruit cocktail? Ten minutes. Twenty bucks."

This time, a shirtless staff sergeant medic wearing sweatpants and sandals took the challenge. Soon after, the first brave Ranger vomited twelve meatballs into a trash bag, to the uproarious delight of a platoon of Rangers.

"What about the meatball sauce? Somebody put that in a canteen cup. Who thinks he can down that? No time limit?"

Matt Commons, a quiet rifleman from DePouli's squad, stepped up.

"I got that, Sergeant."

Commons slurped the thick brown sludge as quickly as he could. He broke out in a noticeable sweat after a couple of full gulps. With four or five simultaneous culinary challenges going, the platoon was having a ball and attracting visitors. I noticed a few SEALs who had slipped into our tent to watch the festivities. One had a head full of orange, curly hair and a thick beard to match. He appeared to be enjoying the show. *That's cool. These guys aren't too good for us Rangers.*

Commons struggled to finish the challenge. Brown gravy spilled out of the corners of his mouth. He heaved twice, turned his head to the trash bag, and rejected the sauce that he had nearly conquered.

The platoon erupted in laughter. Commons stood and waved to his audience, accepting the praise for his worthy entertainment.

Pete and I sat on my cot with a front-row seat to the festivities, enjoying just being with the guys.

30

In all my perplexities and distresses, the Bible has never failed to give me light and strength.
:: ROBERT E. LEE

JANUARY 15, 2002
BAGRAM, AFGHANISTAN

As a nocturnal warrior, I woke up just before sunset. Pete and I decided to go for a run, an activity recently approved by our sergeant major at Bagram. We slipped on civilian workout clothes and trotted out to the airfield. They allowed us to run on an inactive taxiway at the deserted end of the runway but prohibited us from stepping off the concrete because of the area's infestation with land mines.

Pete and I trotted and discussed our separate experiences in our two weeks of combat. I felt a slight tightness in my chest, which I attributed to the change in altitude from our home in Savannah. Less than three weeks ago, we had run together near sea level on Hunter Army Airfield. Now we shuffled along at nearly a mile higher than Savannah. The run featured panoramic views of mountains, rusted hulks of Soviet tanks and personnel carriers, and frequent episodes of aircraft jerking violently into and out of the airstrip in order to miss the mountains and the threat of surface-to-air missile attack contained therein.

Randy Kirby and Matt Commons met us running the opposite direction.

"Keep it up, gentlemen!" Randy said. Commons gave a nod of greeting.

"Sirs," he said.

"*Hooah!*" I offered the all-encompassing Army word, indicating with my tone that I was impressed by their pace. That word must have more than a thousand meanings, all communicated by volume, tone, and context.

After they passed, Randy yelled back at us. "Oh, hey, I got us a chapel!"

"*Hooah!*"

Pete and I ran for another twenty minutes, stopped to stretch, and then walked back to the compound. I took a bottled-water "spit bath" and put on a clean brown T-shirt under my desert camouflage blouse. I met Randy in his tent, and he led me to the empty back half, which had been reserved as extra living space.

"Well, how's this?" he said. "This is our chapel."

"This is awesome."

"As long as it stays vacant," he said. "They told me we could use it until they need it. I'm having one of the guys build a cross to stand outside the door. Just need to run some lights in here."

Another Ranger and another chaplain joined us in the darkening tent. We introduced ourselves, as Randy was our common denominator. Randy opened in prayer, officially consecrating the musty tan shelter as the Ranger chapel. We took turns praying for our families, for the war, for our mission, and for our Rangers. By the time we finished praying, an hour had passed, and we were standing in a tent darker than the night outside.

"Thanks, brothers," Randy said. "I believe this is a holy place. In a dry and thirsty land, this stinky old tent will be a quenching water to the soul."

Randy and I took a walk outside. We talked about the Rangers in the platoon. We talked about the church that was forming with the Rangers in Kandahar, where the rest of the company was stationed. The mountains around us were glowing under the full moon.

"Randy, look at these mountains," I said. "They're really something special. You know, I didn't grow up in the mountains. Where I'm from in Texas, it's mostly plains."

"Yeah, same as Kansas," Randy said, referring to his own native area.

"The first time I saw mountains was on a ski trip to Colorado with my church's youth group. I loved it. I've always wondered what it would be like to live around the mountains. You walk out your door in the morning, and BOOM, there's a huge mountain in front of you."

"Kinda like here," Randy said.

"Exactly," I said. "When I was a cadet at Beast, you know when you march out to Lake Frederick and you go up Bull Hill?"

"I know it well," Randy said.

"We were struggling along, and this chaplain was there, reciting Psalm 121, 'I lift up my eyes to the hills.'"

"Oh, yes."

"Anyway, whenever I see mountains, I think of those verses. Kinda settles me."

"The Maker of heaven and earth," Randy said. He smiled. "Wanna grab an MRE?"

"Let's break bread," I agreed.

The next day, Randy offered to hold Bible study for those interested. Back in Savannah, I had attempted several times to lead an informal, off-duty platoon Bible study. No one attended. Here in Afghanistan, twenty-two Rangers came to Bible study for the first session. The interest continued as the number of Rangers increased daily. Randy asked me to lead the singing, so I typed some lyrics from memory, printed some song sheets, and began leading the music *a cappella*. Rangers new to the Bible study seemed to find it amusing to hear their platoon leader in front of them belting out the high notes.

After a study on the meaning of worship, Randy called me outside under the brilliant stars for a time of prayer.

"Nate, I believe God is calling you," he said. "Your gifts are irrevocable. Nate, I have a word for you. From the book of First Peter: 'Therefore humble yourselves [demote, lower yourselves in your own estimation] under the mighty hand of God, that in due time He may exalt you'" (5:6, AMP).

I let the words sink in with my head still bowed. We finished praying and gave each other a hug.

"Thanks, Randy," I said. "You're a good man."

"I appreciate that," he said. "I appreciate you. I think God's doing something special here."

"Yeah," I said.

"All right, brother, I'm gonna walk down to the Tenth Mountain and see if I can use their phones."

"See ya."

The next day, on Sunday, I awoke to the sound of rustling Rangers. Our medic was putting on his body armor in haste.

"Doc, where are you going?"

"A Marine CH-53 went down," he said. "I'm going."

The Marine helicopter had crashed in the mountains nearby. Some members of our task force responded to the accident and recovered the survivors. Two crew members had died in the crash. Randy postponed the Sunday church service. He moved to the control tower to meet the returning rescue aircraft and to help care for the incoming casualties from the crash.

Randy eventually returned to our compound, and two hours later than scheduled, he gave us Communion with the same hands that had performed last rites on the two deceased crew members.

I sat with a heavy heart on a pile of sandbags in the midst of a throng of Rangers as Randy delivered a powerful message focused on having confidence in Jesus. I found it hard to be confident in Jesus when we'd seen the swift movement of death yet again in this place. *Those two men who perished in the helicopter crash didn't expect to die today. Their families don't even know yet. We could be flying on a similar mission within the next hour. Are we ready?*

Randy concluded with a striking verse. I thought he was speaking directly to me.

"The bottom line is this," Randy said. "Mark 5:36. 'Do not be seized with alarm and struck with fear; only keep on believing'" (AMP).

31

JANUARY 28, 2002
BAGRAM, AFGHANISTAN

Julie's voice had never sounded so sweet. It had been a month since we'd said good-bye, and this was the first communication we'd had. She was at home in Texas with Caleb and our families. I stood shivering outside a tent belonging to the 10th Mountain Division, where we had found a couple of satellite phones that we could use during off-peak hours.

"What time is it there?" I asked Julie.

"Three in the afternoon," she said. "What about there?"

"Nice try, Ju." I said. "I don't even know."

"You can't tell me where you are, can you?"

"No."

"I'll just assume I know where," she said.

"You probably do."

"Why do they try to act like no one knows where you are?" she asked. "The whole world knows that if you're deployed, you're probably in one place."

She was right, but our military was monitoring every bit of communications within several kilometers of Bagram and over most of Afghanistan in the search for bin Laden. I could get in serious trouble by talking about our location or our mission—not to mention the possibility of communications being intercepted.

"Well," I continued. "How was your trip home? How long did it take?"

"Twenty-two hours," she said. "It was interesting. I almost ran out of money."

My heart sank.

"What? How's that?"

"I think it was those boots you bought before you left," she said. "I thought about taking back some of the Christmas gifts we bought so I could have gas money, but I just used the credit card."

"I'm so sorry, Ju. I'm such an idiot."

"It's okay. We made it back. You needed those boots."

"It is pretty cold," I said. I stared up at the stars. They were almost as bright and clear as they were at home in China Spring, where Julie was.

"Your mom was a little shaken up when we got home," Julie said.

"How did you tell her I was gone?"

"I didn't. She and your dad saw somebody at Outback Steakhouse who somehow knew you were gone. They saw your parents and said, 'We heard Nathan is deployed.' Your parents went home without even ordering."

"Is she okay now?"

"Yeah, she's fine. Nathan," she said, "please stay safe. I'm worried about you. I can't stop watching the news."

"Don't worry about me, Baby," I said. "You need to take care of that boy."

"Sometimes I just get so afraid," she said. She started to cry.

"Julie, you don't need to be scared," I said. "Just dream of me. I'll be with you every night."

She didn't answer.

"Ju?"

"I'm here," she said. "Just take care of yourself, okay?"

"I will," I said. "I love you."

A captain exited the tent and nodded at me.

"I gotta go, Baby. They're asking for the phone back."

"I love you," she said.

"I love you, Sweetheart. Give Caleb a kiss."

"I will. Bye."

"Bye."

Julie was right about our location and our purpose for being there. After I hung up the phone, I headed back to our compound for another round of planning for what could possibly become our nation's most important operation since D-Day: to kill Usama bin Laden.

Sergeant First Class Pressburg was waiting for me at my cot. As my platoon sergeant, he was the highest-ranking enlisted man in the platoon. Together, he and I formed the team that led 1st Platoon. He was a dangerously young platoon sergeant, a detailed and vivid storyteller, and arguably the best shooter in the battalion—at least with a pistol. His flamboyant personality, blunt opinion, and aggressive tactics made him a polarizing individual at times. I loved him.

"Coffee and a dip, sir?" Pressburg said. He was referring to our frequent trips to the massive coffeepot in the JOC. There we'd each fill an old half-liter water bottle with coffee, Pressburg would have a pinch of Copenhagen, and we'd discuss tactics, leadership, or the next mission.

"Sure thing, P-bone," I said.

"Sir, you need to lighten up a little bit."

"Sorry. I just got off the phone with my wife."

"No, your attitude's good, sir," he said. "I'm talking about your weight. You're looking a little pudgy these days. It's all those MREs you've been eating. I promise you, I refuse to eat one of those things unless we're humping on a mission and I need the calories."

I didn't reply. For his part, Pressburg was serious about not eating any MREs. He had a running bet with two other NCOs in the platoon to see who could last the longest without eating any MRE products. He had procured a jar of peanut butter, a jar of grape jelly, and several loaves of bread from a buddy at the 10th Mountain Division to sustain himself indefinitely without MREs.

Pressburg's personality attracted attention and invited antagonism. Pete and I had so much fun debating with Pressburg that we spent much of our free time with him. After an involved exchange with him in which we argued whether *Joe Dirt* or *Point Break* was the better movie, Pete and I decided to fix Pressburg. We took packets of peanut butter and jelly from an MRE and secretly squeezed the contents into Pressburg's civilian jars of peanut butter and jelly. The next time he ate a PB and J sandwich, he would unknowingly disqualify himself from the bet. We had our cameras ready for that moment.

Pressburg and I entered the JOC a couple of minutes before the daily update brief—just enough time to fix our coffee. Extra staff officers overcrowded the Ranger area of the JOC, as they had descended upon Bagram to assist in planning the potential mission to kill bin Laden.

"Look, sir," Pressburg said. "Looks like we lost our seats."

"Surprised?"

"Nothing surprises me anymore, sir."

The mission update brief on bin Laden gave me further encouragement that we would actually get to contribute to the war, possibly even in the most profound way imaginable. The target for the mission was given the name "Objective Bison."

Over the next few days, our entire Ranger company crammed into our tiny compound for the mission. We rehearsed our actions, war-gamed contingencies, and studied imagery. A growing number of Rangers stopped by to see Randy Kirby, dropping off letters written to be delivered to their loved ones should they die on the mission. Numbers at the Bible study soared to well over fifty.

Just in time for the mission, one of the Rangers received a package from his grandmother in Brooklyn that made us all feel like we were destined to make history. He opened a large cardboard box to find fifty navy blue T-shirts, half of them displaying the New York Police Department logo and half displaying the Fire Department of New York emblem. *That's why we're here.* I grabbed one with the letters "FDNY" across the chest. We decided right then that we'd wear the shirts under our uniforms on every mission. Objective Bison would be the perfect christening of the T-shirts.

On February 3—Super Bowl Sunday back in the States—we were set to fly on a moment's notice to capture or kill bin Laden. Randy preached a message to fifty Rangers about King David and the secret of his greatness. David was an anointed king; he was a man after God's own heart; he was a warrior.

"God trained David's hands for war; he made his fingers ready for battle, as it says in Psalm 144," Randy said. "David followed hard after God. He thirsted for God like a land with no water thirsts for it. Like this place here in Afghanistan."

Randy held our attention. He was talking to us as warriors. From the Bible. It was strange; I never would have expected Rangers to care about a sermon. But they did. It felt right, that this was the way it was supposed to fit. Warriors who know God. Randy stretched out his arm.

"Later tonight you may be launching in this mission and be in battle," Randy said. "Make peace with God. Come and share in his table."

Rangers took Communion from Randy in silence and moved back to their tents, resolved to meet their enemy. Pressburg and Canon were there. And many brave others.

A few hours later, the mission began to fall apart. Serious doubts and contradictions emerged in our intelligence picture. The high-risk mission wasn't worth it unless we had clear intelligence. The commander told us to stand down, that the mission wasn't going for at least twenty-four hours. Still, we held out hope that we'd hit Objective Bison in the next couple of days.

Given the operational delay, we funneled the energy of our anxious mission preparation into throwing a boisterous Super Bowl party. Rangers pulled out the remaining junk food they had stashed from care packages and cases of nonalcoholic beer that was flown in from Masirah. We switched our TVs from the black-and-white Predator feeds of the empty Afghan countryside to the Super Bowl game, piped in over satellite on Armed Forces Network. The game was broadcast with a few seconds' delay, but we were watching the Super Bowl! In Afghanistan!

Like most of the nation, for a few hours we repressed our obsession with 9/11 and al-Qaeda and the war, watching our "heroes" play sport in front of an audience of millions. But under a thin layer of enthusiasm, we were disappointed. We were relegated to spectator status once again, left watching the Super Bowl via satellite link on the same television that would have provided our commanders a Predator feed of the action, a luxury-box view of Usama bin Laden's demise.

We cheered and jeered and watched the Patriots' kicker, Adam Vinatieri, win the game with a forty-eight-yard field goal as time expired. And then we went back to our tents and to our normal compulsions: checking our weapons and equipment for what seemed the millionth time.

The next day, the dry-erase board in the JOC summed up the state of our lives. Some die-hard New England Patriots fan had posted a color printout of Vinatieri kicking the game-winning field goal, and under it, a victory announcement:

Patriots win 20-17!
Al-Qaeda, you're next!

We were disappointed. Football's Patriots had defeated the Rams, but the Task Force 11 attack on Objective Bison never happened.

32

Contrary to what we sometimes used to think, the spirit is of no avail against the sword, but that the spirit together with the sword will always win out over the sword alone. That is why we have now accepted the sword, after making sure the spirit was on our side. :: ALBERT CAMUS, *Resistance, Rebellion, and Death*

FEBRUARY 17, 2002
KANDAHAR, AFGHANISTAN

With the mission to Objective Bison canceled, we went back into sharpening our warrior skills at a place I had seen many times before on TV. I was never too frightened by the al-Qaeda propaganda videos. The footage of a lone jihadist shooting at a movie screen of Bill Clinton's fifteen-foot face seemed unrealistic. I wasn't alarmed at the images of men wearing black masks and white tennis shoes climbing on an obstacle course at some training camp in Afghanistan. I was now standing at that same training camp, a few miles from the Kandahar International Airport. The camp, known as Tarnak Farms, had been bin Laden's main headquarters during his stays in Afghanistan. This compound had been the birthing place for many terrorist plots over the past few years. Now it was an abandoned and bombed-out pile of rubble, a crumbled ruin of camouflage-painted mud-brick walls.

"Fire!"

The platoon of Rangers commenced firing their rifles and machine guns at dark green silhouette targets along the rough, tan walls. It was good for Rangers to fire their weapons after an idle couple of months, like a yawn and stretch after a solid night's sleep. I had been reluctant to leave Bagram and our mission there, but those who outranked me believed we needed to keep our warfighting skills sharp. We had been sent to Kandahar for two weeks to do nothing but train.

Another benefit of being here was more time with Pete Marques and Randy Kirby, who had moved there after Objective Bison was canceled. We based at the Task Force 11 compound at the Kandahar Airport, which was a half-hour drive to Tarnak Farms. The compound was in better shape than the one in Bagram.

During the first few days at Tarnak Farms, we tweaked our sights and optics. We cross trained with demolitions, grenade launchers, and heavy weapons. We ran the Rangers through buddy-team shooting and maneuver drills. We practiced shooting from a moving Humvee, fully loaded with Rangers. When we weren't training, we stayed at the compound, where we worked out, played cards, and went to church.

I visited Randy's room in the chapel building to get caught up with him. I shared with him the progress of the Bible study in Bagram. We even had a general officer attend earlier that week. Despite joys of witnessing the spiritual growth of the platoon, I was struggling with our presence in Afghanistan. I wanted to see some action.

I needed to talk with Randy about my growing bitterness. I was still upset with the stand-down of the bin Laden mission. I hated my enemy, and I had come to Afghanistan to kill as many as I could. It gnawed at me that we would probably return home with the emptiness of knowing that we, the most elite light-infantry unit in the world, had done nothing to bring our enemies to justice. We could say we had been to the game, but we would have to admit under our breaths that we didn't get to play.

"Randy, what are we doing here?" I asked.

"What do you mean?"

"I mean, here we are, in the middle of Afghanistan, we're in a war, and we haven't shot at anyone. We haven't even *seen* the enemy. We're going to go home after having done nothing," I said. "We're ready for something, Randy. Everyone wants to do *something*. Even the guys from Tenth Mountain have done more than us."

"I know it's hard to be patient, Nate," Randy said. "Just wait on him. Maybe there's more here than doing something. Look at what's happening to these Rangers."

"You mean the Bible study?"

"Yeah, for starters," he said. "We may never know the effect this will have on some of these guys' lives."

"You're right," I said. "Maybe this is another time when I should just let go of it."

"Maybe you *should* just release it, Nate," Randy said. "We all want justice. You're not the only one."

"I guess you're right, man."

"Nate, you mind if I share another thing that I've been noticing in a lot of guys?"

"Sure, man."

"Nate, how would you say you feel about bin Laden and al-Qaeda?"

"Well, you know I want to bring justice to them."

"Yeah, but how do you feel about it?" Randy said. "Do you feel hate toward them?"

"Yes. Yes, I do hate them," I said.

"Do you think that's the way God wants you to approach this?"

Randy hit me hard with his line of questions. We talked for another hour about loving our enemies, about the importance of praying for our enemies, that somehow they'd come to know Jesus. That was a radical concept for me. *How can I want my enemies to know Jesus . . . when I hate them so much?*

Randy was right. I knew what the Bible said. Perhaps I had been harboring anger and hatred for these people, for these aggressors, because I had seen so many murders and atrocities in Kosovo. I needed to let it go, to leave it in God's hands. Just like Psalm 75 said: "God is the Judge" (AMP).

I left Randy's room that evening feeling like I had a good grasp on where my attitude should be for the rest of the deployment. *I'm here. I shouldn't be eager to kill in anger. I am an instrument of justice of the United States government. Even if I don't face the enemy, at least I'm laying the foundation for follow-on forces. Most importantly, I may be influencing Rangers' lives in a very personal and eternal way.*

Randy's clear and direct accountability had given me a general peace about my mission in Afghanistan. It was in God's hands.

The next evening, our Bible study transitioned extemporaneously into a two-hour worship service. It was an amazing experience as Rangers sang praises to Jesus, confessed their sins, and vowed to make God a priority. Rangers knelt in prayer. Some were on their faces. Arin Canon lay prostrate in the back of the room. God was moving in a small band of brothers in Afghanistan, in the midst of a land torn by war and poverty. I thought of Psalm 75 and my yearning to know why God had raised me up to serve with the Rangers. *Maybe this is the reason God called me here. To be a part of this.*

I saw that the time in Kandahar facilitated a much-needed rekindling of our souls as well as our war-fighting skills. We continued to sharpen ourselves against the terrorist camp that was Tarnak Farms. We progressed our training to squad live-fire exercises, and then to a full-platoon assault of a circular riding stable outside the walls of the Tarnak Farms compound.

The platoon's performance was phenomenal. Canon's machine guns poured streams of tracer fire into the corral, just yards in front of assaulting Rangers. Sergeant Lopez's squad dove into a drainage ditch, secured the platoon's flank, and laid down another support-by-fire position, opposite the corral from Canon's guns. The two squads created left and right sheets of lead, which opened like a double barn door to allow DePouli and Wilmoth to charge their squads in between the protection of their firepower. The battalion's mortars isolated the corral, with loads of high explosive rounds and white phosphorous rounds landing to the rear of the objective. Our shoulder-fired anti-tank guns pounded the assault squads' breach points.

Synchronization, accuracy of fires, and communication were at pinpoint accuracy. DePouli and Wilmoth cleared the circular corral with precise movements and shifts in fire. Their squads were swift and violent. The platoon was as good as I'd seen it in eighteen months as its leader.

The only negative thing to come out of the live fire was a broken hand, which came when a chunk of the corral's wall crumbled from ten feet overhead and fell on Drew Phillips, one of Sergeant DePouli's troopers, who carried the M203 grenade launcher. It crushed his hand, and we soon found out that he would return to the States for surgery. Matt Commons, the innocent-looking rifleman who had failed to drink all the meatball gravy in Bagram, was promoted to replace Phillips on the M203.

The next day, we loaded our gear to fly back to Bagram. Randy Kirby caught me just as we were leaving. He pulled me aside.

"Nate, it was great to have you here these last couple of weeks."

"Thanks for everything, Randy."

"Listen, maybe you could talk with Matt Commons when you get a chance," Randy said. "He and I had a good talk last night. He was asking some pretty deep questions, and he prayed to receive Christ. I gave him a little Bible to read. He's excited. I think it would mean something to him if you talked with him."

"Of course, man," I said. "That's amazing."

"See, God has his own purposes for all of us here," Randy said. "Just release it, Nate. See you in Bagram in a couple of days."

"Until then."

We rolled out of the TF 11 compound to the awaiting C-17 airplane that would take us to our home in Bagram. The trip to Kandahar had been worth it after all. We had sharpened the platoon to a razor's edge of lethality, although it wasn't likely we would be able to employ our skills. We had spent some memorable time in Bible study. And as for Matt Commons, he left Kandahar with a newfound faith and a promotion from rifleman to M203 gunner.

33

The legacy of heroes is the memory of a great name and the inheritance of a great example.

:: BENJAMIN DISRAELI

FEBRUARY 28, 2002
BAGRAM, AFGHANISTAN

We had been gone for only two weeks, but I was happy to be back in the rugged, austere environment of Bagram. Much had changed there. The airfield was crowded with large numbers of aircraft— mostly Chinooks. It appeared that the number of soldiers walking around the 10th Mountain area had almost doubled, and when I got to our compound, I saw a new row of tents that did not belong to Rangers.

I linked up with Captain Andy Brosnan, my peer whose platoon had assumed QRF duties for us while we were training in Kandahar. Now that we were back, it was time for us to take over. Andy quickly informed me of the latest operations in northern Afghanistan. As he concluded, I asked about the buildup of forces in Bagram.

"Dude, what's going on here? This place is packed with people. There must be fifty Chinooks out there."

"Oh, that's probably because of Anaconda," he said.

"Because of what?"

"Anaconda. You know about Anaconda, right?"

"No. Dude, I haven't been paying attention to anything in the last two weeks."

"Oh, man, it's a good thing you asked," Andy said. "We're not really involved in it, but let me show you the plan."

He pulled up a few briefings on his laptop and explained to me the concept for Operation Anaconda. Our intelligence analysts believed that a large group of al-Qaeda forces had retreated south following the fight at Tora Bora. They had gathered in a network of defenses in the mountains of southeastern Afghanistan, an area where the mujahideen had stood against the Soviets in the '80s. The plan for Anaconda called for a group of allied Afghan fighters to sweep through a high-altitude bowl known as the Shah-i-Khot Valley. The valley, which itself was at more than eight thousand feet above sea level, was guarded by a crescent of towering mountains on its eastern flank. Elements of the 10th Mountain and the newly arrived 101st Airborne would insert by helicopter at the base of the mountains, encircling and blocking the enemy's escape routes into the mountains to the east toward Khost, and beyond that, into Pakistan. This "hammer and anvil" operation would trap the enemy in the Shah-i-Khot, where American bombers and Afghan fighters would kill them.

"Wow, I'm out of the loop," I said.

"Don't worry about it, man," Andy said. "It probably won't happen anyway. Some people think the mission's been compromised by the Afghan force."

"So what's our part of it?"

"QRF. Just be ready to reinforce TF 11 observation posts, mostly SEALs."

"Got it."

"I need to introduce you to the new pilots."

Andy led me to a new section of the compound, where a row of tents stood in the place where a perimeter wall had once been. Our compound had been expanded in the last couple of weeks to include elements of the 160th Special Operations Aviation Regiment, the Night Stalkers. We'd flown with them many times before, both here and in the States. Andy and I stepped into their operations tent. Andy waded through the tent until he found his guys.

"This is Don, and this is Chuck," Andy said. "These guys are the lead pilots for the QRF."

I shook their hands. Don was a slight man with sunken cheeks. Like most of the pilots, he had a mustache. Chuck was thick and balding. He was clean shaven.

"This is Nate," Andy said. "He's leading your new QRF."

"Which one?" Chuck asked.

"Rangers," I said.

"What about you, Andy?" he joked. "Did you get fired?"

"No, I'm going back south," Andy said. "Nate was here before me, and now he's back. He's up to speed."

"Okay, fine," Chuck said. "It all confuses me. We're supporting QRFs from TF 11, TF Dagger, TF Mountain, and whoever else wants to throw on a QRF. This Anaconda's a nightmare."

"Yeah," Don said.

Chuck turned to me. "So you're the Ranger QRF," he said. "Got it. Where do you sleep?"

"Same place as me," Andy said. "Same tent."

"All right, then. Need anything else?"

"No," I said. "Nice to meet you."

"Same here."

Andy and I walked back to our area. Nearing the tents, we heard the TV blaring. It sounded like gunfire and explosions. Rangers had piled into the dusty equipment tent to watch a war movie. The tent was packed. Many of them stood, peering over others to see the action. It was a movie I hadn't seen before. I tapped the nearest Ranger on the shoulder.

"What are y'all watching?"

"*Black Hawk Down*, sir," he said. "Somebody just got a bootleg copy. It's wicked intense."

I wanted to stay and watch it all, but Andy and I had an update brief soon. I looked around at my Rangers, the flashes of light flickering against their faces. They were watching events depicted on the screen that our friends, colleagues, and from a certain perspective, our big brothers had lived through and had told us stories about. We had become *them*, only ten years later. In Afghanistan, we were the reality, huddled together here watching a depiction of reality, imagining what an intersection of the two would deliver, if it ever came to pass.

The story of those Rangers in Somalia still had a special place in my heart. We were carrying the torch for the Regiment, we were carrying the colors, and we didn't want to let them down. Now being one of them, I was beginning to understand what it was that actually mattered to them. To us. To me.

34

APRIL 2, 1986
ZHAWAR KILI, AFGHANISTAN

Their origins are too ancient to document, and their current location is somewhere between the mountains and the next fight. Stronger men have underestimated them for centuries and have met nothing but death. You cannot kill them—not completely—for they live outside the body. Their desires are as rarefied as the air they breathe. They want nothing more than to protect what little they have, and they'd just as soon kill you as look at you.

They are strugglers. They are the mujahideen.

In 1986, in the Paktia province in eastern Afghanistan, four kilometers from the Pakistani border, the Soviets were trying to eradicate the mujahideen, "to kill the fish by draining off the water," to prove to the world that these scrappy fighters were no match for a world superpower, that their mountain fortress could be taken. The mujahideen had resolved to prove otherwise.

They had built a defensive stronghold mostly underground—an intricate and comprehensive array of caves, tunnels, and passages, stocked and fortified. It was a subterranean city, with a hotel, a mosque, a garage, and a medical center. A handful of royal Saudi militants had financed and overseen the construction in two locations: Zhawar Kili, in eastern Afghanistan, and a region just south of Jalalabad known as Tora Bora. The mujahideen boasted that Zhawar Kili was invincible.

The Soviets had already worked out a plan to withdraw from Afghanistan whenever the political situation stabilized. To facilitate this withdrawal, they urged the Afghan government to take the leading combat role against the mujahideen—and to attack the mountain strongpoint of Zhawar Kili—again. This time, the Soviets would merely direct and support the allied Afghan forces. This time, they would defeat the mujahideen.

The Afghan-Soviet forces moved from the nearby towns of Gardez and Khost to attack Zhawar Kili by ground. They planned a helicopter insertion to vertically envelop the mujahideen in Zhawar Kili by seizing an overlooking mountain—an 11,810-foot peak called Dawri Ghar. This bold tactic reflected an evolving Soviet philosophy of airborne and air-assault insertions in Afghanistan—from previous offset landings to aggressive and precise landings near to their objectives, or directly onto them. The Soviets assigned the Dawri Ghar air-assault mission to an Afghan commando brigade, which would seize the peak in the predawn hours.

The first lift of Soviet-made Mi-8 HIP helicopters carried ten commandos each. They flew over Zhawar Kili, the prize, just before 3:00 a.m. After encountering mujahideen antiaircraft fire during the flight, the commandos were surprised to land unopposed. Upon land-ing, their leader reported that the firing was far away from his location. After radio conversations with headquarters, the commandos realized they were not near Dawri Ghar, but five kilometers inside Pakistan. Headquarters ordered a withdrawal. An hour later, the commandos reported they were surrounded—and locked in combat.

At dawn, the remainder of the commando brigade attempted to capture Zhawar Kili by landing on the open plains and slopes surround-ing the town. The mujahideen were ready. They massed fire on the landing zones, destroying helicopters as they hovered, unloaded troops, and wobbled up into the sky.

Soviet jet aircraft bombed and strafed the mujahideen positions, des-perate to protect the air-assault insertion. The explosions trapped at least a hundred mujahideen inside the caves. The intense close-air support, how-ever, did not repel the mujahideen. Instead of defending their positions, the mujahideen stormed the landing zones and overwhelmed the commandos.

Mujahideen reinforcements, moving from Pakistan to Zhawar Kili, blocked the commandos from the rear, trapping and slaughtering them. In all, the mujahideen captured 530 men. Within a day, the Afghan 38th Commando Brigade ceased to exist.

The rest of the battle was of no substantial consequence. The Soviet-Afghan ground forces seized Zhawar Kili, but only for five hours before the mujahideen counterattacked and drove the invaders from the region.

Within hours of the battle, the mujahideen held a field tribunal for their prisoners, eighty of whom were Afghan officers. The officers had a chance to confess their "crimes" from various battles, crimes that were likely acts of heroism in previous days. Whether the officers confessed did not matter; all of them were executed. The mujahideen *released the conscripted Afghan soldiers after a period of penitent labor, as they assumed the conscripts had been forced to fight.*

The Soviets never disclosed the extent of their casualties. Even so, they had miscalculated the enemy. The mujahideen did not die. They say they shot down twenty-four Soviet helicopters that day.

35

Gallantly will I show the world that I am a specially selected and well trained soldier. My courtesy to superior officers, neatness of dress and care of equipment shall set the example for others to follow.

:: RANGER CREED, Fourth Stanza

MARCH 2, 2002
BAGRAM, AFGHANISTAN

"Wake up, sir. Sir, wake up. Major Mingus wants you in the JOC."

A cold hand gripping my shoulder was not the ideal way to receive a wake-up call. Neither was the constant booming of the helicopter blades from the tarmac two hundred meters away. I rolled over in my thick, black sleeping bag and searched for the tiny face opening.

"What is it?" I asked.

"Anaconda," he said. "Casualties inbound."

"Are you kidding me?" I asked.

He pursed his lips and shook his head.

"Sergeant Canon," I said. "Sergeant Canon."

I sat up and looked across to his cot, wrestling to free myself from a tangle of headphone wires. Canon was not on his cot.

"He's already in the JOC, sir. He's getting an initial dump from Major Mingus."

I hurried to the JOC, glancing at two approaching Chinook helicopters that were likely returning from Anaconda. I swung open the door to the JOC, and the water-bottle counterweight smacked me on the side of the face as I strode through the opening.

"Sir," I said, stepping alongside Major Mingus. He appeared to be finishing up a point with Sergeant Canon.

"Stand by, Nate," Mingus said. "Any questions, Sergeant Canon?"

"Just one, sir, but it can wait until later," Canon said.

I'd heard that tone before. The question Canon had would take some time to answer; that was certain.

"All right. Give me a report when you think they're done with you."

"Roger, sir," Canon replied. He strode out the door I had just entered, obviously with a task in hand.

"Good afternoon, Nate. Here's what's going on," Major Mingus said. He walked me over to the dry-erase board, which displayed grid locations, radio frequencies, and casualty tallies.

"The 101st and Tenth Mountain got hit pretty hard this morning. Mortars, RPGs, machine guns, right on their landing zones. They're taking some casualties, but they're holding their ground."

"How bad are the casualties?"

"Well, there are more than they expected," he said. "I'm sending some of your guys to the airfield to help off-load wounded when they arrive. Aircraft's inbound in about thirty minutes."

Hours later, several Rangers from the platoon trickled into our tents, exhausted and visibly upset. They had handled casualties from another unit, a unit that was engaging the enemy, a unit that was fighting this war.

"This is bull—, sir," Canon said. "These guys are out there getting some and coming back bloodied up, and we're sitting back here playing PlayStation? And then the most we can contribute is carrying their casualties from aircraft to the aid station? Bull—."

Several Rangers sat dejected on the edge of their cots as they removed their blood-streaked blouses and trousers. They felt left out of the biggest battle in the war. I felt the same way. I was jealous, frightened, and embarrassed. Americans were in the thick of a real fight, while I rested in my sleeping bag. We were Rangers, and we were not involved in the fight. Surely there was something we could be doing. My highly trained Rangers were serving as litter bearers for wounded soldiers from conventional units.

Our special mission to kill a select group of high-value targets had precluded us from killing the enemy.

36

I want to know God's thoughts—the rest are mere details. :: ALBERT EINSTEIN

MARCH 3, 2002
BAGRAM, AFGHANISTAN

The ground bounced like a trampoline under my feet. It took me a couple of seconds to realize that it was another earthquake—the second one I'd experienced since we came to Afghanistan, and the second I'd ever felt in my life. The first one had come on January 3, the day before we flew to evacuate the ambushed American near Khost. He died before we could get there.

Arin Canon walked into the tent with a towel over his shoulder and a green canvas shaving kit in hand.

"Whoa, sir!" he said. "You feel that?"

"Yeah, my mind couldn't figure out what it was," I said. "The ground was just bouncing like a plate of Jell-O."

"You remember the last earthquake, sir?" he said. "Day before the Khost medevac."

"Yes, I remember."

"If the earthquakes are any sort of omen here, we should expect something bad to happen tomorrow," he said.

"Whatever."

"Of course, it's also Sunday, and bad things seem to happen on Sundays, too," he said. "Take your pick, some bad s— is gonna happen either today or tomorrow."

"You going to church, Arin?"

"Of course, sir," he said. "I'd never miss a good day at church."

"Good, I'll see you there. I need to brush my teeth."

"Yes, you do, sir, but I wasn't going to say anything."

The church service was about to begin. It was a sunny afternoon, and Randy suggested we roll up the sides on the chapel tent and take some of the chairs outside. A large group of Rangers convened to enjoy the sunshine and Randy's sermon, "The Journey to Easter." It was a happy, upbeat service.

Marc Anderson was there, and he offered up praise to God and thanks for our prayers on behalf of his brother Steve, who was back home in the States battling brain cancer. Steve had made remarkable improvement in the last few days and was believed to be in remission.

We filed by Randy for Communion, and many of us hugged Big A and congratulated him on the news. He had tears in his eyes.

Randy closed the service with a homework assignment for us.

"All right, guys. I've got homework for you," he said. A few

Rangers chuckled. "Go back to your bunks sometime today when you have some downtime and study Psalm 121. Come back and be ready to discuss that at Bible study later tonight."

Randy had chosen the passage of Scripture I had shared with him, one of my sources of strength ever since the march up Bull Hill in Beast Barracks. I didn't need to study the Scripture. It was written on my heart.

I spent most of the day getting caught up on the proceedings of Operation Anaconda. The 101st and 10th Mountain had not made the kind of progress they had expected. As a result, commanders decided to insert more special operators to establish high-altitude observation posts and fill gaps in our coverage of the Shah-i-Khot Valley.

Early in the evening, we were put on alert to possibly reinforce a secret U.S. safe house in Khost. It was appearing that Anaconda wasn't going to be a problem, but the ultra-volatile Khost area could be. Maybe Canon was right about the omen. I scurried to our tents to put the platoon on alert. After three hours of spinning, we were told once again to stand down.

Time for the Bible study approached. I broke away from the JOC to retrieve my Bible from under my cot. Randy was waiting for me.

"Hey, Nate," he said. "I've got a mission for you."

"What's that?" I said.

"I've got to go to the tower to help minister to casualties from the 101st. Can you lead the Bible study for me?"

"I'd love to," I said. "And of all the lessons, Psalm 121."

"Exactly," he said. "And also, I've asked Matt Commons to share a testimony about his faith."

"Awesome, man," I said. "I got it, now you get going. I'm sure they need you down there."

"Right," he said. "And please pray for me in Bible study."

"We will."

Few people showed up at Bible study. We had seven in all. Arin Canon was there. Marc Anderson was there. Matt Commons was there.

We began the session with a couple of songs and moved into prayer time. Commons then shared his new hunger for the Bible, how he'd been looking at a lot of stuff about the afterlife and had talked with Chaplain Kirby about heaven and hell. He explained how excited he was to be learning more. He said that he had accepted Jesus as his Savior in the chapel in Kandahar. His eyes gleamed as he spoke. I don't think I'd ever seen him look so alive.

The Rangers shared some about their families at home. They offered requests for prayer. Matt Commons wanted us to pray for his buddy Drew Phillips, whom he had replaced as the M203 gunner.

"Okay, the best for last and then we'll pray. Who did their homework? Who read Psalm 121?"

All seven of us raised our hands.

"Here, I should just start by reading it," I said.

> I LIFT UP MY EYES TO THE HILLS — WHERE DOES MY HELP
>   COME FROM?
> MY HELP COMES FROM THE LORD, THE MAKER OF HEAVEN
>   AND EARTH.
> HE WILL NOT LET YOUR FOOT SLIP — HE WHO WATCHES OVER
>   YOU WILL NOT SLUMBER;
> INDEED, HE WHO WATCHES OVER ISRAEL WILL NEITHER
>   SLUMBER NOR SLEEP.
> THE LORD WATCHES OVER YOU — THE LORD IS YOUR SHADE
>   AT YOUR RIGHT HAND;
> THE SUN WILL NOT HARM YOU BY DAY, NOR THE MOON
>   BY NIGHT.

THE LORD WILL KEEP YOU FROM ALL HARM—HE WILL WATCH
OVER YOUR LIFE;
THE LORD WILL WATCH OVER YOUR COMING AND GOING BOTH
NOW AND FOREVERMORE. (NIV)

"What do you get from that?" I asked.

Each Ranger answered with his own understanding and application of the passage. I wrapped up the study with my own testimony of how the verse kept surfacing whenever I was operating in the mountains—on Bull Hill, in Ranger School, in Kosovo, and now here in Afghanistan. Psalm 121 was a psalm of ascents, one that the ancient Jews sang on their pilgrimage climbs up to Jerusalem. The psalm had likewise given me encouragement whenever I'd faced a difficult climb in life.

"Guys, when the sun comes up tomorrow, go outside, and if there aren't any clouds, just look around you. The mountains are all around. Think about this passage, Psalm 121. You'll never view mountains the same again. And I bet you'll never forget Psalm 121, either. Let's pray."

37

A timid person is frightened before a danger, a coward during the time, and a courageous person afterwards. :: JOHN PAUL RICHTER

MARCH 3, 2002
BAGRAM, AFGHANISTAN

I burst out of the JOC with a mission in hand. It was still a moonless night in the Hindu Kush Mountains, and with no clouds overhead, the temperature was plunging. I hurried along in the crisp air, the wind muffling my ears, my pace along the familiar path much faster than normal. I knew the stroll well: sixty-five steps from door to flap—that is, from the JOC to my tent, where the rest of the Ranger leaders slept lightly with their clothes on.

I wanted to run to my tent, but it was too dark for that. This former Soviet air base was a dangerous place. A step off the cleared paths could find a lethal land mine and an uncomfortable ride home, if I survived such a mistake. As I neared the tent, my heart was beating faster than my feet, but I somehow gathered myself.

As I transitioned from the gravel underfoot to the wooden-crate sidewalk, I reached for the tarplike flap, outlined by an arch of light escaping from inside . . . fifty, fifty-one—my urgency had lengthened my normally sure stride. After a deep breath, I ripped back the flap and ducked my head through in one motion, startling a couple of sleeping Rangers.

"Get up," I ordered. "We've got a mission."

No one moved.

I was not surprised. We had been operating for more than two months, looking to kill or capture al-Qaeda's top leadership. We had yet to fire a single shot at the enemy. The drill was getting old.

We had all watched in horror on 9/11, readied ourselves for war in Savannah, flown to the other side of the world to set up camp in al-Qaeda's backyard, joined Task Force 11 along with America's most lethal special operators, and were eager to get into the fight. We had grown more frustrated and impatient with each false call or missed opportunity.

We managed to maintain our professionalism whenever we were in our headquarters, the joint operations center; but in our own tents, the men were candid. I shared their frustration, and after a false alert earlier in the evening, their reaction was about what I expected. I turned my attention to my squad leaders, still motionless in their heavy black sleeping bags.

"Get up," I said. "Manifest Alpha. Now."

"Yeah, right, sir," Canon said. "Same as before?"

"No. This one's real. We've got a Razor aircraft down."

With those words, everyone bolted off their rickety cots and began searching for their gear, revealing that they had been somewhat awake and listening. They had just blown their covers, but none seemed to care. Their bodies were in motion before their brains.

Every Ranger knew that our planning priorities as TF 11's QRF clearly included securing a downed helicopter. We'd been the QRF since we'd arrived on New Year's Eve and had thought about nearly every contingency. As such, we knew that any unplanned emergency that could happen would probably become our mission. We were a catchall. Now we had a helicopter on the ground with no protection, and there was no doubt as to who was going to secure it. The question was, who else wanted that aircraft, and how badly would they fight to get it?

"What's going on, sir?" DePouli asked. "A Chinook? How do you know?"

"It's Razor Zero-Three. I heard it on the net. Anderson heard it too. Maintenance problem or RPG fire; they're not sure yet. I'm headed back to the JOC. Thirty minutes."

It was a reminder to the men of our time standard to be stationed at our helicopters and ready to fly. I turned to Canon.

"You got this?"

"Roger, sir."

"Big A's on radio watch in the JOC," I said. "Make sure you get him off."

"Got it, sir."

Eager to return to the urgent radio calls, I chased my thoughts back up the slight rise to our tiny headquarters building, where I could gather my maps and my senses. It was bitter cold. The sky was black, and for a moment in the darkness, I felt very alone. Julie and I had always looked at the moon when we were apart, as if it were some sort of mirror that connected us—like we could somehow see each other's reflection in the lunar seas, no matter how much earth stood between us. Without the connection of the moon tonight, I felt even colder knowing she was at home with our newborn son. Without the moon, she would look to him as the only available reflection of me. I, however, had no such image, no photos, and no moon.

It was so dark I would have passed the door if not for the Navy SEAL who emerged from it just in time. He held the door and quickly stepped aside. Halfway through the door, I locked onto the black-and-white TV screen in the center of the room, which showed a downed U.S. helicopter resting in a valley crawling with al-Qaeda, in the midst of the largest operation of the war.

The live video feed was coming from a Predator unmanned aerial vehicle (UAV), a remote-controlled surveillance drone that seemed to see everything. Having the Predator gave those of us in Bagram a sense of security in knowing that no matter what happened on the ground, someone would be watching; but it was also a little disconcerting knowing that people all over the world could be watching our every move. Little black dots—the men who had been on board the Chinook—scurried around outside the aircraft. That helicopter belonged to Task Force 11—my task force. I wondered if I, too, would soon be a little black dot on that TV screen.

Major Mingus approached and handed me a few warm sheets of imagery. My company commander and battalion commander were both still in Kandahar, 350 miles southwest of us. As the highest-ranking Ranger in Bagram, Mingus was my acting commander. But this was no act.

"Any more radio calls, sir?" I asked.

Mingus gazed at the TV.

"No, we're just watching them on the Predator feed." He paused. "Well, there was one call, but we're not sure about it. There's a missing man."

"Missing?"

"We heard it once," he said. "Not sure who, not sure where—just not sure."

Mingus stared at the screen for a few seconds, then squared his shoulders and leveled his eyes to mine.

"Get to your aircraft. We'll discuss it on the radio while we wait for launch authority," Mingus said. "You've got the grids, right?"

"Yes, sir." I turned to exit the building, not knowing what I would tell my Rangers. I had a hundred meters to figure it out.

As I stepped out of the JOC and looked around at the bowl of mountains surrounding the air base, I thought briefly of our Bible study, focusing on Psalm 121 just hours earlier. I thought of the faces of the Rangers who had been at the Bible study. Looking up into the black expanse above, I briefly prayed that they, too, would somehow draw strength from the Scripture.

By the time I reached our tents and the platoon, I had convinced myself that we would actually fly, that we would actually touch down, that we would do something important on the ground. Before now, I had come to accept that our purpose in Afghanistan was to show our resolve, to prove that we could project power anywhere in the world and that no one could stop us from doing so. But I knew that none of that muscle flexing impressed our enemy. I knew that the only way to prove anything to our enemy was to kill him. I was fine with that. *He thinks I'm weak, and I'm here to end his existence.* I hoped that tonight we'd get that opportunity.

The Rangers looked ready. They were loaded on our desert Humvees, awaiting the order to drive down the narrow dirt road from our inconspicuous compound to the flight line. As I approached the vehicles, I saw that the group of men I had left in the tents just minutes before—groggy, half dressed, and half asleep—had transformed themselves into a band of hulking, fierce warriors, cocked for war. A barrel of burning trash in the background provided a frightening silhouette of the Rangers piled in the backs of the vehicles, a neatly coiled mass of men, canvas, and steel—joined at the hip, their heads separate, distinct, and alert. Each Humvee was like a loaded belt of ammunition, full of Rangers waiting to be blasted at the enemy.

Canon, DePouli, and Wilmoth met me at the lead vehicle in a pair of Humvees. Canon handed me my rifle and informed me that my gear was loaded on the second vehicle.

"Sir, we're just waiting on Matt LaFrenz," Canon said, referring to the medic from Andy Brosnan's platoon. "We forgot that our medic is still in Kandahar."

"Sir, I'm waiting on Commons," DePouli said. "He was just standing around without his equipment, saying he wasn't on this manifest. I told him he's the 203 gunner now. I guess he forgot."

"Okay, guys, here's the mission," I said. "As you know, Razor Zero-Three is down. I just saw the bird on the valley floor on the Predator feed, and the crew was cross-loading to the trail aircraft. No casualties reported, so we may just be securing an empty bird."

"Why didn't they just stay with it?" Wilmoth said.

"I don't know. Doesn't matter. They need us," I said. "The only complicator here is that there's talk on the radio that there's a missing American somewhere on the battlefield. They think he fell out of a helicopter. I don't know anything else about it. Don't know where, don't know when, don't know who."

"Roger, sir, we'll deal with that when we have to," Canon said.

"So, we're either gonna do a CSAR mission or try to find this guy," I said. "They're still working loads on the aircraft, but we should probably take about twenty to the ramp with us."

"We've got twenty-five loaded on these two Humvees, sir," Canon said.

"All right, guys," I said. "You should already have your maps. Same ones from Anaconda planning. Here's imagery from the downed bird. Guys, as you can tell, this one's really unclear. But it's ours. This is our mission."

"Here's Commons, sir," DePouli said. "We're ready now."

Major Mingus walked up to our vehicles.

"Nate, what's taking you so long?" Mingus asked.

"Sir, we're ready," Canon said.

"We're moving, sir," I said to Mingus.

I climbed into a cramped seat behind DePouli and tapped him on the shoulder. It had been more than thirty minutes since our alert, and we needed to get to the aircraft. We would finish our planning on the flight line, if we had time.

Arin Canon leaned out of the Humvee in front of me, glanced over his shoulder, and reported he was leading us to the aircraft.

This mission was developing deep into enemy territory. But it appeared to be more about us than the enemy: a downed helicopter, a missing man, battling the elements and the deadly environment. Getting to and securing the disabled aircraft or finding a missing man would be tough enough, even without enemy contact. In a way, preserving precious U.S. equipment and an even more precious American life seemed nobler and more fulfilling than the remainder of the deployment's prospective missions. It was a chance to get into the fight, to make our time count—to do something that *mattered*—especially to me.

38

When tempest tossed, embrace chaos. :: DEAN KOONTZ

MARCH 4, 2002
SOMEWHERE OVER AFGHANISTAN

We were able to load seventeen Rangers onto two Chinooks and carry along a three-man Air Force search-and-rescue team that I'd never met. I flew aboard the first Chinook, Razor 01, and was the overall ground-force commander for both chalks. Sergeant Canon led the second chalk of ten Rangers aboard Razor 02 but was under my command.

As we screamed along at eight thousand feet in the frigid winter air over southeastern Afghanistan, the sweat streaming down my spine seemed a physiological impossibility. The familiar high-pitched whir of the aircraft's engines should've lulled many to sleep. None slept. It was dark, but a few instrument lights created a muted green shadow over everyone onboard. When I looked to the ramp, the expanse of sky beyond yielded a lighter shade of ambient night.

I shifted many times on the floor, searching for something softer to rest on than the frigid metal deck. I sat on several odd-shaped pieces of equipment, leaned on the outer wall of the Chinook, and rested against other Rangers.

My mind drifted from what was ahead to studying the blurry figures around me, trying to determine their preparedness from their posture and movements. I felt an intense need to defecate, much like the one I felt when I ran hard or stood up while wearing a parachute. I shifted my right leg, which had become numbingly confined under Anderson's body weight and the legs of the guys sitting across from me. I attempted to readjust myself, and needles of pain tingled in my calf. I felt a rush of frosty air sneak up my trousers when I moved.

The three guys across from me were unfamiliar. They were Air Force, and under my command, but I'd never seen them before. Or if I had, I didn't know it. They were already on this helicopter when we loaded in Bagram, as they had just returned from another mission.

I had directed Kevin Vance to sit next to them because he was my embedded Air Force specialist. He was trained specifically to call in bombs from jets. But he was much more than that. He was also a Ranger. He had lived and worked with us in Savannah. *If Kevin's talking with them, it'll be okay. They're all Air Force; maybe they'll get straight whatever it is they need to get straight.*

I'm pretty sure we're gonna do something, even if I don't know what that means. I can't afford to rest or be silent. These men need information, a plan, some guidance. The problem here was that the aircraft's communication systems were arranged such that I couldn't transmit out on the helicopter's radios. I could hear them and talk to the crew over the short-range radio, but I couldn't communicate with anyone outside the helicopter.

I reached into my pocket with a clumsy gloved hand and fished around for the light board. On our flight to evacuate the KIA Special Forces soldier exactly two months prior, I'd learned that I needed an efficient way to communicate with the chalk in a loud, dark helicopter. The light board had a chem-light burning on it, so it was ready to go. I pulled it from the pocket and laid it in my lap. I waited to hear the next few radio transmissions to determine what I would write as my first message on the light board.

When we left Bagram, the mission had two potential tasks: to secure a downed aircraft or to recover a missing American. Or both. I knew exactly where the disabled aircraft was, had maps and imagery of the area, and had the grid coordinates plotted in my handheld GPS. I didn't know where the missing American was, only that he had fallen out of the back of a helicopter and his location and status were unknown. The widespread confusion over our specific mission tasks had led to our standing order to "fly down to Gardez, land, come up on COMMS, and we'll figure it out." Gardez was about an hour's flight south of Bagram and about a fifteen minutes' flight from the Anaconda battle space. As we closed the distance to Gardez, most of the radio chatter centered on the missing American.

"Razor Zero-One, what's the status of the QRF; over?" I recognized the voice on the radio. It was Pete Blaber, a man with a long history in the Rangers and Delta Force. He had served with Colonel Thomas several times before. I trusted him. *If he's in control here, everything will be fine.*

"We're en route," the pilot said. "ETA twenty mikes." Twenty minutes from the target.

"Razor Zero-One, be advised: a MAKO element is nearby the missing individual."

I recognized the call sign MAKO to refer to a SEAL team, specifically the sniper/reconnaissance teams. This was good news. Maybe they had found the unfortunate American who'd fallen out of a Chinook. Lucky for him they got there before the enemy did.

"Ah, it appears that someone has linked up with the missing individual; can't confirm friendly or enemy presence around him; over."

"Seems to be no struggle. A group gathered around a flashing strobe light."

I wrote on my light board and passed it around the Chinook's cabin:

Possible MAKO linkup with missing man.

"Razor Zero-One, send status of the QRF; over."

"We are en route, two 47s with twenty eagles. ETA twenty mikes; over."

"Razor Zero-One, understand twenty minutes. MAKO element is requesting the QRF, in contact with the enemy vicinity of the LZ. Grid to follow."

We're obviously not going to Gardez first. We're going straight in.

As we waited for a grid, the radio traffic switched to the subject of the AC-130 gunship, an armed-to-the-teeth version of the turboprop troop transport from which we parachute. It was a Special Operations favorite for supporting ground troops.

"I say again, request the AC-130 to stay on station," Blaber said. "We need it to cover the QRF's infil."

I couldn't hear the distant station's part of the conversation. It sounded like an argument about whether the AC-130 would stay in the air to support our infiltration—or fly off station and go home. This could be a serious issue. If we lost the AC-130, we'd be without any firepower overhead during our flight into the area.

"Razor Zero-One, this is Shark Seven-Eight." It was our headquarters in Bagram.

"Updated LZ grid follows. Grid, whiskey lima, 193 899; over."

"This is Razor Zero-One, roger; over."

I pulled my map out to plot the new landing zone. I flipped on the LED lip light attached to my headset's boom microphone so I could see the map. As I started to plot the grid, Bagram came back on the net.

"Razor Zero-One, HLZ grid."

"Roger."

"Contact call sign Toolbox for final LZ grid."

"Roger."

I got my light board back and wrote another message:

SEAL snipers in contact w/ enemy vic LZ,
Hot extraction on a hot LZ,
Watch your fires.

I could see the Rangers' excitement as they passed the light board around the cabin. We were finally going to do something important, even if it had nothing to do with the downed aircraft. To recover a missing American was as much who we are as any other mission. And this missing American mattered much more than any piece of equipment.

"I say again, do not allow the AC-130 to break station," Blaber said. He sounded angry.

"Toolbox, this is Razor Zero-One—we need an HLZ grid; over."

"Roger, Razor," Toolbox said. "Grid, whiskey lima, 199 892; over."

"Got it."

"What do you have?" the pilot asked.

One of the other crew members answered.

"193 892, same as Shark."

"Are you sure? It sounded like he said something different. Ask him again."

"Toolbox, repeat grid; over."

"Roger. Whiskey lima, 199 892."

"Sounded the same to me."

"No, I heard it again. You had one of those grids wrong. Read it back to Toolbox."

"Toolbox, I say grid whiskey lima, one niner tree, eight niner two."

"NEGATIVE. One niner *niner*, eight niner two."

"See?" the pilot asked. "Where's this f—— LZ?"

"Razor Zero-One, status of the QRF?" Blaber asked.

"This is Razor Zero-One, two minutes."

"MAKO Three-Zero is requesting immediate insertion of the QRF."

I radioed Sergeant DePouli, who was riding on the ramp. He would be the first man on the ground. I would be near the last.

"One, this is Six," I said.

"One."

"You straight?"

"Roger. Hot LZ. Friendlies nearby. Secure the LZ and conduct linkup."

"You got it," I said.

The crew chiefs held up two fingers and called out the standard time warning.

"Two minutes!" they said.

"TWO MIN-UTES!"

I couldn't believe it. We were going in. I felt like my heart's pounding was about to crack the ceramic plate that protected my chest.

On my right, Marc Anderson slapped David Gilliam, his nineteen-year-old assistant machine gunner, on the back. He gave Gilliam a thumbs-up and leaned close.

"Today I feel like a Ranger!" Anderson said, a measure of his excitement and the relative importance of the day.

Gilliam was twelve years younger than Big A, who had taught the younger man everything he knew about being a warrior. As a machine-gun team, the two were a perfect match of experience and youth. Gilliam groped along the cold floor to squeeze Anderson's leg. As long as Big A was there, everything would be all right.

I was starting to feel sick to my stomach. I closed my eyes and prayed for the mission.

"Razor Zero-One, be advised: BMNT is expected in five minutes."

BMNT—before morning nautical twilight. That meant that the sun wasn't quite up yet, but the dawn was upon us. A daylight landing.

We're screwed.

★ ★

NO GREATER LOVE

★ ★

39

When soldiers have been baptized in the fire of a battle-field, they have all one rank in my eyes.

:: NAPOLEON BONAPARTE

04 0614 MAR 02 (DELTA TIME ZONE)
SOMEWHERE OVER AFGHANISTAN

"I've got an RPG—one o'clock! Three o'clock! Engaging!" The door gunner shouted, opening fire with his M134 Gatling gun. I heard the aircraft's M60 machine gun joining fire.

Too late.

The *schussssss* of an incoming RPG round pierced the chill mountain air, followed closely by a *thump* as the charge exploded into the Chinook's right engine. A second grenade ripped through the cockpit windshield, spraying hot shrapnel over the flight crew. The helicopter jolted downward, and my stomach dropped with it.

We're going down.

I slammed into the deck. My head bounced off the frozen floor, breaking my night-vision goggles off their mount and onto my nose. My eyes were watering. My nose was numb, the smell of a punch in the face. The impact rolled me onto my back, crashing me into the side of the aircraft and leaving me faceup in a stupor. I saw streaks of light passing overhead.

Thungk! Thungk! Thungk! Machine-gun fire sounded like someone beating the aircraft with a ball-peen hammer as it punched through the helicopter's riveted skin. Glowing lines of tracer bullets zipped just above my head, zigzagging their way through the aircraft, shredding the insulation off the inner walls and leaving a confetti-like residue hanging in the cabin.

I turned to see the minigun's smoking barrels swivel to rest over a crumpled mass of fleece and canvas in a pool of blood. The right-door gunner was down. The left-door gunner fell at my feet, grunting as a bullet hit his survival knife and splintered blade fragments into his leg, fracturing his femur.

Another RPG blew into the cabin, exploding on an oxygen tank directly above me. Sparks blossomed and fell, searing my pale uniform. The oxygen tank caught fire. I rolled to my stomach, staying below another burst of machine-gun fire that thumped the cabin. I looked toward the ramp and saw a mangled heap of bodies—no movement. Groans came from the pile. Judging from the amount of incoming gunfire, I knew several were wounded or dead.

The pilot emerged from the cockpit, his limp hand suspended by tendons and bone; he was holding the wrist together with his good hand. Blood shot between his fingers in arterial spurts. He was stuck in the companionway to the cabin as another RPG blasted the cockpit, peppering his backside with more shrapnel. I heard voices shouting outside the aircraft. They spoke in languages I didn't know.

I crawled as fast as I could to exit the bird, over my comrades. Other Rangers fought to free themselves of their safety lines, jerked taut by the landing and the aircraft's nose-up attitude.

Another explosion rocked the helicopter. The gunfire was in a crescendo, coming from multiple directions. *If something doesn't change drastically, and soon, this helicopter will become a multimillion-dollar coffin. I'm the senior Ranger on the aircraft, and with the fate of twenty-one Americans still undecided, I know it's up to me to make the difference.*

It was still 6:14 a.m., and the sun remained just below the horizon. My life had changed in twenty seconds. I had the sick feeling that I'd be here until nightfall, if I lived that long. Our Ranger forefathers taught us to live by the Creed, to never leave a fallen comrade to fall into the hands of the enemy; and they made great sacrifices to keep that promise. We, too, had made that promise—to Rangers past and present and to the missing American we'd come to retrieve—and we were here to make sure we honored it. But as I scrambled to the ramp of the aircraft, one question pressed at the corners of my mind: who would keep that promise for us?

40

Nothing fires the warrior's heart more with courage than to find himself and his comrades at the point of annihilation, at the brink of being routed and overrun, and then . . . :: STEVEN PRESSFIELD, *Gates of Fire*

04 0614 MAR 02 (DELTA)
TAKUR GHAR
10,240 FEET

I crawled over my own men to get out. Their faces showed desperation. It wasn't really a crawl, more like a series of falls on all fours, strung together to propel me rearward in the aircraft. Machine-gun fire continued to ping the helicopter. *I'm selfish to crawl over them. I'm saving myself. This helicopter is about to blow up. But they'll see me and know to get out too. I've got to get out.*

The helicopter wobbled left and right as it settled into the snow. The rhythmic twin rotor blades pulsed weaker with each turn, tips drooping with the last few instinctive twitches of the dead bird. The aircraft's engine gears whined lower in a slurred chromatic scale—down, down, down.

A few feet from the ramp, I saw a pair of boot soles facing the sky. They were on the ramp, and the man wearing them was face-down in the snow. He didn't move. I didn't look close enough to identify him, but I was alarmed to see his arms at his side, as though he hadn't tried to brace his fall.

Beyond him three Rangers lay prone in the snow, shooting to the left side of the helicopter. I made it to the open back end of the Chinook and tumbled headfirst over the last few bodies, off the ramp, and into the snow, next to the facedown Ranger and half on top of Specialist Aaron Totten-Lancaster, the fastest man in the platoon. He was on his back, struggling to right himself.

I looked back into the helicopter. There on the ramp, eye to eye with me, inches from my face, was Matt Commons. He was lying in the way, across the ramp. *He looks so alive—he is—he can't be. Does he think he's still alive?* A red pool spilled under his head. *That can't be blood; it's too thin. It's too bright.* It was dripping off the ramp, into the fleece-white snow.

Why are these Rangers down?

I saw hydraulic fluid dotting the snow alongside the helicopter. I saw a few cedar trees dotting the snowy landscape. I smelled the cedar.

I sucked in a gulp of cold, thin air. My nose, throat, and lungs stretched wider to find more of it. I couldn't get enough.

No way two of my men are dead. At this point, I knew that three men were dead—one of them I'd never met, but two of them I knew well. Take a lifeless body and replace its face with that of someone you recognize, someone you love. So close to life, yet none of us can bring it back to them. They had no idea they were going to die. Even as it happened, they had no idea, no warning, no expectation that it would be them. *And I have no expectation that I will die either, nor will I realize my own error even if I am proved wrong. There will be nothing. Or something. To die like that is to never know.*

As a group we were like knights toppled from our horses into the fray of men-at-arms—where the biting, gouging of eyes, clubbing, and pulling of extremities make men more equal.

I heard clicking above my head. My mind interpreted the sound as someone snapping fingers above my head. I heard throaty rifle bursts. *Is someone shooting at me?*

Cli-cli-cli-cli-cli-click.

"Lancaster, move!" I pushed his shoulder. "Get up there."

"Shoot him, Sergeant!"

Lancaster and I crawled uphill a few feet from the ramp through the snow along the right side of the bird, our knees kicking up powder into our own faces, desperate to find cover.

"Move. Move. Move. Farther."

I heard an American rifle firing on full auto behind me, just off the ramp.

I leaned against the black skin of the aircraft's right fuel tank, which bulged like a love handle along the length of the fuselage. Graphite-gray hydraulic fluid gurgled from bullet holes along the helicopter's sides. Lancaster lay on his stomach fifteen feet to my front, just under the refueling probe, which pointed to the top of the slope. We had found what seemed to be a safe place.

Just beyond Lancaster, I saw a bearded face peeking over some rocks.

"Lancaster! Front!"

Lancaster rose to one knee with his M249 Squad Automatic Weapon (SAW) and fired three quick bursts, the recoil easing him back with each blast.

I swung my M4 rifle up into the natural pocket between my deltoid and chest—just off my body armor—flicked the selector lever to *semi*, and squeezed off five rounds over Lancaster's shoulder.

Did we hit him? Where did he go?

"Lancaster, lock that down."

"Roger, sir." Lancaster has such a soft voice that anyone who didn't know him would think he was scared. I knew better than that.

As I got my bearings, I saw that the helicopter was resting in a shallow bowl of snow, with a horseshoe of high ground ringing the front and sides of the helicopter. The back of the helo was tilted down toward a valley that dropped thousands of feet below. The enemy was in an ambush around us, firing down from the horseshoe of high ground.

I rolled to my side, looking over my shoulder down the slope to the rear of the aircraft. Across the valley to our rear, several rows of taller mountains stacked higher, as if reinforcing each other. The sun was one-quarter above the peaks.

The Rangers just off the ramp were still firing up to the left side of the bird. Those Rangers had crawled over two bodies already, without stopping to look at or care for them, instead moving right into the jaws of a machine gun. Ray DePouli was in the center, bent over on both knees, changing a magazine. He had already burned through one magazine.

"Whatta ya got, sir?" DePouli asked.

"I don't know," I said. "I'm trying to figure it out."

We must be surrounded. How did we get here? Who tricked us? This isn't the right spot. Get back to the bearded man—security first.

I turned back to my front, looking up to the top of the slope. Lancaster was looking in the same direction. The M134 minigun hung limp in the front window, pointing straight at him. That multi-barreled machine gun operated only on the aircraft's electrical power, which appeared to be down. Still, I felt uneasy about six barrels aimed at Lancaster's back. *He should move, but asking him to move right now is possibly a greater threat to his safety.*

The terrain cupped the helicopter, with high ground on both sides. We were in a saddle less than a hundred yards from the peak of a mountain. *Somebody made a big mistake in telling us to land here.*

Dink-dink-dink-biddlat-blat.

Gunfire sailed above my head, impacting the side of the bird. Lancaster and I returned fire to the top of the mountain. I heard someone using a fire extinguisher inside the helicopter.

I saw the bearded man again, peeking over a boulder at the top of the peak, the two o'clock direction from the nose of the aircraft. I rose up and fired several rounds at him without aiming, hoping that my speed would catch him. He disappeared. I stayed on one knee, eager to see his face again, holding my rifle high and ready. *Come on. Come on. Show yourself.*

An orange flash erupted next to the boulder under a short, piney tree. I dove into the snow. Another burst. *That's a machine gun under that "bonsai" tree.* I lifted my head. I couldn't see a target. *If I can't see them, they can't see me—or can they?* Rangers from the rear of the helicopter fired past me up the mountain. I felt safe, deep in snow that covered most of my body. *That won't protect you. Find cover.*

I knew I couldn't lie there and stay pinned down. I had to get away from the helicopter. *Battle Drill 1A: Return fire and seek cover. Locate the enemy. Suppress the enemy. Attack.* I felt hot in my gear. Hot in the snow.

I heard the sound of a bottle rocket set off near the boulder. I looked to the boulder and saw a dark capsule—an RPG—plunging down on me. I turned my head away, to the helicopter. *Here it comes.*

The RPG slammed into the rock just beneath the snow and detonated to my right. I felt a deep impact on my right thigh—like a hammer—and then a sharp driving prick in the same place. *I've been hit.* I heard Lancaster grunt.

"Agh!"

"You all right?" I asked. "Everybody all right?"

"Sir, I've been shot."

"No, it's shrapnel," I said. "Where?"

"It's my calf."

Lancaster was still lying on his stomach. He tried to lift his leg. "Hmph."

He was in pain. He turned, reaching for his calf. I lost sight of security to our front for a moment, watching him grope at his leg.

Battle Drill 1A: Return fire and seek cover. Locate the enemy. Suppress the enemy. Attack.

I spotted a pile of clothes in the snow fifteen yards from the right side of the aircraft, just in front of a large rock. A puffy blue ski jacket with spots of feathery down peeking out. I assumed it was an enemy fighter. He had a metal tube half hidden under his body. It looked like a rocket launcher. *Is he dead? Is he playing dead? He sure is close to us.*

"Has anyone checked this guy?" I asked, taking my hand off my rifle to point. "We need to check this guy."

"I put about a hundred rounds in him, sir," Sergeant Joshua Walker said. "He ain't a problem."

"Sergeant DePouli, let's move," I said.

"Roger, sir; we're ready."

We stood, firing at suspected enemy locations, executing basic tasks. Trapped in the low ground in the middle of a well-laid enemy ambush, we fought for our lives—operating from muscle memory and reflex from countless hours of training—to break through the inertia of being shot down and to gain back some of the momentum.

One Ranger moved ahead, trudging up the slope in the snow.

Bdat. Bdat-dat. Bdat. Bdat-bdat-dat-dat-bdat.

I bounded forward, firing. The energizing smell of gunpowder filled my nostrils. I raised my knees high, stepping over the snow and the hidden scree underfoot. I saw a boulder in front of me: good cover. My wounded leg felt fine for the moment. All I felt was the trigger. We moved as a synchronized unit, just as in training: forward one man at a time, each man in his own lane. *These are basics. Fire and move.*

The natural response would be to cower, to hope it would all go away, certainly not to move toward the threat. But we were living out the purpose of the Infantry—to close with and destroy the enemy. We were actively bringing the fight to the enemy—instinctively, not as an individual has instincts, but as a group, with a collective instinct.

Three of us convened behind an egg-shape rock big enough to hide us. I was in the center, with Sergeant Walker on my left and Kevin Vance on my right. Lancaster was still near the nose of the bird.

I looked at Sergeant Walker—and kept looking. His helmet appeared to have been hit in at least three places, but with grazing shots. He turned toward me, apparently concerned by the expression on my face.

"You good, sir?" he asked.

"Yeah. Are *you* good?"

"I'm fine, sir," he said. "You had me scared for a minute."

The top of his tan helmet was frayed and fuzzy, the jagged white cross-fibers splayed upward like fiberglass when it breaks.

"Moving!" Sergeant DePouli called from the ramp of the Chinook. On instinct, we provided a wave of suppressive fire to cover his bound to us. DePouli dove behind a pile of rocks to our right, on top of the body that had been freaking me out. He rolled the body over and out of his way.

Pfft-pfft-pfft-pfft-pfft!

Machine-gun rounds pelted the snow around our positions, followed by the muzzle blast from the peak. We crouched behind the boulder and returned fire, hunched behind our rifles to stay low. Each round I fired sounded simple and abrupt. *Plat. Plat.*

We ceased fire. The guns' barking reverberated through the mountain range in long, exhaustive tones. I remained in a crouch, swaying my barrel left and right, scanning, centered on the boulder and what I called the bonsai tree. *Try it, come on.*

Suddenly, another bearded face peeked from behind the bonsai tree. *I've got him.* My red dot reticle floated center mass of his green jacket. *Squeeze the trigger straight back.*

Click.

No round fired, no recoil. Just the clicking of the firing pin against an expended casing already in my rifle's chamber. I dropped to the ground. My rifle had malfunctioned, and I had to clear it. *I can't believe I missed him. You idiot, you didn't clean your rifle. This is your fault.*

I pulled the reticulated cleaning rod free from the plastic zip-ties holding it in place alongside my rifle barrel. We carried the rods exposed on our weapons for just this purpose, to serve as ramrods should we need to clear the barrel. I slid the rod into the barrel from the muzzle end, in the opposite direction that a bullet travels. The rod hit the spent casing. I rammed it once. Nothing. I rammed it again. *Crack.*

The rod had broken off in my hand at one of the thin metal threaded joints. I'd need a tool to remove the round now. *There's no time for that; I need a weapon now. The casualties.*

I turned and ran low back to the ramp with my rifle in hand, my night-vision goggles hanging from a lanyard on my body armor, bouncing in the snow between my legs behind me. The lanyard caught my legs and tripped me. I fell short of the ramp, eating a faceful of snow, my rifle flying out of my hands and banging into the side of the helicopter.

Cli-cli-cli-click.

Another burst of gunfire just over the ramp—a burst likely aimed at my back just before I tripped on my lanyard. Crawling now to the back of the Chinook, looking for an extra rifle, I found one lying on the ground beside the facedown Ranger, his feet still on the ramp. I recognized him from the back of his head and his hair. It was Sergeant Crose. He hadn't moved since I last saw him. *He must be dead.*

There were other bodies in the snow around him. Their pain-filled groans left no room for pride. They were grown men, hard men, deep in pain. I picked up Crose's rifle and ran uphill to the rock where I'd had the malfunction. I did not fire, wanting only to get back to cover.

I dove into the void between Sergeant Walker and Sergeant Vance, safe behind the big rock and between their active guns. Vance wore a heavy black North Face fleece under his body armor, looking like he got off the wrong ski lift. Lancaster was still lying near the nose of the helicopter with his SAW. Beyond him, I saw a pilot deep in the snow under the bubble nose of the Chinook, peering up the slope through the bare-iron sights of his M4 rifle. He wasn't even wearing a helmet.

"Hey, you okay over there?" I called. "Pilot, you okay?"

"I think my leg's blown off," he answered. It was Chuck, the pilot I had met in Bagram a couple of days before.

"You need to move?"

"No, I'll stay here for now. I've got this side covered."

"Totten, get over here," Sergeant Walker said to Lancaster.

"I don't think I can stand up," Lancaster said. "My ankle is numb."

"Just get over here. Crawl or something."

Lancaster began rolling from the helicopter to our boulder. An explosion rocked the ground to our front, between our position and the peak. I felt the concussive thump.

"What was that?" I asked. "Are they throwing grenades at us?"

"Who the f— do they think they are?" Walker said. "Aw, naw, naw, naw."

Sergeant Walker pulled a grenade off his body armor and removed the safety pin. "Cover me."

"Go for it," I said.

We crouched and fired as he stood, balanced, and threw the grenade. His body armor restricted his throwing motion, and the grenade flew a mere twenty feet. We hit the deck and waited for the explosion. *Thwump.*

"That's not gonna work. They're at least fifty meters from us . . . and uphill."

"I can get it there, sir."

Sergeant Walker repeated the grenade-throwing drill. Twenty-five feet. *Thwump.*

I heard another rocket rip off from the peak. An RPG screamed over us and skipped off the ramp with an ear-grating metallic scrape. It did not detonate.

Sergeant DePouli spotted something on the peak. He came to a knee and aimed. *Kerplat.* Still aiming. *Kerplat.* Still aiming. *Kerplat.* He lowered his rifle and eased back into the snow.

"I got him. I got him. Got that RPG f———."

I looked directly to my left, where the helicopter sat, its blades long since stilled. Just next to the limp minigun, I saw a faded red Maltese cross painted on the fuselage, with the letters "FDNY" inside the cross, underscoring the reason we were here fighting for our lives. It was watching over us as a reminder. A statement to our enemy.

I didn't even know where we were. We were warriors in a faraway place, here for them. It had been six months since the Twin Towers fell in New York, but it felt like we were born for that day—to meet our nation's enemies.

41

The last thing a woman will consent to discover in a man whom she loves, or on whom she simply depends, is want of courage. :: JOSEPH CONRAD

**04 0621 MAR 02 (DELTA)
TAKUR GHAR**

I've heard it said that threat clears a man's head.

I believe that to be true up to a certain threshold. But in matters of extreme threat, I believe it's possible for a few images to dominate a man's mind, even to the disastrous point of total dysfunction. My own mind's preoccupation in thin air under extreme duress was with my young family—with Julie and Caleb.

I didn't believe I would die in that moment, but I thought about their future without me. In an obtuse way, I confronted the possibility of my death through seeing my wife and four-month-old son alone, without a husband and a father. But I never thought I would die. My instincts were denying my mind's practical conclusion—that I could die there—in a way that removed any fear. Still, I recognized how sad it would be for Julie and Caleb to be alone, searching for another man to take my place.

42

But by the all-powerful dispensations of Providence, I have been protected beyond all human probability or expectation; for I had four bullets through my coat, and two horses shot under me, yet escaped unhurt, although death was leveling my companions on every side of me!
:: GEORGE WASHINGTON, In a letter to his brother John, July 18, 1755

04 0621 MAR 02 (DELTA)
TAKUR GHAR

"Sir, we need to bring the machine gun up here," DePouli said.

He had caught me in midthought, staring at the boulder in front of me.

"What's that, Ray?"

"I'm gonna get the 240 up here so we can get some suppression."

"Yeah, that's good."

"Gilliam, you ready?"

"Roger, Sar'nt."

It was odd to me that DePouli was asking Gilliam, the youngest man on the mountain, to employ our most casualty-producing weapon.

Gilliam? Where's Anderson? Why is Gilliam bringing the machine gun? I just saw Anderson. He was sitting right next to me on the bird.

We stood and provided a heavy burst of rifle fire, allowing Gilliam to trudge up to DePouli's location with his twenty-eight-pound machine gun and several hundred rounds of ammunition. Lancaster stayed prone on the left end of our boulder, scanning to the front of the bird. I noticed it was difficult to aim my new weapon—Sergeant Crose's weapon. Operating his rifle should've been instinctual, because he had configured it exactly like mine: laser on top of the barrel, foregrip under the barrel for my left hand with two pressure switches—one for the laser and one for the mounted tactical flashlight—and a parallax-free, floating-red-dot aiming sight on top of the receiver.

I realized that the problem was with the red dot. I couldn't make it out. There were several red dots. I pulled the rifle away from my face. It was spotted with blood. I took a knee to clean the rear lens of the sight and returned to suppress the enemy.

Gilliam settled in next to DePouli, rolling the dead RPG gunner out of the way again.

It was always a major decision to commit a machine gun to the fight, a decision usually reserved for the platoon leader. Putting a machine gun into action was an investment in at least three ways: it told the enemy just how serious we were, it told the enemy what kind of force he was up against, and once committed, was hard to pull back. Here, suppressing with a machine gun could possibly deter the enemy's ambitions to attack us or exploit a flank. I didn't know how many casualties we had, but I only saw five from our bird that could move and shoot. It was clear to me that emplacing the machine gun was more than a show of force. We needed the extra firepower.

"Let's get that thing rocking and let them know we're here," I said.

Gilliam ripped off a long burst.

Doh-doh-doh-doh-doh-doh-dohn. Seven rounds, just like Anderson had taught him.

"Hit it again," I said.

Doh-doh-doh-doh-dohn. Gilliam was performing like a thirty-year-old, like Anderson. Gilliam was a bushy-haired kid from eastern Tennessee. He had a baby girl of his own at home named Skila. *Is Gilliam thinking about his daughter right now?*

I rolled to my back so I could survey the landscape to our rear. I was looking for other Americans, other skirmishes. We should've landed in the middle of Operation Anaconda. I saw no evidence of other Americans. We were alone.

The terrain to the east behind us dropped to a steep and narrow valley a couple thousand feet below and then back up a mountain taller than ours. That distant peak appeared to suspend the bright morning sun just above its tip. The sky was cornflower blue and devoid of clouds.

I pulled out my GPS, a pocket-size civilian model by Garmin. It wouldn't turn on.

"Sergeant Walker, you got your Garmin?" After his GPS locked on a few satellites, I took out my Russian-made map and marked our location on top of a mountain saddle. The peak was labeled "Takur Ghar."

A few of the aircrew members had gathered at the ramp of the Chinook, some of them lying on their backs. *These guys are wounded. One of the pilots had to have lost his hand.* The helicopter crew was easy to spot. They wore solid tan coveralls with black fleece, black body armor, and black harnesses over their torsos. They had no gear for a ground fight. One of the crew members saw me looking in their direction.

"Team Leader!" he said.

"Yes," I said.

"What do you need us to do? On the ground we fall under you. Just tell us what you need." It was Don, the air mission commander. I wondered if he recognized me from Andy's introduction in Bagram. It didn't matter.

"We'll need you to gather any extra 7.62 ammo from the helicopter."

"We've already got it. Where do you need it?"

"At the gun on my right," I said, pointing at Gilliam and DePouli. "And any extra magazines from the wounded we'll need up here too."

For the next ten minutes, Don and a redheaded crew member with a mustache sprinted up to our forward positions with arms full of ammunition, wearing no equipment, no helmets, carrying no weapons. We covered their movement with suppressive fire. After four such runs, they had more than supplied us to sustain the fight. They gave me thirteen magazines. I replenished the three I had already expended, replacing them in my personal gear pouches in case we had to move quickly. For the immediate fight, I stacked the excess ten magazines on the rocks to my front.

The crew members' bravery left me humbled, but seeing them run in the snow, unencumbered by eighty pounds of equipment, made me jealous. It occurred to me how obsessed we Rangers had been with lightening the loads we carried. "Ounces make pounds, sir," my men would say, justifying arguments to lessen amounts of food, water, clothing, and even body armor on certain occasions. When we expected to operate at high altitudes, the NCOs pleaded to leave the body armor behind in favor of greater endurance and speed. Even I wasn't wearing the ceramic back plate issued to me. "Mobility equals survivability, sir."

Despite the obsession with a lighter load, the one thing we never neglected was ammunition. Most Rangers carried well beyond the standard seven magazines, each magazine holding thirty rounds. Some Rangers carried twice the basic load, hauling fifteen magazines on their body armor. Here, with ten extra magazines stacked on the rocks to my front, I realized that in a fight like this, where I'd actually shoot more than my basic load, there was plenty of extra ammo lying around.

Thwump. The enemy was throwing grenades again.

"This is bull—," Walker said. "I'll be back."

Sergeant Walker turned and skipped down the slope to the ramp, leaving his rifle leaning on the rock next to me. I looked at

Vance, who was shaking his head. Sergeant Walker returned out of breath and carrying another rifle with a grenade launcher mounted beneath the barrel. It was the weapon Matt Commons had carried into the fight, the weapon he had inherited from Drew Phillips at Tarnak Farms. Walker laid a canvas rig full of gold-domed 40-mm high-explosive grenades against the rock.

Walker slid open the breach, inserted a grenade, and raised to a knee.

"They want to throw grenades?"

Foomp. Walker's shot sailed over the boulder and detonated down the other side of the mountain. His next two shots did the same. Because we were below the enemy, the only way to get the grenades to detonate was to shoot them short or almost straight up in the air, and the latter option would've been too dangerous to us. Walker tried to shoot the grenades short, with no effect.

"Why don't you try to hit the top of the tree or the side of the boulder?"

Walker's next shot exploded on the boulder, spraying shrapnel into the bonsai tree. *Foomp . . . Fa-RUMP!*

Just as I was about to assume that Walker's shot had been effective, another few rounds cracked over our heads.

43

As soon as there is life, there is danger. :: RALPH WALDO EMERSON

04 0642 MAR 02 (DELTA)
TAKUR GHAR

The vast snowfield to the rear of the helicopter looked less peaceful to me with every passing minute. Our exposed backside worried me.

We had everything focused up the mountain at the bonsai tree, with almost no security to our rear. I had assumed risk there for the time being. Our defensive posture was akin to my body armor, with guns and breastplates and eyes to the front and no protection to the rear. A vulnerable gaggle of casualties, medics, and aircrew lay just off the ramp of the helicopter, exposed to the elements and possible enemy flanking attempts. I needed to establish better security.

"Sergeant DePouli, who's covering our rear?"

"Miceli's got it, sir," he said.

"Where is he?"

"He's down there in that rock outcropping."

I squinted at a knob of brown rocks jutting out of the mountain and snow. I couldn't locate him.

"I can't see him, Ray," I said.

"You can't, sir? I sure hope you can see the enemy. He's got it covered, but all he's got is a rifle."

"Where's his SAW?"

"It got shot up in his hands on the ramp. He's lucky he's alive."

"Is he wounded?"

"Nope. He's a lucky b——."

"Nobody can kill Miceli but Miceli, Sar'nt," Walker said with a smile.

"Nice," I said. "Well, if he's our only rear security, let's get him a SAW."

One of the crew members again volunteered to shuttle our equipment, this time retrieving Lancaster's SAW (squad automatic weapon) and carrying it down to Miceli's position. Miceli was covering half of the perimeter by himself from the rock outcropping. As a whole, we were blind to our left flank, as the left rim of the saddle loomed thirty meters away. If we tried to flank that way, we'd be cut down by the enemy near the bonsai tree.

"You want to check out our flank, Ray? We need to move," I said.

"Which one, sir?"

"Go right."

"Roger. I'll take Miceli with me."

"All right, give me a call when you get close and we'll suppress. Shift fire on FM COMMS."

Sergeant DePouli crawled downslope. The redheaded aircrew member, whose name I learned was Brian, moved into DePouli's position alongside Gilliam to feed the machine gun's ammunition belt.

I had learned over the past year and a half as a Ranger platoon leader that I didn't have to motivate my squad leaders to do anything. Rather, the problem was keeping them reined in. Their aggressiveness was a high-octane example of the U.S. military philosophy in training and previous wars: to stay on the offensive. We weren't very good defenders, in part because we never trained it, but primarily because we were wired to attack. Every Ranger on that mountain wanted to assault and kill. I wanted to assault just as badly, especially with so many guys bleeding. DePouli's voice came over my radio.

"Sir, we can't use this flank. It's a sheer cliff," he said.

"So there's no way? The enemy couldn't use it, either?"

"No way," he said.

"Okay, come back up here and we'll try something else," I said. "No, wait; do you think there's enough room in that rock outcropping for all of us?"

"The whole chalk?" he asked.

"Yeah, to move all of our casualties there and strongpoint around those rocks."

"No, sir, there's not enough room," DePouli said.

"Sir, I found something else down here—a recoilless rifle's down here."

"You think we could get it up here?" I said. "Maybe fire it?"

"Sir, it's a long way down here," DePouli said. "It's pretty big, too. Anyway, I don't see any ammunition down here."

Sergeant Walker had an idea.

"Sir, we have some rounds right here," Walker said.

"Where?" I asked.

"Right there," he said, pointing at the dead RPG gunner near Gilliam.

"Those are RPG rounds, Sergeant Walker."

"What's that, then?"

"That's an RPG, but it's full of holes. It's like Swiss cheese."

"Okay, well—what does Sergeant DePouli have?" Walker said.

"A recoilless rifle."

"Yeah, that thing. What's that?"

"It's like a big bazooka or something," I said.

"So you can't use them rounds in that recoilless rifle?"

"No."

I wasn't sure if Walker was truly confused or if he was just messing with me.

DePouli came back up on the radio. "Sir, I think we got something down here, some kind of enemy position," he said. "I'm gonna clear it."

"No, wait for us to establish better security."

"Sir, it's just right here. We've got it."

I knew that when Ranger NCOs got something in their heads, it was nearly impossible to change their minds. I realized that if I resisted an idea and they remained adamant about it, then they were usually right anyway.

"Okay, One," I said to DePouli. "Go ahead."

Bdot-dot-dot. Bdot. Bdot.

Gunfire from Miceli's position. *Oh no.*

"One, this is Six; over," I said.

"Yeah?" DePouli said.

"Whatcha got?"

"I don't know, some sort of sleeping position. But there's an American rucksack down here. I'm gonna check this out."

This doesn't make any sense. Why would there be American gear up here? Maybe we were double-crossed. Did somebody lose this gear? Is the enemy wealthy enough to buy the same stuff we have?

"Gilliam, fire a couple of bursts at the bonsai tree," I said. "I don't want them getting any ideas."

Gilliam handled the machine gun well. His new assistant, Brian, fed the ammo belt into the machine gun with his left hand, using his other hand to muffle the blast in his right ear. He still wasn't wearing earplugs or a helmet. He looked like he'd been snatched out of a crowd and put into a firefight, but in the past hour, Brian had done some very brave things.

Gilliam came off the machine gun and made a statement, which was rare.

"Sir, I found some binos over here on this enemy," he said.

"Throw them here; I could use them to scan our rear."

Gilliam threw the optics to our group, and Vance leaned out from behind the boulder to retrieve them. He handed them to me. They weren't binoculars. They were night-vision goggles—expensive goggles. I tapped Vance on the shoulder.

"Kevin, look at these," I said.

"What are they, NODs?"

"Yeah, and good ones," I said. "These are better than ours. These are like the ones the SEALs and aviators use."

Why would these former mujahideen fighters have night-vision goggles like this? Either someone has betrayed us or someone was captured here.

DePouli ran back uphill to his position with Gilliam, drawing enemy fire while he moved.

"Hey, sir, you gotta see that position down there," he said. "It's like a sleeping position and a little mosque down there. And I found this."

He threw me a black radio the size of a brick, just like the two I was carrying on my gear. It was a Multi-Band Intra-Team Radio, or as we called it, the MBITR. I turned it over in my hand to see a white label taped to the back of it: "RED 1S." I recognized the call sign. It belonged to SEALs.

Maybe we didn't land in the wrong spot after all. The SEALs were requesting us in the vicinity of a "hot LZ." *But where are the SEALs?*

"Okay. We'll figure all this out later," I said. "Right now, we need to get moving."

44

War is very simple, direct, and ruthless. It takes a simple, direct, and ruthless man to wage war.

:: MARTIN BLUMENSON, *The Patton Papers*

04 0718 MAR 02 (DELTA)
TAKUR GHAR

"Team Leader."

"Yeah," I said, looking over my back to see who was calling. It was another mustached fellow in a plain camouflage uniform with a Vietnam-era equipment rig over his body armor. He was fifteen yards downslope from us, just to the right of the ramp. He knelt behind a rucksack with an antenna exposed and a handset pressed to his ear. His helmet's chinstrap was hanging loose under his chin. He was an Air Force combat controller (CCT). His job was to talk to aircraft.

"All right, I'm working close air support right now," he said. "Looks like we'll be in business in a couple of minutes."

At the mention of CAS, I finally noticed that there was no AC-130 flying overhead. It must have gone off station before we even landed. The CCT worked to get us aerial coverage, but we would have to settle for whatever happened to be flying overhead at the time.

"Let me know when you get them on station," Vance said.

"Roger," the CCT said. "Bossman, Bossman, this is Slick Zero-One, controller in contact; over."

It was 7:18 a.m. In a fight against this type of enemy, engaging in direct contact and intense fire for anything beyond a few minutes is not normal. We had been on the ground just over an hour. Now we were going to get some help.

Walker tapped me on the shoulder. I looked at him, but was distracted by the splattered flecks of blood on his face, blood mixed with oil from the rifle he was firing, the rifle Matt Commons had carried into battle.

"Sir, what are them rocks for?"

A column of fist-size rocks stood a few feet in front of our boulder, protruding above the snow line. It seemed strange enough to me, it seemed man-made, just like the trail markings my dad had taught me about while camping in the woods. The application here in Afghanistan, as my intelligence officer had briefed us, was that the enemy stacked rocks to mark their firing lanes, their sectors of fire. If this was the case, we were dead in the center of a prepared and sighted-in ambush kill zone.

"Team Leader, I've got CAS on station," the CCT said. "F-15s with five-hundred-pounders ready to fly."

The idea of dropping bombs in this fight seemed ludicrous. Vance stepped in.

"We're not using bombs, Jeremy," Vance said. "Talk to them about guns."

The CCT, apparently named Jeremy, went back to work on the radio.

"Twister Five-One, this is Slick Zero-One—request gun runs; over," Jeremy said. "Roger, stand by."

"They're good with guns," he confirmed.

Vance looked to the top of the mountain to check his bearings and then eyed the sun's position. These jet fighters were not designed to support troops in close contact, but they did possess 20-mm cannons, and we needed them.

Vance looked at me. "Sir, can you pick up my sector of fire? I need to coordinate this CAS run."

"Of course, Kevin," I said.

Vance pointed with an extended hand along his envisioned flight path.

"Tell them to come in at a 220 heading," Vance said.

"Roger," he said. "Twister Five-One, Slick Zero-One. Target description: Do you see a black helicopter? Okay, from the nose of the helicopter, go one hundred meters, direction two o'clock. You should see a tree on top of the mountain . . ."

Two minutes later, I heard the dry, scratching sound of a pair of F-15E Strike Eagles inbound. Vance scanned to our rear, looking for the jets.

"I got him. I got him," Vance said. "Tell him to abort, abort! I don't like it!"

The F-15s ripped over the mountain peak, banking hard right, leveling, and then darting up and away, pumping bright yellow flares from their undersides.

"Bump them more to the west, to a 245."

"Got it!"

"Twister Five-One, this is Slick Zero-One—adjust attack heading to Two-Four-Five."

The jets came in again, this time more from our rear. I felt like I was at an air show as the jets again sped by the peak.

"That's good," Vance said. "Clear 'em."

"Twister Five-One, that is a good attack heading," the CCT called. "You're cleared hot; over."

"Everybody, heads down. Gun run in thirty seconds."

We tried to wiggle deeper in the snow and brace ourselves for the close air support. We were only seventy-five yards from the intended target. I prayed for steady hands in the cockpit, hands that would be releasing their rounds several thousand yards away. I put my head down.

I raised my head. I had to look. I wanted to see the jets in action, and I was nervous that they might hit us. I knew that once they squeezed that trigger flying at more than five hundred miles per hour, they couldn't get the bullets back. If they were going to hit me, at least I wanted to see it.

I saw the lead fast mover roll out of a long right bank over the taller eastern mountains. He leveled his wings at us. A moment later, a brown dust cloud appeared beneath his jet, looking like he had just sprung a leak in his exhaust pipe. In a half-second, the ground to our front erupted like a pond in a hailstorm. The brown dust cloud under his plane was hundreds of spent 20-mm shell casings.

Sheew-shew-PHUM-PUM-PUM-PUM.

The first gun run from the F-15s pounded the ground between the enemy position and us. I couldn't believe how close it was.

"Whoa!"

"What was that?"

"Machine guns. Don't worry about it. Just keep your heads down," I said. I turned back to Jeremy. "Again."

"Twister Five-One, adjust another twenty meters farther away from the downed helo; over."

The Strike Eagles turned tight over the eastern peaks, the trail jet moving on an inside arc to take the lead. Within a minute, they were hammering the peak again.

The guys around me burst into a cheer.

"Whoa! You hit it! Smell the pine, baby! Good run."

"F— you, al-Qaeda! There's a little U.S. Air Force on your ass!"

I felt embarrassed at our childish levity in the midst of such dire straits. But I couldn't keep from smiling.

"Was that good?" Jeremy asked. "On target?"

"Yeah, Jeremy. Have 'em hit it again," Vance said.

"All right, they've got one run left," he said. "And by the way, my name's not Jeremy; it's Gabe."

I looked at Vance in disbelief.

"*What*, sir? I thought his name was Jeremy," he said.

After another on-target and nonfratricidal gun run, the F-15s broke station. Minutes before, we had become instantly all-powerful when the jets arrived with their earsplitting engines and menacing weapons. Now they were gone, leaving us to the feeble protection of our precipitous cocoon of able Rangers, to the sound of wind at ten thousand feet.

We're still here, we still have guys dying, and we still can't move. How do we get out of this?

A dreadful feeling sank over me, like I had decided to go for a swim in the ocean and found myself five miles out and exhausted: I dreaded having to swim back, but I had no choice.

Either I do it, or I die right here.

45

You cannot stay on the summit forever; you have to come down again. So why bother in the first place? Just this: What is above knows what is below, but what is below does not know what is above. One climbs, one sees. One descends, one sees no longer, but one has seen. There is an art of conducting oneself in the lower regions by the memory of what one saw higher up. When one can no longer see, one can at least still know. :: RENÉ DAUMAL

04 0801 MAR 02 (DELTA)
TAKUR GHAR

I heard the distant rumble of jet aircraft approaching. In a few minutes, we again would be all-powerful. The CCT spoke up to inform me of what I already knew: we had another sortie of CAS.

"Team Leader?" the CCT said.

"Yeah."

"Sortie of F-16s on station, four five-hundred-pounders each, ready for tasking."

"Have them hold tight for now," I said. Gun runs with 20-mm cannons was one thing; five-hundred-pound bombs were a greater risk.

Okay. It seems that we've beaten the enemy back some, even if they're still alive and holding the top of the mountain. I have five guys. I could attack. If only I had more shooters.

Chalk 2.

"Sergeant DePouli, did you see what happened to Chalk 2?"

"No, sir. I lost 'em about a minute out."

"Me, too," I said. "We sure could use them right now."

"Sir, unless they landed right here, it's gonna take them a while to get to us."

He was right. We needed to act. We couldn't sit here all day and let guys bleed to death.

"Controller, get the F-16s up," I said.

"Sir, are you sure?" Vance said.

"We need to get some suppression and prep an assault," I said. "Let's have 'em do gun runs again."

Gabe took five minutes to give another full CAS check-in briefing to the new CAS sortie of F-16s. Everything the F-15 pilots had learned flew away with them to an air base or a refueling tanker hundreds of miles removed from the peak. I trusted the F-16 pilots just as well as the F-15s, even though the only thing they had in common was the airspace they occupied. New pilots introduced new risks.

"Guns in thirty seconds," Gabe said. "Everyone find cover."

The F-16 pilots needed a full shooting pass of the mountain in order to adjust on target, but before they ran out of bullets, they, too, put effective lead on the target—the bonsai tree. They made at least four shooting passes of the mountain.

"Sir, they've got bombs if you're ready for them," Gabe said. "We could withdraw from here and call 'em in."

I again looked at Miceli's rock outcropping. I was tempted to break away from the enemy and develop a stronger defense.

I was a Ranger leader. I had made up my mind. I looked at De-Pouli.

"Okay, let's get ready to assault," I said.

"We're ready, sir," DePouli said.

"All right, let's go," I said. "Gilliam, suppress."

The young machine gunner began rocking the suspected enemy positions, assisted by Brian, the air-crew member. Walker, Vance, DePouli, and I stood from behind our rocks and began firing. Gilliam increased his rate of fire. We began walking uphill in the snow. Walker was on the far left. I was between him and Vance. DePouli was on the far right. Everyone had a grenade in his off-hand except me. Walker fired a grenade from Commons's M203. We kept moving upward to the bonsai tree.

Slow is smooth. Smooth is fast.

As a platoon leader, I'd never been a part of a Ranger fire team. My job was to coordinate and synchronize assets, affect the fight outside the platoon, set conditions, and anticipate the enemy. That was the graduate-level definition of leadership I had learned to live by. But here on the mountain, my presence as a mere soldier was a necessity. As we assaulted the enemy, our team of three NCOs and one officer wasn't a group of leaders. We were Rangers, plain and simple. We were shooters. We were leading with our muzzles.

Bdat-dat. Bdat. Dat. Dat. Dat. Bdat.

We were closing the distance nicely. No sign of the enemy. We were nearing hand-grenade range, which for everyone except Walker was usually at thirty-five meters.

Almost there. We're about to end this thing. Gilliam's shifted. Good.

I saw a bearded face flash from behind the bonsai tree and fire two short, poorly aimed bursts from a machine gun at the base of the tree. He disappeared behind the tree. He was in a waist-deep hole. My eyes naturally swung past the tree . . . to see the wall of a bunker, logs roped together and covered with fresh branches of evergreen foliage. Gilliam's gun had been firing into the side of that bunker all morning.

Where had he gone? His muzzle could be in that foliage and I'd never see it.

Dug in. Overhead cover. Machine gun. Bunker.

It all seemed wrong to me, a potential disaster.

"Bunker! Bunker! Bunker!" I said. "Get back, get back!"

The trio of NCOs hesitated in a moment of disbelief, fumbling with grenades, and then followed the order. We bounded back as a group, stopping to suppress over our shoulders as we retreated to our safe protective rocks.

We just retreated. I can't believe it.

"Everybody okay?" I asked.

"Roger."

"I'm good."

"What happened, sir?"

"That was a hard bunker," I said. "A machine gun. It just seemed wrong."

"F—, sir. We were almost there."

"I know. It just wasn't right," I said. "We need more guys. If we try that again and don't make it, nobody can defend this crash site."

If the enemy bunker was built as well as it looked, then our 7.62-mm machine-gun rounds would have little effect on it. And even after the jets' gun runs, it appeared that some of the enemy fighters had survived. I needed heavier weapons. We had failed to bring our antitank missiles along with us—a costly oversight.

I heard the casualties groaning in pain. I overheard someone near the ramp say we needed to get off the mountain as soon as possible.

Staring up the slope where I had just been, where we were so close to reaching that bunker, I wondered if I would ever see the top of the mountain. The memory of our Bible study last night hovered just beneath my conscious thought. *Psalm 121. The faces of Marc Anderson, Arin Canon, and Matt Commons.*

There had been only twenty-one men on our helicopter. We had more than ten casualties, only five trigger pullers, and we'd already tried to assault once. We couldn't bring CAS any closer without risking fratricide, and there was no way anyone would send us another helo before sundown.

Do these guys think they're gonna make it home? If we're going to make it home, I have no idea how. If we're going to make it home, who will get us there? Does the outcome rest on me? God, help us.

46

Never shall I fail my comrades. I will always keep myself mentally alert, physically strong and morally straight and I will shoulder more than my share of the task whatever it may be. One hundred percent and then some. :: RANGER CREED, Third Stanza

04 0832 MAR 02 (DELTA)
TAKUR GHAR

In my mind, I had no need to talk to my higher headquarters—at least not yet. We had been on the ground for almost two hours. We were fighting for our lives. I could spare only one guy for the radio, and that was the CCT. And if his effort on the radio hadn't been directly impacting the fight, I would've had him pulling a trigger too. I knew several high-ranking individuals must've been angry that they hadn't gotten a report from me. But what could they do for me? Send me CAS? Already had it. Send me reinforcements? How would they get here? They sure couldn't land on this LZ, because it was fouled by Razor 01. The decision was easy for me: shoot now, report later.

"Team Leader, I just got a report that the QRF landed southwest of us," Gabe said.

"What do you mean, the QRF?" I asked. "We *are* the QRF."

The radio in my ear came to life for the first time since De-Pouli had shot up the enemy mosque and found the mysterious U.S. equipment.

"Six, this is Four."

Four? That's Canon's call sign. Surely that isn't right.

"Six, this is Four; over." It was definitely Canon.

"Four, this is Six; over," I said.

"Roger, I'm on the ground. Moving to your location now with Chalk 2," Canon said. "Pilots said they dropped us eight hundred meters southwest of you."

"Okay, if you're southwest, then we have the mountain between us. Just head northeast up the mountain and stop short of the peak. We'll suppress from here, and you can assault the enemy positions up here. We're pretty banged up."

"Roger, Six," Canon said. "Can you throw up a flare so I can get a fix on your location?"

"Sure. Stand by." The M203 grenade launcher could launch some nice signal flares, if we had any.

"Sergeant Walker, do you have any flares for the 203?"

"Roger, sir; I've got three green ones."

"Four, this is Six. We're gonna launch a green flare." Sergeant Walker fired the flare above our position.

"Do you see it?"

"Negative," Canon said.

Hmm. That's not good. Maybe he's farther away than he thought.

Walker fired another. Still no visual confirmation. Something had to be wrong.

"Four, this is Six; can you send me your grid location?" I asked.

Canon sent an eight-digit grid location, which was accurate to ten meters. I checked my map, looking for his position relative to the pencil mark I had made on our own location. His position wasn't southwest of us, but northeast of us. He'd been looking in the wrong direction for the flare.

"Four, Six. You're to our *northeast*," I said. "All you have to do is follow the valley to your south into the mountain pass and then turn right, up the first big mountain. We're near the peak, gathered around our bird."

"Roger. We'll be there," Canon said.

"How long?"

"I estimate about forty-five minutes," Canon said.

"Good," I said. "Glad you made it."

"Roger, sir."

I smiled at DePouli and made an announcement.

"Guys, Chalk 2 is on the ground to our north in that valley," I said. "Watch your fires in that direction. They're moving to our location now. Forty-five minutes."

Canon came back on the radio.

"Six, this is Four. I've got a linkup with MAKO Three-Zero."

How is that possible? If it's true, that would mean Canon's linking up with the missing guy.

"Four, this is Six," I said. "You say you've linked up with that MAKO element?"

"Negative; I've got a SEAL officer with me here. We picked him up in Gardez. He wants us to go with him to help extract his guys. He says you can move down here to our LZ."

Move down to help extract his guys? "No, you're coming up here," I said. "I've got an LZ right in front of me, and we're not moving anywhere. He can go to his guys. They're fine. We're still getting shot at up here. Tell him I need you *here*."

"Roger, Six. En route."

"If you come up the mountain from that eastern valley, you'll come up right behind us."

"Roger."

Woomp. Woomp.

We all heard the unmistakable sound of mortar rounds leaving their tubes somewhere to our rear, in the taller eastern moun-

Nate and his squad of fellow New Cadets take a break on the march
back from Lake Frederick *August 1994*

AN OFFICER IN THE MAKING

◀ LEFT

A lieutenant in cadet's clothes *May 1998*

Julie offers Nate a congratulatory kiss
after pinning his lieutenant's bars
with MAJ Eric Schacht (left)

➡ BELOW

RIGHT ▶
Cadet Nate Self and his
fiancée, Julie Wenzel
Grad Week, 1998

◀ LEFT
Newlyweds Nate and Julie Self at the Clifton House in Waco *June 1998*

Julie and Caleb at home in Texas during Nate's deployment to Afghanistan
➡ BELOW

◀ LEFT
SSG Ray DePouli and SSG Harper Wilmoth
Tarnak Farms, February 2002

CPT Nate Self and CPT Pete Marques
Bagram, April 2002

Matt Commons takes the challenge to drink a canteen cup full of T-ration meatball gravy, to the delight and uproar of his Ranger platoon *January 2003*

◀ **LEFT**

1st Squad:
(Clockwise from front left)
SSG Ray DePouli
SPC Aaron Totten-Lancaster
SGT Brad Crose
PFC Brent Akin *(face not pictured)*
PFC Matt Commons
PFC Yuma Barnett
PFC John Phillips
PFC Nicholas Mosca
SPC Anthony Miceli
SGT Joshua Walker
Bagram, January 2002

RIGHT ▶
LT Dave Blank and LT Nate Self at
Camp Monteith, Kosovo *early 2000*

★ ★ ★ ★ ★ ★ ★ ★ ★ ★ ★ ★ ★ ★ ★ ★

TWO FAMILIES

★ ★ ★ ★ ★ ★ ★ ★ ★ ★ ★ ★ ★ ★ ★ ★

Nate Self with Caleb at 6 months old.
Welcome Home Ceremony, Hunter
Army Airfield *Savannah, Georgia*

CPT Nate Self with Kurdish children
of Al Qosh, Iraq *late 2003*

SSG Ray DePouli briefs upcoming squad
tactics before breaching a mud wall
Tarnak Farms, February 2002
➥ BELOW

➥ ABOVE
Nate Self and Chaplain Randy Kirby talk
just before loading aircraft to fly back to
the United States *Bagram Airbase, April 2002*

★ ★

RANGERS LEAD THE WAY

★ ★

◀ LEFT
CPT Pete Marques and
U.S. Air Force Staff Sergeant
Kevin Vance, *Bagram*

SGT Eric Stebner
➥ BELOW

RIGHT ▶
CPT Nate Self
Tarnak Farms, Afghanistan

◆ LEFT
SGT Josh Walker (left) and
SPC Anthony Miceli

SSG Arin Canon (left) and PFC David Gilliam *Tarnak Farms, February 2002*

CPT Nate Self and SSG Arin Canon aboard an MH-47 Chinook

★ ★

★ ★

➡ **BELOW** An abandoned Razor 01 a few days after the battle

Looking down the barrel of SPC Randy Pazder's M240B machine gun during the enemy counterattack. The ridgeline in the foreground is the enemy's launching point.
March 4, 2002
➡ **BELOW**

⬅ **ABOVE** Downed Razor 01 *March 4, 2002*

SGT Philip Svitak

U.S. Navy Petty
Officer 1st Class
Neil Roberts

U.S. Air Force
Technical Sergeant
John Chapman

U.S. Air Force
Senior Airman
Jason Cunningham

★ ★

TAKUR GHAR

Still capture of Predator
video feed, Razor 01
Takur Ghar, Afghanistan, March 4, 2002

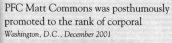

◀ LEFT
PFC Matt Commons was posthumously
promoted to the rank of corporal
Washington, D.C., December 2001

RIGHT ▶
SPC Marc "Big A"
Anderson
Kandahar, Afghanistan

⬆ ABOVE
SGT Bradley "Danger" Crose
Bagram, Afghanistan

NEVER FORGOTTEN

SPC Jonas Polson, CPT Nate Self,
SGT Eric Stebner at the TF 11
memorial ceremony
March 2002

tains. Those sounds signaled the outset of a protracted period of agony, of waiting for the mortar rounds to reveal their destinations. Even a gust of wind could determine the difference between safety, wounds, or death.

The incoming mortar rounds sounded akin to a subway—the metallic railing of train cars rifling down the tracks, like they were being sucked through an enormous straw. The sound grew louder.

An explosion spit rock and snow skyward, twenty meters off the nose of the helicopter at the top of the peak.

"Was that one of ours?"

"No, that was enemy indirect," I said. "Probably 82-mm mortars."

It made sense to me that the enemy's first mortar volley hit so close to the top of the peak and so close to us. I was trained to plot artillery targets on key terrain—mountaintops, intersections, and prominent buildings. Mountain peaks like this one were easy to see. Adjusting fire from such noticeable terrain was simple. And because it was key terrain, it was likely that all combatants involved would want to drop ordnance on it in order to deny it, to repel forces from it, or to kill anyone stubborn enough to stay on top of it.

Woomp. Woomp.

Another volley of mortars. The mortar attack prompted the medics at the ramp to move our casualties back into the helicopter, despite it being the most noticeable target. The helicopter provided more protection from an area weapon such as mortars than did thin air.

It occurred to me that both we and our enemies were calling in large amounts of ordnance in the same places, but with much different intentions. This simple coincidence alone underscored the geospatial proximity of our two forces, and how borderline insane it was for us to be dropping bombs and mortars in the same place, which, for both of us, was literally on top of ourselves.

When I heard the rounds incoming, I lay as low as I could,

splayed flat, and pushed my face into the snow. I imagined the mortar rounds falling through the air. Where would they land?

Fa-RUMP! RUMP!

The mortars landed to our rear, down the mountain about two hundred meters. The first rounds had been over us. This volley was short. *They've got us bracketed.*

We understood from the basics of shooting indirect fire that the next set of rounds would be right on top of us.

47

One ought never to turn one's back on a threatened danger and try to run away from it. If you do that, you will double the danger. But if you meet it promptly and without flinching, you will reduce the danger by half. :: SIR WINSTON CHURCHILL

04 0845 MAR 02 (DELTA)
TAKUR GHAR

I had not anticipated the psychological effects of being under mortar attack. On this mountain, it was easier to duck from the enemy fighters' line of sight than it was to hide from the mortar threat directly overhead. The time of waiting, that time between audible launch of mortar rounds and the haunting sound of them incoming, ratcheted my nerves with each second.

I needed reinforcements soon. Chalk 2 had to be getting close to us. Doubling the force on the mountain would allow us to mass our force and assault the enemy bunkers.

"One-Four, this is One-Six; over," I said.

Ten seconds of radio silence. I looked at DePouli. *Why isn't Canon answering?*

"Four, this is Six."

"Six, this is Four; over." Canon sounded out of breath.

"Four, we're taking mortar fire up here. What's your ETA?"

"Wait one," he said, apparently pausing to check his bearings.

"Six, Four," he said.

"Go."

"We're moving pretty slow down here. It's much thicker than I thought. We really need a fixed rope to make some of these steps."

"How long?"

"Forty-five minutes," he said.

I needed to move soon to get away from the mortar threat. The only way to knock out the bunkers was to bring in something bigger. *I can't wait on him.*

"Gabe, you still got those F-16s?"

"Yeah, but all they have is bombs," he said. "I still have the F-15s for a little while too."

"That's fine; I need something bigger to knock out those positions," I said. "Get them ready."

I turned to Vance. "Kevin, what do you think?"

He thought for a moment.

"Well, if we can walk the rounds up the other side of the mountain, we'd probably be safe," he said. "I'm not sure how close we can bring them."

"Go work it out with Gabe," I said.

Vance scurried down to the CCT's position, grabbed his own rucksack and radio—which he had left at the ramp in order to join the gunfight—and attempted to raise our higher headquarters. Vance and Gabe discussed the best place to drop the bombs to affect the enemy and to protect us. I looked at my quick reference card, which listed the distances at which I could expect certain percentages of friendly casualties. We were well inside all the safe-risk distances on the card. *These distances are for flat open areas, anyway. We're behind some rocks down a steep slope. Surely it'll be safe.*

Miceli spotted a group of three people walking in the valley to our rear. He was sure they weren't Americans.

"Hey, sir, Miceli thinks he's got eyes on some enemy in that valley," DePouli said. "He wants to engage."

"Is he sure they're not friendlies?"

"He's pretty certain, but they're a long way off."

"Those guys could be the observers calling in the mortar rounds."

"All right, tell him to engage."

Miceli began shooting bursts from the SAW, but he realized the suspected enemy fighters were much farther away than he estimated. He tried aiming well above them in order to compensate for the extra distance, but eventually decided he couldn't reach them.

"All right, everybody, we've got a big one coming in," Gabe said. "Brace yourselves."

Here we go.

"Twister Five-Two, you're cleared hot," he said. "Okay, roger. Stand by. Team Leader, I need your initials."

"What?"

"Your initials. All three, or first and last. Doesn't matter," he said. "The pilots need your approval to drop it this close."

They wanted me to take full responsibility for decisions such as this.

"NES," I said.

"Twister Five-Two, this is Slick Zero-One; initials follow," he said. "NS."

"Okay. Bombs are away," Gabe said.

The incoming GBU-12 bomb sounded like ripping paper as it closed the final distance to the mountain. The ground bumped beneath us. A rich and deep explosion drove a taupe dust cloud high above the peak. *Oh, the power of a radio.*

"Do it again," I said. "Closer."

Gabe and Vance continued to work together to ensure their calculations were correct. They had the F-16s on for this run.

"Clash Seven-One, this is Slick Zero-One; initials NS; over."

The F-16s delivered another successful and safe bombing run.

"Closer again," I said.

I had to do something to escape the mortar threat. Chalk 2 wouldn't be with us anytime soon. I couldn't leave everyone out in the open area to be cut up by high explosives falling all around. *Should we assault again? Should we move away from this helicopter? Should we retreat down the mountain and hide? Could we get another helicopter in here to pick us up?*

"Team Leader, we need to take this hill and get the casualties out," Don said. "We need a bird."

My heart felt pulled in their direction—to the casualties and those treating them—but I couldn't succumb to the temptation to put them above all else, at the risk of compromising the safety of every American on the mountain. Besides, I knew we weren't on that short of a timeline. The enemy dominated the LZ to our front. Even if we killed the enemy on the peak, it seemed that the LZ on the mountaintop was a mortar target anyway, and therefore useless. We'd be lucky if anyone went home while the sun was still up. I called Don to my location to discuss our options.

"Don, what do you think about trying to move everyone to another LZ?"

"I think it's a good idea," he said. He looked over his shoulders, quickly assessing the surrounding terrain for use as a landing zone.

"What about there?" he said. Don pointed at a tiny shelf down the mountain, 150 meters behind the helicopter. The flat area was shielded to the east by a steep ridge that would obscure our position from possible enemy mortar observers. And because it was downhill, it would be easy to move the casualties away from the helicopter and the enemy bunkers.

I looked at the ridge again. I thought I saw a concrete or cinder-block structure at one end of the ridge, wedged against a giant boulder under a tree. It couldn't have been much bigger than an outhouse. *There's no way that's a man-made structure out here in the middle of nowhere.*

"Do you think they could get a Chinook in there?" I said.

"Oh, yeah," Don said. "They can do it."

A couple of the other crew members disagreed.

"I *know* they could get in there," Don said. "I could do that easy."

The only problem with Don's confident recommendation was that he wouldn't be flying that aircraft. He was lying in the snow next to me.

"Are you sure?" I said.

"Positive," Don said.

"Okay. That sounds like a good plan. We've gotta get away from these mortars. Tell the medics to get the casualties ready."

"Team Leader, we've got another bomb incoming," Gabe said. "Take cover; bombs away in fifteen seconds."

The last bomb impacted just off the peak, close enough to the enemy positions to scare them, but unlikely to have inflicted casualties. It jolted my internal organs. I could feel it deep inside. Chunks of gravel rained down around us.

I decided it wasn't worth the risk to bring the bombs closer. I didn't believe the bombs were accurate enough to knock out a single bunker so close to us—at least not without serious risk to ourselves.

"All right, let's hold what we got for now," I said.

I needed to coordinate for a helicopter to pick up our casualties once we moved them to the flat area to our rear. I called down to Vance, who was working next to Gabe.

"Kevin, have you been able to reach Higher?" I asked.

"No, sir." Vance said. "I called Bagram and Kandahar. Bagram didn't answer, and Kandahar answered at first, but then stopped talking to me for some reason."

Seemed that it didn't matter if I wanted to talk to our higher headquarters or not. We couldn't get through even when we tried. Maybe Gabe could relay the request through the aircraft overhead. I turned to Gabe to place the request. He was engaged in a radio call, so I waited for him to conclude.

"Roger. Wildfire Five-Three, Wildfire Five-Three, this is Slick Zero-One; say again; over," Gabe said.

Wildfire. I know that call sign.

I had an idea.

48

Creative intelligence is and always has been the supreme requirement in the commander . . . coupled with moral character. . . . The best hope of tilting the scales and of overcoming the resistances inherent in conflict lies in originality—to provide something unexpected that will paralyze the opponent's freedom of action. :: B. H. LIDDELL HART, *Thoughts on War*

04 0944 MAR 02 (DELTA)
TAKUR GHAR

The nature of warfare that I was experiencing in Afghanistan was far removed from traditional combat. Even as we possessed the world's most powerful military and economic backing, we deployed to Afghanistan without armored vehicles and without artillery. What we lacked in traditional heavy-hitting equipment, we hoped to replace with Special Forces teams on horseback, mercenary Afghans, UAVs, and Joint-Direct Attack Munitions (JDAMs)—GPS-guided bombs designed to fly themselves to the target grids after being released.

The UAV that orbited a few thousand feet overhead sounded like a remote-controlled toy about to run out of gas. And that's exactly what it was. The type of UAV overhead and most used in Afghanistan was the RQ-1, known as the Predator. It very well could've been piloted by an airman behind a joystick in Kuwait or Saudi Arabia or Missouri, since the fifteen-foot, prop-driven plane beamed pictures anywhere in the world; relayed radio communications; and, on CIA-owned versions, fired Hellfire missiles directly onto targets of choice.

"Gabe, who are you talking to?"

"Right now?" he asked. "It's the Predator. I'm trying to get eyes out to the east."

"No, I need you to wait on that," I said. "What was the call sign?"

"Wildfire Five-Three."

"Find out if it's armed," I said.

"What do you mean?"

"Just find out if it's armed. Some of the Predators have Hellfires," I said.

Because Gabe was not a member of Task Force 11, he hadn't been given access to the levels of information that I had absorbed in the hours of planning in the JOC. The fact that some Predators were armed was secret and privileged information at the time.

Gabe came off the radio. "Team Leader," he said. "It is armed. Two Hellfires."

"On the bunker," I ordered.

Vance spoke up. "Sir, don't do that. Hold him," he said. "We're really close."

I turned back to Gabe and the Predator. "Gabe, what do we have?"

"Just working up the target location," he said. "Couple of minutes and we'll be in business."

I pulled the weapons data reference card from my pocket and scanned through the lines. *Hellfire . . . fifty meters.*

"Kevin, we're good. This says fifty meters."

"Sir, I don't know."

I remembered hearing UAVs overhead in Kosovo when I ran night border patrols with the Scout Platoon. The UAV's mere presence there caused me to think twice about our every action, as I imagined my battalion's leadership watching us on a TV at Camp Monteith. Even now, I still had never seen a UAV. Here on the mountain, I didn't take the time or effort to locate the Predator overhead, nor was I worried about what my commanders were seeing on their TVs. I wasn't interested in looking good—I was interested in killing.

"Oh, I forgot to tell you that somebody passed me the frequency to a MAKO team nearby." Gabe said. "That make any sense to you?"

"Yeah," I said. "Those are the SEALs. They're probably wondering where we are."

"Also, I've got a radio report from Juliet Zero-One," Gabe said. "They've got eyes on the back side of the peak," Gabe said. "They see at least two fighters alive and moving around under a tree. They say we should just assault, that they're just sitting there."

"Where's Juliet?" I asked.

"They're to our north across the valley."

"What do you think, Kevin?"

"I don't like it."

"Team Leader," Gabe said, "the Predator has eyes on the bonsai tree. He's got the target. He's right on it."

"We gotta get away from these mortars," I decided. "Gabe, hit the bunker."

"Sir, we're ready to rock," Gabe said.

"All right, everybody, CAS incoming."

Again, we lay as low as we could, awaiting the Predator strike. The prop engine droned above, sounding like an old lawn mower cutting through the sky. Its monotonous idle revealed no intent to attack, no throttle increase, nothing but the same consistently drowsy tone from hours before.

"Away!"

The Hellfire tore through the air with a high-decibel scratching sound that triggered a reflex of anger in me. The mountain shook. A puff of smoke and dust rose from the north slope of the mountain. The missile missed its target by at least two hundred meters.

"Gabe, what was that?" I said.

"Not sure."

"Well, we only have one more chance," I said.

Canon came over the radio. "Check fire! Check fire! Check fire! I say again, cease fire!"

"Four, what's wrong?"

"Whatever you did, that almost hit us down here," he said. "And MAKO is even closer to that target."

"No, they're not," I said. "They're lower."

"No, they're right *there*," Canon said.

Either Canon was closer to us than I thought or that Hellfire was farther off than I thought.

"Gabe, where did you say that MAKO team was?"

"About 150 meters to our north," Gabe said.

"Four, Six," I said. "Just keep moving. It's a whole lot closer to us than it is to you."

I was more concerned about wasting another Hellfire than I was about hitting Chalk 2 or MAKO. Maybe I had become emboldened by the successful CAS runs earlier in the day. Maybe I had been lucky not to hit my own force. Maybe I considered it an unacceptable alternative to be sitting there, bleeding, doing nothing.

"They screwed up the Hellfire," Gabe said. "They've got a second one ready."

"Hit the bunker," I said. "Make sure they don't miss."

"Got it."

Come on, hit it. We need this.

The next Hellfire missile split the bonsai tree in half. I didn't even have to look. I had spent so much effort staring, shooting, and assaulting that enemy position that I could feel exactly where it was. I knew the missile was on target.

"Yeeeoww!"

The Predator buzzed on, with an intermittent engine hiccup. The irony of Hellfire missiles on a glorified toy that struggled to stay aloft struck me as amusing.

I took a moment to replay where I was in my decision-making process. *Casualties. Tried to assault. Need reinforcements. Incoming mortars. Can't wait for reinforcements. Need to assault again to get away from these mortars. Predator suppression. Now we should be ready to assault again. What happened to the enemy mortars? They had us bracketed. Why aren't they firing their mortars?*

"Kevin, how long has it been since we took mortars?"

"At least five minutes, sir."

"That's strange," I said.

As if on cue, the mortar fire renewed.

Woomp. Woomp.

49

If you can keep your head when all about you

Are losing theirs and blaming it on you

. . . Yours is the Earth and everything that's in it

And—which is more—you'll be a Man, my son!

:: RUDYARD KIPLING

04 0958 MAR 02 (DELTA)
TAKUR GHAR

"Guys, take cover," I said. "We've got another set of mortars incoming. Get yourselves ready to assault that bunker after these rounds impact."

I wasn't sure in my mind if we'd all be able to assault after these mortar rounds impacted. *They had bracketed us before. This volley should be right on top of us.* We'd be lucky if we still had our four able Rangers to assault two minutes from now.

"Sir, this one's gonna be close," Walker said.

"I know."

I realized that even if we survived the next set of mortar rounds and successfully assaulted the bunker under the bonsai tree, it would take us a considerable amount of time to move everyone out of the targeted area.

The faint sound of falling mortars grew louder. Our previous brief but intense experience of taking mortar fire had given me an internal sense for when the rounds should be upon us. The crescendo of the rounds leveled off. Instead of hearing the mortars screaming down overhead, I heard them impact in the same vicinity where the errant Hellfire hit. Somehow, they missed.

"Sir, you gotta stop shooting at us!" Canon protested over the radio.

"Four, this is Six. That's not us. Those are mortars."

The radio fell silent. Then, "Roger, Six."

The enemy had apparently discovered Chalk 2 moving toward us. The mountain fighters were attempting to hit a moving target. *Why would they do that?* I contemplated the enemy's actions and intent. It occurred to me that the enemy was attempting to isolate us, to seal us off from our reinforcements. We were prey already in their grasp; they could come back for us at their choosing. *They're trying to cut us off.*

"Four, this is Six," I said. "Keep moving. They're trying to isolate us."

"Roger."

"Four, what's your ETA?" I said.

"Twenty minutes," he said.

"Got it."

I decided that I would hold my force in place until Chalk 2 reached us or the mortar threat resumed and forced me to assault the peak. I moved to Gabe's position to try to call my higher headquarters again. Since the last Hellfire strike, we hadn't taken any gunfire from the peak.

"Kevin, come down here and try to reach Higher again," I said.

It was only a matter of time before the enemy did something to us, either with mortars or reinforcements. I called Canon to speed his approach.

"Four, this is Six; over," I said.

"This is Four," Canon said. I sensed frustration in his tone.

"Okay. We're in trouble here. Lots of casualties, and we're also under a mortar threat," I said. "Is there anything you can do to lighten your load?"

"We've already dropped some nonessential gear and cross-loaded some stuff," he said. "The machine gun is slowing us down."

"You have a machine-gun team?"

"Yeah, we've been cross-loading as much as we can," he said. "Everybody's got their share of the suck. Aside from dropping ammo or back plates, there's not much we can do."

"Drop your back plates," I said. "We need you here."

Radio silence.

"Roger."

"Let me know when you think you're ten minutes out, and we'll work on the linkup," I said.

"Wilco," he said.

Even as I gave that order, I thought of the movie that my Rangers had watched a couple of days before, how the absence of back plates in Somalia may have cost lives. *Have I just exposed my Rangers to a greater likelihood of dying?*

The desperate men who worked with the casualties spoke up again.

"Team Leader, Team Leader, when are you going to assault that position?"

"As soon as this other chalk gets here," I said. "Not until then."

"Kevin, you stay here and work the radio to Higher," I said. "Make sure both of you use the Slick Zero-One call sign to avoid confusion."

I ordered Walker to fire up another flare to give Canon a fix.

PPHHHEW! The flare curled up and popped. The burning green ball swung underneath a tiny white parachute, floating and drifting over the peak.

"Four, this is Six; do you see the flare?"

"Roger, Six."

"Can you give me an ETA?"

"Forty-five minutes," he said.

I decided not to tell anyone else on the mountain that Chalk 2 would be later than expected. I was tired of managing expectations and letting everyone down.

50

Readily will I display the intestinal fortitude required to fight on to the Ranger objective and complete the mission, though I be the lone survivor. :: RANGER CREED, Sixth Stanza

04 1020 MAR 02 (DELTA)
TAKUR GHAR

"Six, this is Four; over," Canon said. "I think we're getting close."

I hoped this time he was right.

"Let's start working our linkup signals," he said. "Wait, I think I see you. Just stay there. We've still got some distance to go."

If Chalk 2 was approaching from the east as planned, they'd be climbing the slope behind the helicopter. The nearest Ranger to them would be Miceli.

"Sergeant DePouli, let's get Miceli looking for Chalk 2," I said.

"I'll just go down there with him, sir," DePouli said.

"Great. You guys just work the linkup yourselves over the radio."

Sergeant DePouli crouched as he retreated down the slope to Miceli's position. After he settled in between the rocks surrounding Miceli, he called Canon on the radio.

"Four, this is One; over."

"Four," Canon said.

"Great to hear you're joining us," DePouli said. "I'm at the linkup point down from the helo."

"Roger, I think I see you guys," Canon said. "I see a couple of tan helmets in the middle of some boulders."

"Yep, that's us," DePouli said. "I can't see you, though."

I chuckled at the situation: Canon already knew what they were wearing, and most Americans in the Shah-i-Khot would be wearing similar tan uniforms and helmets. Surely we could be more sophisticated than this.

"Okay, I'm looking right at you," Canon said. "There's two of you. Wave at us."

"Can't see you," DePouli said.

"Okay, now I see you waving at us," Canon said.

"Well, you told me to wave."

"Look down," Canon said. "Wave back."

I turned to see DePouli's position with Miceli. Both of them were facing to the south, facing the opposite direction of Canon's approach.

"One, this is Six; turn to your left," I said. "They're coming up that way."

"Roger."

"You see me now?" Canon said.

"No."

"Wait, we're gonna throw some snow," Canon said.

I couldn't believe the comedy developing in a simple linkup during broad daylight. I looked at Sergeant Walker next to me.

"Can you hear this?" I said, hoping that someone else could share in my delight.

"No, sir. What's up?" Walker said.

"Never mind. They've almost linked up."

"Sorry, sir, I wasn't listening to your conversation, sir," Walker said. "But I do gotta take a dump."

"Are you kidding me?"

"No, sir, I really gotta go," Walker said. "What, a guy can't take a dump in the middle of combat?"

Sergeant DePouli made physical linkup with Sergeant Canon and the rest of Chalk 2 a quarter hour later, augmenting our beleaguered force by ten Rangers. Under Canon's leadership, Chalk 2 included another two-man machine-gun team, a six-man squad led by Staff Sergeant Wilmoth, and the Ranger medic, Matt LaFrenz.

"That's it, I can't wait any longer," Walker said.

Walker rolled to his back and started unfastening his belt, right in the middle of us.

"Aw, come on!"

Lancaster scooted his wounded leg away from him. As if I hadn't had enough motivation to move to Chalk 2, I had plenty of reason to move now. I started to crawl downhill.

"I'm headed down to Chalk 2," I said. "You guys enjoy your time in the latrine."

I was excited to see the other half of our QRF. I felt like we'd just won the battle, even though the fight was far from over. I was again in awe of the men I led, and although they fell under my command, I looked up to them as much as they looked to me for direction.

I saw Sergeant Stebner first. He was a wiry team leader, just like Walker and Crose but taller, probably weighing less than the equipment he carried. He was searching through the sleeping area and field mosque that DePouli and Miceli had cleared hours before.

"Sir, have you been down here?" Stebner asked.

"No, I've been up by the bird the whole time."

"I found a skateboard helmet down there by that rucksack," Stebner said. "It had a bullet hole in it. There was also a Nalgene water bottle with *Fifi* written on it. It's definitely American gear."

Stebner looked tired. His uniform was wet. He wore canvas desert boots, which were also wet. I scanned around at the men of Chalk 2 gathering around me. They all looked exhausted, faces flushed and pale, uniforms sweat through. Some sat on the rocks to catch their breath. Sergeant Wilmoth was the lone exception. He was the most physically fit man in the platoon and showed no effects of the three-hour hike two thousand feet up the mountain under mortar and sniper fire. I found out he was one of the few Rangers who hadn't jettisoned his ceramic back plate.

"Good to see you, sir. How's it going?" Wilmoth said in a carefree tone, just as if we were meeting in the produce department of a supermarket in Savannah.

"I'm fine, Harper," I said with a grin. "Great to see you, too."

Canon and DePouli joined us. I was there with three squad leaders in a quorum of the QRF's leadership at Miceli's rock outcropping.

"Sergeant Canon, how's Chalk 2 doing?"

"We're better now, sir," Canon said. "We're here."

"We're good, sir," Wilmoth said.

"Sir, I've got one guy a little out of it right now," Canon said.

"Physical or emotional?" I said.

"I'm not sure. It's Vela. He carried too much stuff, and he refused to cross-load."

"Well, keep an eye on him," I said. "Tell your guys to catch their breath, drink a little water, and get themselves ready to fight."

"Roger, sir."

"Five minutes," I said. "Let me know when you're ready."

I moved across the slope toward the helicopter to Gabe's position, where he and Kevin continued to monitor aircraft overhead for observation and close air support.

"How's it going, guys?"

"Doing all right," Kevin said. "I tried headquarters again. Couldn't get anyone to answer me."

"What call sign did you use?"

"I used his: Slick Zero-One."

"Yeah, they wouldn't know that one," I said. "Still, you'd think they'd answer."

"I'm talking back to Masirah right now," Kevin said. "Champ Two-Zero. They want to know if we've linked up with Chalk 2 yet."

"Tell them we have," I said. "Gabe, how's that other Predator coming?"

"I'm working it up right now," Gabe said. "What's next, boss?"

"Another assault. We've got plenty of guys now," I said. "I'll probably be hanging back here with you from now on."

"Fine by me," he said.

Vance came off his radio. He looked frustrated.

"Sir, they're asking again if we've linked up with Chalk 2," he said.

"Look man, they're all around us," I said. "Tell them we have."

"They're not believing me," Vance said. "And they don't want us firing any more Hellfires."

"Are they in charge here?" I asked.

"It appears that they are," Vance said.

"Gabe, let me know when you get that Predator up," I said. "We can hit the bunker again before we assault."

"Will do."

We now had fifteen able Rangers on the mountain, triple the number we'd had all morning. I realized that I should fall back to a place where I could lead the unit, where I could see and hear and talk on the radio. Almost five hours after being shot down, I finally stopped serving as a rifleman to focus solely on my duties as a platoon leader.

Canon, DePouli, and Wilmoth came to my position near Gabe to report they were ready to assault.

"All right, guys," I said. "Real simple. Sergeant Canon, take your other machine gun and put it into action next to Gilliam. Sergeant DePouli will show you where."

"Roger."

"Harper, take your squad and assault from Sergeant Walker's position straight to the top of the peak. Just go the same way we went before. Walker will point it out to you. There are bunkers up there. Sergeant DePouli, move your squad to protect our flanks."

"Got it."

"We're trying to get another Hellfire strike on the bunkers up there before we assault. After that, we'll maneuver."

I felt total empowerment as I watched Ranger NCOs depart with a clear mission and the resolve to make it happen. The Rangers of Chalk 2 crept up the slope to their assault positions. They were eager to shoot somebody. I could see them conversing with Chalk 1 Rangers who had been fighting on the mountain. *Learn all you can, boys.*

A cry of pain erupted from the front lines.

"Aaahh!"

"Stebner, what's wrong with you? It ain't gonna hurt you."

I looked to the boulder where Walker had apparently followed through with his talk of defecation. Walker and others formed snowballs to clean the feces from Stebner's sleeve. *Unbelievable. We're fighting for our lives and guys are acting like a bunch of poop-smearing monkeys.*

"Sir, when are we ready?" Canon asked.

I wanted the Hellfire strike first. *Protection through firepower.*

"Stand by, Four."

"Gabe, what's the deal with the Predator?"

"They told me another fifteen minutes," Gabe said. "If they approve it."

"We're not waiting on that," I said. I keyed my radio.

"Okay, guys, let's hit this."

"What's the signal to initiate?" Canon said.

"Just start shooting."

51

The pleasure of risk is in the control needed to ride it with assurance so that what appears dangerous to the outsider is, to the participant, simply a matter of intelligence, skill, intuition, coordination—in a word, experience. :: A. ALVAREZ

04 1101 MAR 02 (DELTA)
TAKUR GHAR

Wilmoth's squad stood and poured an extreme volume of gunfire on the peak, so much so that the casualties and aircrew yelled frantically that we were shooting too much.

"Hey! Slow down! You're gonna run out of ammo!"

"They're wasting everything! They'll have nothing left!"

I ignored the crew members. If ever we needed firepower, it was now. Canon sat between two "talking" machine guns. Gilliam and Specialist Randy Pazder alternated bursts at the bonsai, maintaining constant suppression for Wilmoth's squad. They were firing more than usual, more than in training, more than I expected here. It was beautiful. It was good for the Rangers to light it up. They needed to exercise their full lethality, to stretch themselves, like any world-class athlete would.

Sergeant Wilmoth walked uphill with one fire team as his other team supported from the boulder with heavy fire. LaFrenz, the medic, assaulted with the lead fire team. Sergeant Walker assaulted with them, now abandoning his task to secure the flanks with his own squad. They walked slowly, smooth and confident. Within half a minute, the squad disappeared over the peak.

I felt guilty for not assaulting with them. My men were covering the ground that I hadn't been able to control earlier in the day. I was perched one hundred meters back, watching them close with the enemy.

Wilmoth's Rangers continued firing beyond the bonsai and boulder down the western face of the summit. Canon shut down his machine guns and followed.

WUMP! WUMP!

Explosions. I wanted to know what was going on, but I waited for the Rangers to culminate the assault. We members of Chalk 1 were now alone again at the crash site. *Security.*

"Sergeant DePouli, watch the flanks!" I said.

"Got it, sir!"

A massive explosion rocked the far slope, much more than could be accounted for by grenades. *Someone must be wounded.* I waited.

Eventually Canon came over the radio with a report.

"Six, this is Four; over."

"Go ahead."

"I think you should get up here. It looks like we have a casualty up here."

"What do you mean, a casualty?"

"You just need to come see this," Canon said.

My stomach felt heavy. I needed to move forward.

"Come on, Kevin. Let's go," I said. "Gabe, stay here."

I moved up the mountain, over the same path as our failed assault, over the same path as Wilmoth's successful assault—at least, I assumed it had been successful. Vance followed with his rucksack and radio. Canon called a warning from the peak.

"Sir, don't come any further," Canon said. "Don't look at them if you don't have to. If you don't need to look at them, don't look at them."

Nearing the boulder and bonsai tree, I saw pieces of flesh lying around on the ground, cut bone fragments with blood and skin and hair still attached.

I saw the black, knobby soles of a pair of boots facing me. They were high-quality, Vibram-brand soles. I recognized their distinctive yellow octagon logo. My own boots had the same soles. This casualty was most likely American.

I continued toward the body. The boots led to a desert camouflage uniform, a bright red beard, and a gruesome wound that had nearly decapitated the casualty. *The Hellfires. I killed him. Was he a prisoner? Was he trying to assault? What have I done?*

I had to look away. I tried to find Canon. "Arin, where you at?"

"Here, sir," he said, stepping up from another bunker beyond the bonsai tree. "I almost blew myself up just now. I threw a grenade in a bunker over there. It was full of RPG rounds. I almost killed myself."

"Was that the explosion I heard?"

"*Oh*, yeah," he said. "Sir, did you see that casualty?"

"Yeah, was that the casualty you reported?"

"Yes, sir," he said. "There's another one over there." He pointed near the bunker under the bonsai tree, which was buried over and covered by layers of broken logs, rope lashings, and evergreen foliage.

My mind began to attack itself. *The Hellfire must have blown this bunker apart. What have I done? Did I kill two Americans with the Predator strike? What were they doing here? Were they hostages? Have I been shooting at them all day?*

I looked at the capsized bunker. I could see a hand, a green camouflaged sleeve, a beard, and an AK-47 Kalashnikov assault rifle.

"How many people are under there?" I asked Canon.

"A couple of enemy fighters and the American," he said. "This red-headed chap was unarmed. I found his service pistol in his butt pack, but it hadn't been fired. Looks like somebody hacked at his throat."

"Well, we fired Hellfires into this spot a little while ago. . . ."

"Who knows, sir?" Canon said.

"Before we do anything else, let's get the rest of this objective cleared, and then we'll consolidate," I said. "We need to clear back to the south, across the saddle to the other side of the bird."

"Roger, sir. I'll get Harper on that."

I was confused about the presence of Americans at the bunker. I stood in the center of an enemy strongpoint that I had dueled for hours. Now I was as puzzled as I'd been at the beginning.

"Let's take a second, Kevin," I said to Vance. "Just a second to think."

We climbed across the prominent boulder, which had been our reference point for most of the fight. We sat down next to the body of a short, dark-haired enemy fighter. His legs below the knee were cemented deep into the snow, his feet curled under his butt, his body splayed backward in an uncomfortable-looking contortion. An empty RPG tube lay across his chest and his knit skullcap rested three feet behind his head, containing the top quarter of his skull. *That's the RPG gunner DePouli shot. That's the man who wounded me.*

My right thigh was cramping with a deep, dull pain. I looked at my trousers. No blood. I rolled to my right side to keep the wound numb in the snow.

Wilmoth's squad swept past us, across the front of the helicopter, and up the other side of the saddle peak. They cleared the left flank of the bird, the side from which we had taken such intense fire on the ramp upon landing.

Specialist Oscar Escano fired his M203 grenade launcher at a tree twenty meters to his front, startling the other Rangers in his squad.

"Escano?!" Polson said.

"I was just clearing that tree."

I smiled at Vance. It was funny to see Rangers policing each other in typically blunt fashion, but I appreciated Escano's aggressiveness.

When Wilmoth's Rangers reached the southern saddle peak, they opened fire and threw grenades. They leapt into action, taking cover in craters created by the mortar rounds, the bombs, and whatever else had been dropped on the mountain before we arrived. The Rangers spotted an enemy fighter hiding past the crest overlooking the left side of the Chinook. Wilmoth's men cut him down in an instant. They found another body and an RPG launcher.

"Sir, this is Two," Wilmoth said over the radio. "Objective secure."

Those words signaled success: We had taken the mountain. We now owned the terrain that had owned us for so long.

We had been fighting for five hours.

52

Energetically will I meet the enemies of my country. I shall defeat them on the field of battle for I am better trained and will fight with all my might. Surrender is not a Ranger word. I will never leave a fallen comrade to fall into the hands of the enemy and under no circumstances will I ever embarrass my country. :: RANGER CREED, Fifth Stanza

04 1114 MAR 02 (DELTA)
TAKUR GHAR

For the first time all day, I was certain we would all make it home. Several had already given their lives on the mountain, but we had eliminated the close-in enemy threat, greatly reducing the risk of taking further casualties. It seemed that we had discovered two additional American bodies that we'd need to carry back to Bagram in addition to the right-door gunner, Sergeant Crose, and Corporal Commons. I wasn't sure who else had been wounded or killed.

I was still confused by the presence of two American bodies mixed in with the bodies of al-Qaeda fighters. I needed to clarify some things. I called Sergeant Canon to my position at the boulder, which I had established as the platoon command post.

"Sergeant Canon, we need to start moving the rest of the force up here to the summit for protection," I said. "And you and I need to figure out who these dead guys are." Canon nodded.

"Well, I got this guy's ID card from his butt pack," he said, pointing at the red-bearded body lying outside the bunker. "Let me check the guy in the bunker."

Canon reached carefully through the foliage and debris, fishing around in the American's pockets to find some personal effects. He lifted a transparent plastic wallet.

"This guy's Air Force," Canon said. "His name's Chapman. The redheaded guy is Roberts. He looks like a SEAL. Stebner said he saw him in Bagram, that he came to hang out sometimes. He thought they called him 'Fefe.' That's the name from the water bottle Stebner found."

I thought back to the redheaded SEAL who had watched us challenge Rangers to eating games. *Could this be him? Commons was there that night, too, and now he's dead.*

"But why are they here?" I asked.

Gabe arrived at our new command post and sat next to Vance. I wondered what Gabe and Vance thought of seeing a fellow Air Force CAS specialist lying dead in front of them.

"Were these guys a part of our force?" Gabe asked.

"No. We're trying to figure out who they are and where they came from," I said.

"Do you know their names?" Gabe said.

"Chapman and Roberts."

"Wait one," Gabe said, sliding the black bricklike MBITR radio from one of his pouches. He turned away to make a radio call. I looked down the western slope of the mountain to the valley. Billows of green and purple smoke rose from the village of Marzak, one of the main objectives for Operation Anaconda. I assumed the 10th Mountain and the 101st Airborne were having more success than in previous days.

"Got it," Gabe said. "Those two guys belong to the SEAL team in the draw."

"What do you mean?" I asked. "Did they leave them here?"

"One of them's the guy that fell out of the helicopter, and one of them was fighting with his team up here. Roberts was the MIA."

Everything seemed to rush into focus all at once. My mind finally recognized what my eyes had been seeing and perceiving incorrectly all day. The American rucksack, radio, helmet, night-vision goggles, and water bottle—the SEALs had been *here*; Roberts had fallen out of the helicopter *here*. He wasn't an unfortunate private from the 101st Airborne. He was a Navy SEAL. He had been executed before we arrived. We had found our missing American.

"Arin," I said, "we found our man."

"I know, sir," he said. "Too bad we got here too late."

I took a moment to myself just to make sense of what was going on. I replayed the major steps that brought us to a mountain that would be on some of these men's gravestones. We crash-landed right on top of them. Right on top of the enemy. *Just like Son Tay.*

Colonel Thomas had told me to read *Spec Ops* when I got to Savannah. In it I read about the helicopter assault into northern Vietnam to rescue seventy-five POWs from the Son Tay prison camp in 1970. The assault force consisted of only thirteen men, just like Razor 01. They crashed their helicopter directly into the enemy camp on purpose, in order to achieve surprise. *Maybe that's what we did here. Maybe it's better we didn't fight our way up this mountain.* The prison camp at Son Tay had been empty. The man we were sent to rescue now lay dead next to me.

"Arin, let's sit down and talk about this," I said to Canon. "Okay, I'm not sure how this is all gonna go down, but we need to think about exfiltration. Maybe we could get one bird for our casualties."

"I'll start getting them moved up here," Canon said.

"Kevin, start working an extraction plan with Higher," I said. "And see if you can get a medevac bird in here ASAP. Put the LZ just off this peak, on the west side. Have them approach from the west."

"Roger, sir."

Matt LaFrenz was already preparing a spot for the new casualty collection point less than twenty meters from my new command post.

"Sergeant Wilmoth, we need litter bearers!" I said.

Sergeant Stebner and Specialist Escano moved down to the crippled hulk of Razor 01 to carry casualties from the helicopter to the mountaintop. They teamed with two aircrew members to begin their task of carrying heavy men uphill in the snow at over ten thousand feet.

One of the Air Force pararescue jumpers was helping Lancaster hop up the mountain. Lancaster draped one arm over the PJ's neck, looking like an injured football player limping off the field.

My head ached just behind my eyes. Any number of factors

could've contributed to the headache: the altitude, lack of food, intense combat stress, dehydration. The muscles around my neck and shoulders were tense. I needed to relax, to regroup. *We're not home yet, but we've made it through the worst.*

I saw Sergeant Canon walking back toward the peak from Wilmoth's position with his eyes set on me.

I sensed he wanted to talk to me alone. I got up to meet him. His face was stern and angry looking, but he held his rifle at the low ready, with the posture of an expert marksman.

"Sir, I've got an initial casualty report coming from LaFrenz in a few," he said. He hesitated. "Sir, where's Big A?"

I hadn't seen Anderson all day, not since I'd squeezed him on the shoulder during our final approach.

"I don't think he made it," I said. "I think he's done."

Canon's eyes looked full of anger. His lip quivered. He squinted hard and fought back tears, shaking his head.

"Sir—" He was starting to break down.

"Arin, let's go, man; not now," I said. "We've got stuff to do. I *need* you here. Hold it down. We'll have the rest of our lives to think about this. Let's just do our jobs here and get our boys home."

"Roger, sir," he said. Sergeant Canon stood straight and rolled his shoulders, almost visibly discarding his emotion. He set his jaw, turned down the slope, and walked toward the bird.

"LaFrenz will have you a casualty report soon, sir," he said.

God, I love these men.

I turned away and walked to the western slope of the peak, where the open Shah-i-Khot Valley stretched below, where I could be alone. I wept bitter tears.

53

In war, you win or lose, live or die—and the difference is just an eyelash. :: DOUGLAS MacARTHUR

04 1131 MAR 02 (DELTA)
TAKUR GHAR

One of the priorities for a commander in a defensive posture is to "troop the line," an age-old practice of moving about the perimeter to inspect security, emplace key weapon systems, and check on the men. With the enemy fire doused and al-Qaeda bodies strewn around, I thought it was an opportune time for me to walk the line.

"Kevin, keep working on those helos. I'm gonna check out our security," I said, standing to stretch my stiff body and wounded thigh.

"Got it, sir," he said. "They've got me talking to Masirah *only* now. Bagram's not involved anymore."

"Whatever."

I could only imagine the angst at the various levels of command, where they likely saw our predicament on the silent video from the Predator but couldn't talk to anyone on the mountain. Vance was now talking to an air-conditioned command tent fifteen hundred miles away on Masirah Island, just off the coast of Oman. That tent housed the staff for the two-star general in charge of the Joint Special Operations Command (JSOC). A platoon would normally take orders from a company commander, a captain or major, at least four pay grades removed from a two-star. The benefit to me was that I had direct access to almost any asset I deemed necessary.

I looked down the slope to see Rangers struggling to pull two casualties uphill in the snow. Four men, one at each corner of a Skedco litter, heaved independently in the general direction of the peak, straining to keep the litter moving.

I walked from the boulder across the peak to the south to check on Wilmoth's squad, which had taken up defensive positions on the opposite point of the saddle. I heard a strange noise a few feet away, in the direction of the helicopter.

Teeewang! Phhht. Phhht. Dink. Dink. Dink.

I dove for cover, but there was none. I fell into the thin snow atop the mountain, looking at the nose of the helicopter downhill from me. The PJ who had carried Lancaster stumbled between the helo and the peak and scrambled to make it up the slope. Heavy machine-gun fire ripped up the mountain at us. It was coming from a couple hundred meters behind and below the helicopter to the east, along a knife-edge ridge topped with trees. My paranoia with our exposed rear area had been well founded; now we needed much more than Miceli to secure to our east.

Pazder laid down a long burst of machine-gun fire at the ridge, maybe fifteen rounds. Gilliam did the same, firing over other Rangers downhill from him. Enemy machine-gun and tracer fire ricocheted, skipped, and tumbled throughout our positions, concentrated on our casualties at the ramp. The ground around me seemed to explode in a thousand tiny random places, kicking rock spall all over. *I need to find cover.*

I rolled left and down the western reverse slope to shield my movement from the gunfire, looping around and back to the boulder where Vance and Gabe hunched low, talking on their radios.

"Gabe, fast movers!" I said.

"Working the target now, sir," Gabe said.

I jumped into the dugout area behind the boulder and peeked over the rock. At least a handful of al-Qaeda fighters had combined and co-ordinated their counterattack from our rear, from the lower ridgeline, including some from the cinder-block structure I thought I had seen earlier. That structure must have been a bunker or a cave entrance.

I knew it. I've been worried about our rear area all day, and now look at what I get.

Because the counterattacking enemy fighters were below us, their weapons achieved effective "grazing fire," wherein the bullets stay about a meter off the ground throughout the target area. Every bullet they shot was a threat to us.

Two casualties on litters were lying in the open—abandoned halfway up the slope when the Rangers carrying them sought cover.

These guys are gonna be slaughtered out there.

Sergeant Stebner sprang from behind a rock and grabbed the corner of one of the litters. He attempted to drag the casualty farther upslope by himself. Another barrage of gunfire ripped over Stebner's head, forcing him back behind cover. The casualty lay in the open. Stebner again abandoned his covered position to pull the casualty along, this time partway into cover.

This guy is amazing. He has no fear.

Our perimeter, an asymmetric amoeba, bulged and morphed as Rangers fine-tuned their positions. Within a minute, we had formed a rough circle of fire in two tiers, one at the top of the mountain and one ringing around the back of the helicopter and over to Miceli's rock outcropping. Rangers at the top fired over the helicopter and over the lower group of Rangers and casualties, enveloping the soft center of the perimeter with a blanket of overhead fire. It looked like two rows of gunfighters firing from a grandstand. This was definitely something I'd never seen before: an in-depth support-by-fire position from echeloned elevations.

Specialist Polson was lying a few feet from us at the top of the mountain, firing over the Rangers below. His SAW malfunctioned every couple of rounds, requiring him to pull the charging handle to the rear every few seconds. The M249 SAW was a weapon that we had come to know as temperamental. Only the more seasoned Rangers could handle it, as it required massaging, tilting, and even holding your mouth just right. Sometimes it just didn't matter how good you were; the SAW just needed to be replaced. Polson seemed to be arguing with his SAW. Every time the SAW went *ka-chunk*, he replied with an expletive.

A white puff of smoke rose from the ridge as an RPG streamed at us, the smoky trail behind the RPG outlining its flight to kill. The round hit and skipped near the helicopter, just where Lancaster, Walker, Vance, and I had been earlier in the battle. The RPG bounced to the top of the peak, detonating just a few feet from our CP.

Ka-WUMP!

Most of the shrapnel blew over the peak. We were safe.

"Gabe, where are the bombs?"

"I was working a B-52 with Jaguar, but it hit way off," he said. "I'm working other options."

"What other options?"

"F/A-18s with 500-pounders or the Predator."

"Do something."

Gabe listened intently to his radio.

"All right, I got CAS inbound in thirty seconds," Gabe said. "Hellfires."

"Guidons, guidons, CAS incoming. Take cover; over," I said.

54

Everything in war is very simple, but the simplest thing is difficult. :: CARL VON CLAUSEWITZ

04 1206 MAR 02 (DELTA)
TAKUR GHAR

I heard the distant rumble of jets approaching. As the sound grew louder, the enemy gunfire subsided, then ceased. These guys were smart. They knew what was coming.

Gabe was performing well. He was targeting the bombs from the Navy F/A-18 Hornets on the reverse slope of the enemy's ridge, where the enemy was likely moving or hiding, and where the knife-edge ridge would protect us from the effects of the blast pattern. He was good enough to know what I wanted even before I said it and bold enough to advise me when I wanted the wrong thing. He and Kevin Vance made a great team.

The five-hundred-pound bomb sounded like a jet on a kamikaze run into the ridge. It burned in parallel to the mountain we occupied, flying to the north. The finned bomb flashed across my field of vision clearly enough for me to recognize what it was, but I was astounded that I could actually see something moving so fast.

I felt the concussion deep within my chest. A gray-brown mushroom cloud shot up from the enemy's ridge—towering and drifting and smearing to the northeast.

"Gabe, let's do that again," I said.

"Sorry, sir, they've gone off," he said. "We've got another check-in coming soon."

"All right, let's get ourselves straightened out."

I called DePouli, Wilmoth, and Canon to report. "Guidons, guidons; over."

"One."

"This is Two."

"Four; over."

"Let's tighten our perimeter. Get ready to fight another counterattack," I said. "It's gonna be awhile before we get all of our casualties moved."

"Six, this is Four; over," Canon said.

"Yep."

"We've taken more casualties," he said. "They're here at the ramp. They're new casualties; over."

I couldn't bring myself to answer. After all we had overcome today, we get hit with a cheap counterattack.

"Who?"

"A couple of the guys who were working on the casualties," Canon said. "Not sure if they're crew members or what. I'll get you a better report; over."

Gabe spoke up again.

"Sir, they're passing me a grid to a target location now," he said. "They've intercepted some radio communications that the enemy is trying to get a video camera and tape the fight."

"Unbelievable," I said.

Kevin Vance's radio was turned to max volume, so I was able to overhear the next call from Masirah.

"Slick Zero-One, this is Champ Two-Zero; over."

"This is Slick Zero-One; over."

"Okay, I am the ground force commander; over."

"What?" I said. "How's that possible? He's not even here."

Vance picked up the handset and put it to his ear.

"Sir, they're asking again if we've linked up with Chalk 2."

"Again? Tell them yes, we have," I said. "Sergeant Wilmoth! Let's get these guys moved up here!"

"They want us to count everyone," Vance said.

I thought for a moment to make sure I gave them the right number. *Twenty-one from Chalk 1, on Razor 01. Ten from Chalk 2. Two additional Americans dead here on the peak.*

"Tell them we have a total of thirty-three," I said. "That includes Chalk 2 and these two bodies we found."

The Rangers who were dragging the first two casualties uphill finally reached the summit. Most of the litter bearers were from Wilmoth's squad in Chalk 2, which meant they had raced two thousand feet up the mountain to reinforce us, assaulted the peak, and carried the first load of casualties. They dropped all around us. They were spent from physical exertion. But the casualties were still not in a safe place.

"Guys, take those casualties over the peak to the reverse slope, away from that counterattack," I said. "You leave them there and they'll get shot."

Those who had just plopped to the ground labored to stand, heads and shoulders hanging low, and dragged the casualties another twenty feet to our new casualty collection point. With the first two casualties in place, the Rangers who carried them sat down and sucked water from their CamelBak hoses. They couldn't move anyone else.

"Sergeant Wilmoth," I said. "You're gonna need to replace these litter bearers. Get some fresh ones."

"Roger, sir."

Matt LaFrenz received his first casualties at the new collection point. Gilliam arrived with his machine gun and took up a position near an idle enemy antiaircraft gun facing the west. Canon moved Pazder's machine gun to a craggy point just below Miceli's rock outcropping.

"Kevin," I said, turning to Vance. "What's the deal on the medevac bird?"

"Last I checked they were working it up. They're looking at bringing in reinforcements for us."

"Reinforcements?" I said. "We don't need reinforcements. We need aircraft. *Reinforcements?* Where are we gonna put them?"

"I don't know, sir. They said they were sending seventy to reinforce us."

"Tell them I don't want a seventy-man reinforcement," I said. "I've got no place to put them. We've got a small LZ here. There's too much risk. Just tell them we need a medevac."

"Roger."

Canon came back up on the radio to clarify the casualty situation at the helicopter.

"Sir, this is Arin," he said. "I've confirmed two more casualties. They're both medics. One is a PJ and one is from the flight crew. They're pretty bad."

I didn't have a clear picture of the overall casualty situation. Whatever our total number of casualties, it had just increased by two. And, in a cruel turn of multiplicity, the enemy had taken away half of our medical treatment capability. Two more casualties, two fewer medics.

"Sir, I'm gonna get LaFrenz down here," Canon said.

"Roger," I said. "Get those 240s plussed up for the next counterattack. They're not done with us; you can bet on that."

Lancaster stood on one leg in the same bunker below us, holding his wounded leg off the ground behind him. His good leg was ankle deep in a pool of water. He looked like a camouflaged flamingo, perched atop the mountain, peering down the barrel of a rifle.

"Lancaster, why don't you move out of that water?" I said. He looked down as if he was unaware of the puddle and hopped to the side until his foot was on dry ground.

The PJ who had helped Lancaster to safety sat on a rock a few feet from me, staring into the distance in a daze. He looked fatigued, removed, indifferent. I didn't even know him. He was part of Gabe's team, the team I'd met on the Chinook.

"Gabe, is he okay?" I asked.

"Maybe just give him a minute," Gabe said.

Polson returned to our position without his SAW. He carried a special M4 rifle equipped with a scope and silencer, spray painted tan and green. It was not a Ranger weapon. I assumed he got it from

Chapman's body; the Air Force Special Tactics guys usually config-ured their gear and weapons however they wanted.

Another team of Rangers trudged uphill with a litter casualty, their weapons slung across their backs. This part was not glori-ous, not exciting or cerebral—it was just hard work. We needed to move the bleeding men, and the only people to move them were men already completely exhausted from previous desperate exertions.

Canon approached me to give another report.

"Sir, here's the lowdown. In the next ten minutes, these teams will have three litter casualties over the peak at the new casualty collection point."

"Good."

"Now we've got two more litter casualties at the bird."

"The medics?"

"Yes, sir," Gabe confirmed.

"This is gonna be tough."

"And we've got four bodies on the bird, including Anderson."

"This'll take forever," I said. "How are we gonna do it?"

"We'll do it, sir," Canon said. I believed him.

"What a day, man," I said. "We all wanted to see combat. Well, here it is."

"Yep, in all its glory," he said.

"Be careful what you ask for, right?"

"Yeah," Canon said. "'Cause you just might f—— get it."

55

When a man is injured, longevity is measured in minutes, and the quicker you can get him into the hands of medical personnel, the better. :: WILLIAM WESTMORELAND

04 1422 MAR 02 (DELTA)
TAKUR GHAR

Those Ranger medics were something special. Their skill set made other medics look like elementary school nurses. They were advanced EMTs, graduates of the demanding Special Operations Combat Medical Course; they regularly worked in live-tissue labs, and some had treated wounded Rangers in previous conflicts and in training. I'd once had three cysts removed from my scalp by a Ranger medic back in Savannah. He performed the surgery in thirty minutes—on a whim.

Matt LaFrenz was no exception. In fact, LaFrenz had something extra. He was as proficient a Ranger—in the role of rifleman or team leader—as any other. In several people's opinions, including mine, he could've served as an Infantry leader in the Rangers, the SEALs, or in Delta Force if he truly desired it. LaFrenz's war-fighting skills were an asset in a gunfight, but with one of the PJs and the flight medic now wounded, we had a dire need for his medical expertise.

Sergeant LaFrenz reported to me on the peak, where he had helped Wilmoth's squad clear the bunker system. He projected a flat, emotion-free expression.

"Sir, I owe you a casualty report," LaFrenz said. He raised his hand to waist level, where he read from a palm-size notebook.

"Right now we've got four KIA at the bird, plus two here, right?"

"Yeah, these two were already here," I said.

"So, six KIA," he said. "We've got five litter casualties and a few walking wounded."

"How bad are the litter WIA?"

"I've got three that are urgent surgical," he said. "They need to get out of here soon. What'd they say about the medevac?"

I looked at Vance for an answer. He gave Sergeant LaFrenz the answer I expected but didn't want to hear.

"They're saying they're working it right now," Vance said. "They want to send a reinforcing package to us. They're assembling in Gardez or at FARP Texaco, I'm not sure what they said."

LaFrenz pursed his lips and stared at the horizon. "These guys need to get out of here. They've lost a lot of blood already. There's not a lot I can do for them out here."

"Are you getting the help you need?" I asked.

"Yeah, I've got a PJ working with me," he said. "We just need to keep those litters moving up here to safer ground. And we'll need to find a way to keep the wounded warm."

"All right, we'll work it, man," I said. "Just keep me posted."

LaFrenz walked over to the new casualty collection point to check on the two casualties. The team that carried the second casualty uphill was resting. A quick look down at the helicopter revealed that we didn't have an active litter team.

"Sergeant Wilmoth, let's get another aid and litter team rotated in," I said.

"Sir, there's nobody fresh," he said.

"We've got to keep them moving," I said.

"Roger."

A few Rangers shuffled positions on the peak to form the litter teams, adjusting some to spots they'd not seen before. As if giving guys a rotational tour of the mountain would check their weariness.

One of the Rangers approached our command post and saw the

dead RPG gunner a few feet from us, the body still bent backward with a void between the open skull and knit cap. He walked by and, as if to check for responsiveness, kicked the enemy fighter in the head and kept walking, without breaking stride.

Amazing. These guys are comfortable with dead bodies after a few hours of fighting. The Ranger's actions were a nonchalant version of the cautious, lockstep method with which we cleared enemy bodies, yet I couldn't blame him. Even to me, the same ripped and mutated bodies that littered the field had become mere terrain features, just a part of the landscape.

Gabe came off his radio.

"Do we have any targets right now? I've got a sortie that needs to refuel."

"No, we're okay right now," Vance said.

"Hey, sir," Gabe said. "What should I do if I gotta go to the bathroom?"

"Just go right over there somewhere."

"By the way, I got a report of an enemy force moving toward us from the south," Gabe said. "They're saying it's seventy enemy."

I was confused and suspicious that we were getting reports mixed up. *Seventy-man reinforcement or seventy-man enemy force?*

"Gabe, are you sure they're not talking about the reinforcing package?" I asked.

"They said it came from a radio intercept," Gabe said.

"Kevin, did they say who the seventy-man unit was?" I asked.

"Not real sure, sir. They said something about SEALs."

Truthfully, I just wanted more Rangers. I thought about my battalion commander, Tony Thomas; my company commander, Joe Ryan; my buddy Pete Marques; and our chaplain, Randy Kirby. *Those are the guys I want here with me. If we need help to make it through this, I want to do it with my Ranger brothers.*

Gabe returned from relieving himself to find someone calling him on his radio. Whatever the message, by the look in his eyes, it seemed to interest him.

"Sir, I've got a report of an enemy 250-man reinforcement moving toward us," Gabe said. "This is from Jaguar One-Two, another CCT to our south. He's on an observation post with Aussie SF. I'm going to coordinate fires with him so we can cover this area better."

Interlocking eyes. Good. The most likely enemy counterattacking forces in my estimation would come from the south or east. We'd already been hit once. If the enemy really was moving toward us in greater numbers, we'd need help. They smelled wounded prey on the mountain and were moving in to finish us off.

Suddenly, the seventy-man reinforcement seemed like a better idea.

56

Never interrupt your enemy when he is making a mistake. :: JOHN MILTON, *Samson Agonistes*

04 1527 MAR 02 (DELTA)
TAKUR GHAR

The enemy attempted another counterattack during the lull between close air support. This time, we were ready for it.

Pazder and Vela defended from their position. Canon spotted targets and directed their fires. Every time the enemy crested the ridge to shoot at us, Rangers poured gunfire on them. The semifresh litter bearers moved their casualties up the slope during the counterattack, but they adjusted their route in order to use the helicopter as a shield. They moved their path straight off the nose of the bird, using its massive body as cover.

Gabe had a new sortie of CAS on station immediately.

"Sir, I've got Tomcats," he said.

"Do it," I said.

Gabe gave the Navy F-14s a quick terrain overview and an emergency call for fire.

A minute later, a bomb screamed closer. Rangers took cover. The bomb roared into the middle of our perimeter, detonating inside our ranks. I was terrified: I saw it fly just thirty meters away from the ramp of the helicopter. Its deafening explosion engulfed us in a dust cloud.

Oh, no. Somebody's gotta be dead.

I fumbled for my radio handset.

"Everybody okay?" I said over the radio.

"Cut that out, sir!" DePouli said. "Just stop it."

Once the dust blew away, I saw the same Rangers who had just been fighting a counterattack, now brushing debris from their shoulders and straightening their helmets. One Ranger picked up his helmet from the ground and placed it back on his head.

"Guys, what was *that?*" I asked.

"It must've been a stray, sir," Gabe said.

"Sometimes that happens," Vance said.

For a moment I considered how fortunate we'd been up to this point with close air support, and how close we'd just come to killing ourselves. If we had been dropping ordnance at targets a kilometer away from us, a little mistake would be no big deal. Just fewer enemy would get killed. But as close as we were to dropping bombs on ourselves, the slightest error could be fatal. A single bad bomb was one too many.

The litter bearers continued with the casualties to the top of the peak and, once again, took a break just like the first group. LaFrenz shouted to me.

"Sir, what're they saying about that medevac?"

Gabe made the call right away.

"Champ Two-Zero, this is Slick Zero-One; status of medevac?"

"This is Champ Two-Zero; we're working it at Gardez. It'll have a response time of thirty-five minutes. What is the status of your patients? What is your total number of KIA?"

"Hey, Sergeant LaFrenz," I said. "Can you come here?"

LaFrenz climbed over the rise from the casualties to the command post, his hands smeared with blood.

"Matt, they want to know the status of our casualties," I said. "I want to make sure they hear it from you."

"Okay, sir," he said. He took the handset. "What're the call signs?"

"Champ Two-Zero, and we're Slick Zero-One."

"Champ Two-Zero, this is Slick Zero-One; over," LaFrenz said. "Go ahead."

"Roger, I have five litter patients and two ambulatory. Three of the litters are urgent surgical. I have six total KIA."

"Roger; over."

LaFrenz lowered the handset, seemingly surprised at how simple and uncomplicated the exchange was. Perhaps that wasn't a good thing. He looked at me.

"Sir, if we don't get them out soon, two will die and one will lose a hand," he said. "Maybe worse. Just make sure they understand that."

After LaFrenz departed, I got back on the radio to clarify.

"Champ Two-Zero, this is One-Six; over."

"Champ Two-Zero."

"Three need surgery; two of them won't make it unless we get a bird in the next hour or two."

"Roger, we're working it."

During the next half hour, the enemy attempted to counter-attack again but met substantial resistance from the Air Force over-head. We began collapsing our perimeter to protect ourselves from the jets' bombs. Gabe and Vance worked up grid coordinates for one-thousand-pound JDAMs.

The enemy countered the bombs with poorly aimed mortars, which landed well to the east and downhill from the Razor 01. We reported the mortar attack to Masirah.

"Champ, this is Slick Zero-One; status of medevac; over."

"Slick, wait on medevac. We need you to prosecute some time-sensitive CAS targets; over." They proceeded to pass us grid loca-tions to enemy mortar positions, command and control nodes, and troop concentrations.

What about the medevac?

As Gabe and Vance began controlling jets all around, I went back to work on the medevac request with Champ.

"Champ Two-Zero, this is One-Six; over."

"Go ahead."

"Request status of the medevac," I said.

"We're working an exfiltration package right now to remove the whole force; over."

"What's the hit time; over?"

"We'll brief the plan at 1500 Zulu."

That's 6:30 p.m. local. Three hours from now. These guys will die.

I wanted to somehow reach through the radio and squeeze their hearts, the way mine was being squeezed. I tried again.

"Champ Two-Zero, just want to reiterate the serious nature of our casualties."

A long pause. Another voice came on the radio.

"This is Champ Zero-Two."

I knew this call sign. It was the second-in-command of JSOC. The subtle change in order of two digits—from Champ 20 to Champ 02—was a substantial change in authority.

"We understand what's going on up there. We're not gonna be able to send a medevac bird. Exfiltration will happen on the time-line."

The handset seemed to float away from my ear. I don't recall answering the radio.

Three more men will die here today. That's a certainty.

57

There seems to be four degrees of courage and four orders of men measured by that standard. Men who did not feel fear; men who felt fear but did not show it; men who felt fear and showed it but did their job; men who felt fear, showed it and shrinked. . . . The story of modern war is concerned with the striving of men, eroded by fear, to maintain a precarious footing on the upper rungs of that ladder.

:: LORD MORAN, *The Anatomy of Courage*

04 1606 MAR 02 (DELTA)
TAKUR GHAR

Our mission had begun early that morning having two possible objectives: to secure a downed helicopter or to recover a missing American, or perhaps both. We had secured Roberts and his team-mate Chapman, and at a great price; but we couldn't have imagined that the helicopter we would secure would be our own.

Had our mission been to secure Razor 03, Roberts's helicopter, somewhere in the valley below us, one of our essential tasks would have been to sterilize the helicopter. This meant we would remove, disable, or otherwise destroy all weapons, maps, imagery, documents, and radios aboard. After moving all the casualties from the vicinity of Razor 01, including the four killed there, we needed to sterilize our own helicopter.

Rangers continued to rotate shifts as litter teams as they carried the dead bodies of our brothers up the slope from the helicopter. They laid the KIA on the far end of the casualty collection point to keep them separated from the wounded and facilitate an efficient loading onto the extraction aircraft. I saw Marc Anderson's huge body there in the sun. He wasn't wearing a shirt.

It must be really cold lying in the snow bare chested, I thought. And then I realized that he was gone. He didn't feel anything. Pairs of Rangers trekked to and from Razor 01, retrieving food, radios, ammunition, clothing, and flight documents. They tore insulation from the helicopter's inner walls and carried the heavy quilted panels to the casualties to keep them warm. A growing pile of optics, broken weapons, snow gear, and miscellany formed near the command post. I saw my rifle in the pile. I had forgotten about leaving it at the helicopter. Sergeant Crose's weapon had not malfunctioned on me once.

The final task in our consolidation was one of the most gruesome: we needed to recover and position the bodies of Roberts and Chapman for exfiltration. I started to discuss it with my squad leaders. Some of the aircrew overheard our conversation.

"Wait a minute; what if they're booby trapped?"

"Well, we have to move them," I said.

"I don't know about that. That is probably not a good idea. I don't think that's a good idea at all."

I turned to Sergeant Wilmoth.

"We've got to clear them somehow," I said.

"I know, sir, I just don't know how," he said.

Don Tabron, the heroic air-crew member, stepped into the conversation.

"We have a rope on the bird," he said. "We could probably pull them out."

"Go get it," I said. "Everyone take cover while we move these bodies."

A small team of Rangers rigged the rope around Roberts's ankles and moved to a defilade position over the peak. They began to pull. I was afraid dragging Roberts's body over the rocky ground would cause further damage to his upper body, but they pulled him all the way to the casualty collection point without any problems.

They repeated the process with Chapman but routed the rope around a boulder and to the other casualties in an L shape to avoid dragging his body into the bonsai bunker and getting it snagged there.

Gabe, Vance, and I returned to our command post near the bonsai bunker. I gazed into the valley to the west. I could see the allied Afghans' main objective for Anaconda, a smooth oval-shaped ridge that was labeled the "Whale" on the briefs I'd seen. It looked small from my position on the mountain. I saw bombs going off in the valley between the Whale and our position.

Our whole northern flank was covered by Lancaster alone. He was still standing on one leg. He needed some company—he'd been alone too long for his mind's health.

"Gilliam, bring your machine gun over here and get in this bunker with Lancaster," I said. I wanted to ensure any attempts at our feeble northern flank were met with heavy resistance.

Don sat near me on the boulder. Last time he and I had talked alone, we'd agreed to move the casualties downhill behind the Chinook to a shelf just below the knife-edge ridge—the ridge where the enemy had launched its counterattack. Had we executed that plan, it was possible that no American on this peak would be breathing right now.

Don was a hero. He was one of the crew members who had ferried ammunition and weapons through harrowing enemy fire, moved casualties throughout the battle, and defended the soft casualty collection point as the two medics were shot. He looked haggard and shell-shocked. He slipped the black knit skullcap off his head and looked at me.

"Well, how are you doing?" he said.

"I'm doing fine."

"Well, let's take a look at this." He held out his right hand, which was covered with an extra mitten over his flight glove.

"D— thing shot off the end of my finger." He pointed at the natural wrinkled folds in his desert camouflaged Gore-tex parka along his right forearm and elbow, where the bullet had ripped through at a few places, just as if he'd folded and cut it with safety scissors, like a child making paper snowflakes. The thought made me think of my son, Caleb. *I sure hope I get to see my son make a snowflake someday.*

"That was one bullet?" I asked in disbelief.

"Yeah," Don said, allowing a fatigued chuckle. "That's what they call a million-dollar wound."

"You're lucky, man," I said.

"You know, I can do without a Purple Heart."

"Yeah, we all could," I said. "I understand, man. We'll get out of here, don't worry about it."

"I can't believe what just happened," Don said.

"I know."

"Twenty-six years, I could live without that," he said. "I didn't need that."

Don teared up. His face contorted and reddened. All the emotion and tension bubbled to the surface.

"I'm the air mission commander," he said in a shaky voice. "I'm the *air mission commander*. I'm responsible for *this*." Don sobbed quietly.

"It's not your fault. And don't you think that it was. We didn't know. It's nobody's fault. Don't worry about it, man. Don't think about that right now. Think about it tomorrow. Do it tomorrow."

Do it tomorrow, I had told him. Just like I'd told Canon: *We'll have the rest of our lives to think about this.*

Don squeezed the black knit cap in his good hand, resting his elbows on his knees, looking at the snowcapped broken rocks between his feet.

58

Mountains are not fair or unfair—they are just dangerous. :: REINHOLD MESSNER

04 1723 MAR 02 (DELTA)
TAKUR GHAR

The group of men I had seen lying in the aircraft and off the ramp when we were shot down were now in a similar arrangement on top of the peak. Sergeant LaFrenz had organized the new casualty collection point and had stabilized what casualties he could. But without surgery, two of the casualties would probably die; another would lose at least a hand, and now he, too, was fading due to blood loss. We were now prepared for medevac and exfiltration aircraft, but none was coming until after dark.

One of the urgent casualties was the young PJ who had sat across from me in the cabin of Razor 01; I remembered him removing his night-vision goggles just before the thirty-second call. Another of the urgents was the flight medic. Both men had been shot in the abdomen while treating casualties at the ramp during the initial enemy counterattack. The third man needing surgery was the pilot whose hand had appeared to be shot off when we were first ambushed. Everyone else appeared to be stable.

We further collapsed our perimeter to tighten security and to utilize greater air assets. The enemy continued to attempt attacks from the same knife-edge ridgeline below us. It was hard to comprehend why the enemy continued to use the same terrain that we continued to pound with bombs. Most of the trees that had lined the top of the ridgeline were gone. The ridge had gone from looking like a Mohawk hairstyle to one more like Kojak's.

Gabe worked on getting bigger bombs on the enemy. He had a B-52 and a pair of Navy F-14s on station ready to drop JDAMs.

"Sir, do you want me to keep hitting these guys?"

"Yeah, I'm sick of them thinking they can screw with us," I said.

After passing the target to the aircraft, an errant thousand-pound JDAM hit on the forward slope of the bald knife-edge ridge instead of the enemy-held reverse slope. The total blast force was deflected toward our position.

"Get down!"

A massive shard of metal—a long section of the bomb's skin—flew at our soft group of Rangers.

Whum-whum-whum-whum-whum.

The chunk looked like a bedpost flying through the air and made a low, whooping sound. It was at least a meter long, moving end over end like a huge boomerang. It rocketed a hundred feet over our heads, moving like something in the movies, propelled into space and not slowing down.

We turned our heads and watched it fly at least a couple of kilometers into the center of the Shah-i-Khot Valley toward the Whale. I said a quick, fervent prayer that it wouldn't hit anyone. It was one of the most impressive things I'd ever seen.

I decided to stop calling for bombs, realizing that they posed a greater threat to us than the enemy did.

I want to kill the enemy so badly, I almost killed my own men.

59

Short is the little time which remains to thee of life. Live as on a mountain.

:: MARCUS AURELIUS, *Meditations*

04 1808 MAR 02 (DELTA)
TAKUR GHAR

Matt LaFrenz tried to keep the casualties calm and comfortable. He assured them that the medevac was en route, that it was all planned out, that we were taking care of them. Meanwhile, the lucid casualties from the aircrew insisted that no one else would fly to the mountain until well after dark.

The young PJ, Jason Cunningham, was fading fast. His bleeding was deep inside his pelvic region, requiring swift and expert surgery to control it. LaFrenz had given him extra whole blood, which Jason had innovatively carried into combat on his own, but his body couldn't hold it inside. After several hours of care and encouragement, Jason took a drastic downward turn.

"Jason. Jason. Stay with us, Jason."

"Doc . . . Doc!"

"Jason!"

LaFrenz and others attempted to revive him through CPR and other means, but it was clear they couldn't save him. Those who had worked all day along with Cunningham to save others now watched him pass away right in front of them. Several men broke down with grief.

I looked up for a moment. Don was moving away. Someone was attempting to console him. The other PJ, Jason's team leader and fellow pararescue jumper, sobbed.

LaFrenz trudged over to the command post, his face and eyes red with tears, his nose running. He wiped his cheek with the back of his bloody hand and sniffed.

"Sir, you can tell *them* that our KIA count is now seven."

I looked away from Matt's eyes to the ground at his feet. He walked away. Kevin handed me the radio.

"Champ, this is One-Six."

"Champ; over."

"Champ, our KIA count is now seven."

There was no response.

60

How much of human life is lost in waiting. :: RALPH WALDO EMERSON

04 1920 MAR 02 (DELTA)
TAKUR GHAR

Finally, after three delays, the plan for exfiltration went out over the radio. Several elements involved in the extraction called in from all over Afghanistan and beyond. MAKO 30 and I weren't in the best location to be following an hour-long brief over the radio, but we were encouraged by the subject of the brief: our ride home.

During the brief, Gabe and Kevin continued to receive requests to observe close air support and control it in the destruction of known and suspected enemy positions around the Shah-i-Khot. Masirah and command-and-control aircraft overhead were feeding Gabe, Kevin, and Jaguar 12 more targets than they could prosecute. They handled terminal attack guidance for one-thousand- and two-thousand-pound JDAMs like they were flipping pancakes. The continued bombing runs and radio conversations nearby made listening to the plan more difficult.

"Kevin, can you help me copy this stuff down?"

"Sure, sir," he said. He pulled a small spiral notebook from his pocket. I wrote key phrases, times, call signs, frequencies, and grid locations in marker on a laminated 3x5 card I pulled from my pocket.

The sun was dropping in the sky, and the wind began to blow. I began to feel cold. I stopped writing every detail and hoped that Vance was doing a good job of taking notes. The brief concluded after an hour.

"Okay," Champ said. "One-Six on the ground, read that back for everyone's benefit."

I couldn't believe it. He was asking me to brief back the whole plan.

"Roger, sir," I said. I grabbed Vance's notes with mine and began to replay what I'd just heard. After fifteen minutes of talking, I had repeated everything we had written down and I had remembered. I concluded with what I believed to be the most important part of the plan: "Approach heading Niner-Zero, landing heading One-Tree-Five. Mark northwest corner of LZ with an IR strobe." We would finally be able to use our infrared devices for the first time since Razor 01 had been in the air. "First bird is the casualty bird. Second bird is for KIA and nonwounded."

"Okay, thanks," Champ said. "Any questions?"

When I got off the radio, Rangers on the mountain were eating. They had found what little food was on the helicopter and divided it among everyone, giving priority to those who needed it most. A Ranger squatted next to me and handed me one fourth of a rock-hard peanut butter PowerBar. I gnawed on it and washed it down with water from my CamelBak.

"Sir, MAKO Three-Zero says they're turning off their radios," Gabe said. "They're running low on batteries. They gave me their grid and said, 'Don't shoot at us.'"

"Nice."

Rangers moved around the peak to find sparse patches of lingering sunshine in order to stay warm. They pulled out ponchos, quilted poncho liners, and other cold-weather gear.

"Sergeant Canon, let's make sure these guys are in buddy teams before dark," I said.

"Already done, sir," he said.

"Sir, would you be my buddy?" Vance said.

"Of course, Kevin." We were already sitting back to back.

Several Rangers began unfolding their tarplike escape and evasion maps to use as ground cloths. They placed the waterproof and tear-proof maps on the snow and lay on top of them, their every adjustment amplified by the rigid maps and the snow. They changed socks and T-shirts to keep their bodies as dry as possible.

I kept my leg in the snow to keep it numb. I could feel blood starting to ooze through my long underwear. If it were to soak through to the surface, I didn't want anyone to see it.

LaFrenz, with help from the other PJ and others, crafted lean-to shelters over the casualties using logs and foliage from the bunkers, space blankets, aircraft insulation, and clothes from our dead brothers.

And lying there beside them in the open were the shirtless, lifeless, and hopeless bodies that a short time ago had housed the souls of men we loved.

61

We are the Dead. Short days ago
We lived, felt dawn, saw sunset glow,
Loved and were loved, and now we lie
In Flanders fields.

:: JOHN McCRAE

04 2000 MAR 02 (DELTA)
TAKUR GHAR

The presence of daylight was the single greatest obstacle preventing our departure from the mountain. Those who were making the high-level decisions many miles away had been very clear: the Night Stalkers would not fly back to the Shah-i-Khot to get us until after dark. Now, with the day's azure sky and blinding snow replaced with a black overhead expanse, we collapsed our perimeter to the size of a golf green and waited for aircraft. It had been fourteen hours since we'd flown into the valley in the darkness of another night, since the men on Razor 01 had removed their night-vision goggles for the day.

The pulsing breeze whistled through my helmet, intermittently muting the conversations of Rangers in their buddy positions. The temperature must have been hovering just above freezing. Kevin Vance and I huddled close together for warmth. We Rangers had no pride when it came to staying warm. We had learned in Ranger School to use each other to block the wind, to share the heat generated by our bodies and exhalation, and to take turns scanning a shared sector in order to allow a buddy to rest. Yet even with Kevin's warmth, my abdominal muscles were sore from shivering.

"Kevin, you awake?"

"Mmm?"

"You droning there?"

"I'm still here, sir," Vance said. "What's up?"

"Nothing," I said. "Good job today."

They'd all done a good job. Snapshot images from the day's events passed through my mind. Such brave men. Such pure motives. Such deep sacrifice. I sat shivering and bleeding among a motley band of America's most recent heroes—assembled from some of America's most diverse locales but drawn together by a common purpose and a shared sense of duty.

Eventually the drone of turbopropeller-driven airplanes could be heard, growing louder. The familiar sound of the C-130 Hercules airframe caused us to stir on the peak. We knew they were gunships. The same type of AC-130 gunships that had been ordered off station during our infil that morning were back to provide fire support to us if we needed it. From their orbits several thousand feet above, our tight group of Rangers must've looked as minute and insignificant as the hole on the top of an ant mound.

"Slick Zero-One, this is Nail Three-One, on station to provide direct support to your egress; over."

"Roger, Nail; over."

"I'll be covering the mountain around you and to the north. Nail Three-Two will work everything outside the mountain and south, controlled by Jaguar One-Two; over."

"Roger."

"We're gonna do some shooting to tweak our guns. No need to control; over."

Two AC-130s. Two security blankets. If anything moved toward us, it would die before it even entered the grid square we occupied.

I looked at my watch. 1645 Zulu time; 8:15 p.m. local time. *The extraction helicopters should be here any minute.* Five Chinooks were en route, escorted by Apache helicopter gunships, A-10 Warthog fighters, and a few sorties of regularly scheduled CAS.

The flight lead Chinook called us on the radio.

"One-Six, this is Razor Five-Four; three minutes; over."

"Roger, do you see our IR strobe?"

"Contact."

The AC-130 began thumping rounds into the mountainsides to our east. The familiar sound brought back memories of training with the AC-130 at Fort Knox. It sounded like a giant popgun overhead, with the 40-mm cannon's impacts a split-second delayed.

Thum-BOOM, thum-BOOM, thum-BOOM, thum-BOOM.

"One-Six, Razor Five-Four; one minute; over."

"Roger; we're burning the LZ now."

We called the Predator overhead to "burn" the LZ next to us with its infrared spotlight, which we had sighted in minutes before. This technique was our insurance against the lead Razor bird landing in the wrong spot, an error that had occurred on previous missions.

"I see the burn; over."

I looked to the southwest, where the lead Chinook lumbered up the valley, flickering its IR signal light to confirm our location. The bird approached slowly, seemingly floating like a hot-air balloon. I had asked the pilots to land with their ramp next to our casualties to expedite our loading of them. The lead aircraft's nose approached our position on a heading that would require it to turn completely around in order to land as I had requested.

"Sir, he ain't turning," Canon said.

"He'll turn it around over the LZ," I said. "I told them I wanted their ramp right on top of our strobe."

The aircraft flared over the peak, blasting us with rotor downwash and stinging our exposed skin with tiny rocks and snow. I looked overhead to check his landing heading. My tired eyes, one of which was looking through a monocular night vision device, interpreted the aircraft's silhouette as facing just how I'd requested it. But from my vantage point it could have been facing either way. Though I was certain, I actually couldn't tell *which* way he was turned.

"He's turned the wrong way, sir!" Canon said over the din of the rotors.

"No, he's good," I said. "He's perfect!"

The Chinook settled onto the ground. I could see the muted green glow of instruments and night-vision goggles inside the cockpit and the bird's refueling boom a few meters from our perimeter.

He's turned the wrong way.

The reinforcing SEALs aboard the lead Chinook were meant to load our casualties onto the aircraft; instead, they exited the bird and took up positions on the vacant southern end of the saddle. For the next ten minutes my exhausted Rangers, who had fought all day, traversed the loose western slope of the peak, carrying casualties around the tilted Chinook and loading them onto the ramp. Razor 54 was on the ground for more than ten minutes waiting for us to finish loading.

Sergeant DePouli's squad got on the Chinook after the wounded casualties. The helicopter whined higher and flew over our heads to the north. The sound of wind at ten thousand feet.

The SEAL team leader made his way to my position, where we exchanged pleasantries and essential matters of information before I handed over control of the peak. I called the second Chinook to ensure the pilots landed with the ramp near our casualties so that we could load the dead more easily.

The second Chinook approached low from the north. The bird popped over the peak and our position and landed along the correct heading, the black cavern of the cabin inviting us to enter. Again, the Rangers began dragging casualties to the aircraft. They struggled to lift the bodies to the ramp.

I grabbed the SEAL team leader on the sleeve and squeezed his arm. I thought of Anderson's knotted shoulder that I'd squeezed aboard Razor 01.

"Thanks for this," I said. "I appreciate it. See you all back there in a little bit. Need anything else?"

"No."

The Rangers and crew members stacked and lined the KIA along the centerline of the aircraft's cabin. I hobbled to the bird last along with Vance. I climbed up onto the ramp, which was hanging over a slope. My heart jolted in my chest when I saw Jason Cunningham near the ramp, lying there with no shirt and the look of a silent scream on his face.

I inched through the cabin along the wall toward the front of the aircraft. Canon was already seated between the front door gunners. I walked on toward him.

"Sir, you don't want to go any farther than this," Canon said. "Just stay where you're at."

The last time he had told me to come no farther, I had seen something I could never forget. This time I obeyed.

I sat against the wall, across from where I had sat when we were shot down on Razor 01. The bird wobbled and wiggled as the engines whined higher. And then we were airborne.

Despite the wind rushing through the open windows, the aircraft held a repugnant smell. It sickened and saddened me to realize that the odor was caused by my dead brothers who were stacked around me like pieces of equipment. *They deserve more honor than this.*

Ten minutes later, the temperature in the cabin rose over the course of a few seconds, and I realized we were landing. The crew chiefs signaled for us to stay seated, so I figured we weren't yet in

Bagram. I didn't know where we were landing, or even why. Several individuals whom I did not know loaded on our aircraft carrying what I assumed to be sensitive items from another aircraft—a couple of miniguns, several radios, and other heavy objects I did not recognize. *Maybe they're the crew members from Razor 03, the bird we originally intended to secure.*

I moved to sit with Canon to provide the newcomers additional space, to get warmer, and to find some comfort with one of my guys. He and I sat facing the ramp. I leaned back on his chest as he straddled me. Aircraft were scarce, and they were trying to use all available space to ferry people and equipment back to Bagram. Had I not been so tired, I would have been upset that they were using the Chinook—which carried my heroic, battle-fatigued soldiers and the precious cargo of our dead comrades—as a taxi.

We flew away and landed again twenty minutes later. Again, the crew signaled for us to stay seated. I heard Sergeant Pressburg talking over our platoon radios, which meant he was near the aircraft. I couldn't understand why he was there, wherever it was we had landed, but I was too exhausted to even bother finding out.

Sergeant Canon started talking with Pressburg over the radio, giving him a casualty report. I could sense anxiety in Pressburg's voice.

"Hey, Canon," he said. "Where's One-Six at?"

Maybe he thinks I'm dead.

"I'm in between his legs," I said over the net.

"Good to hear you, sir," Pressburg said.

"You too, P-bone."

We lifted off again and landed again to take on more fuel, and then flew back to Bagram on the final leg of a flight that totaled more than two and a half hours.

A few minutes away from Bagram, my left foot went numb. It

had fallen asleep under someone else's leg again. I tried to move it, but the Ranger whose leg was on mine must have been asleep, because he didn't even try to help me move my leg or move off it.

I finally wrested my leg free. It had been under the lifeless body of Marc Anderson.

62

He who climbs upon the highest mountains laughs at all tragedies, real or imaginary.

:: FRIEDRICH NIETZSCHE, *Thus Spake Zarathustra*

04 2245 MAR 02 (DELTA)
BAGRAM, AFGHANISTAN

Sometimes familiar places seem foreign when seen from a new vantage point. We landed at our home air base in Bagram, but on a side of the base that I didn't recognize. The Chinook set down across the main runway from our compound, and although I saw the dim yellow lights glowing from the control tower, I didn't realize we were in Bagram.

The crew chiefs motioned for us to off-load the Chinook. Two steps off the ramp, I stopped to bask in the hot turbine-engine exhaust blowing from the twin cylinders atop the cabin. I opened my eyes to see that everyone else was doing the same, then turned away from the eye-stinging fumes. Taking deep breaths of the bird's toxic exhaust and ignoring the choking sensation it triggered, I enjoyed the warmth inside and out. What a bittersweet way to breathe. What a bittersweet day to live.

I must have stood by the bird for at least five minutes without knowing or caring who was there with me. A Humvee rolled alongside the Chinook. Sergeant Canon got out of the passenger's seat.

"Listen, Rangers, if you're not on this Humvee, you're walking back," he said.

Half a dozen Rangers climbed into the open back of the Humvee, and just as many began waddling across the broken tarmac to the corrugated steel apron and onto the dry dirt road leading to our compound. I limped back, following the leaders. I still didn't know where I was.

I didn't recognize the gate to our compound until I walked through it. Fresh Rangers from another platoon were on guard duty, Rangers who must have flown into Bagram from Kandahar during the day. They hadn't been there when we'd flown out the night before.

On the way to my tent, another unfamiliar Ranger nearly ran me over.

"Oh, hey, sir, how's it going?"

"Pretty good."

I walked along the wooden-crate sidewalk to my tent, walked to my cot, and took off my body armor. Lifted from my shoulders, the weight I'd carried for the past twenty hours made my body feel light enough to take flight on its own.

I needed to report to the joint operations center. I left my gear scattered on my bunk and walked back outside. A Ranger NCO walked briskly past me, stopping after he recognized my face.

"Hey, sir, where's the JOC?" he said.

"There," I said. "That door over there. That's the JOC."

"Thanks, sir."

I stopped in the middle of the compound and looked around at the faint white mountains encircling the air base. No moon overhead. The oppressive droning of diesel generators felt familiar. Nothing here seemed to have changed. Yet for me, everything had.

Another lost Ranger walked by. "Hey, sir, where's the pisser at?"

"It's up over there."

And life goes on.

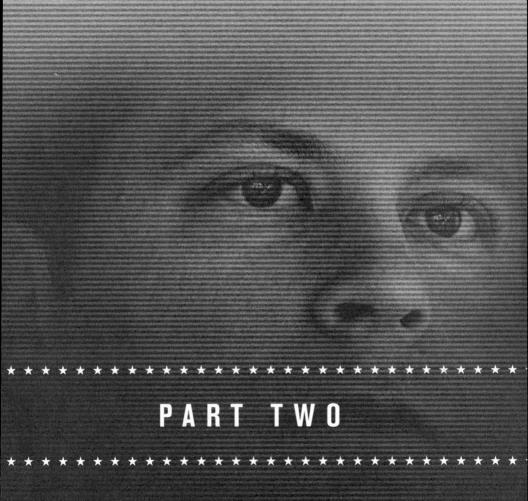

PART TWO

★ ★

RECOIL

★ ★

63

In the days following our return to Bagram, I found myself at the receiving end of a serious allegation from one of my Rangers.

"Sir, you *said* it. I heard it come from your mouth. You were swearing out there."

"That's impossible. I know I didn't say anything. That's not me."

"I know it's not you, sir. That's when I knew it was bad. When you cussed."

"What did I say?"

"You said, 'Jesus Christ.'"

"Impossible."

"Whatever, sir. I'm pretty sure of what I heard."

I went back to my cot angry. The accusation had me fuming. And hurt.

Had I cried out the Lord's name in vain under fire? I couldn't believe that I had. I'd never uttered it before. *Ever.* When I was in junior high, I know I had said a bad word or two. But the guilt from that was too much for me. So I kept it clean after that. I stuck to the quasi–curse words that I saw as acceptable—*freakin'*, *crap*, *crud*, *dang it*—weak substitutes for the real thing.

Because I never really cursed, I'd take extreme offense whenever somebody said that I did. I felt wronged. It made me mad just knowing that someone else *thought* I had cursed.

I had a coach once who made boys do push-ups for failing to say, "Yes, sir," or for wearing a baseball cap indoors, or for swearing, or for anything. Grave offenses got fifty. One time, he thought I said something that I didn't, and he tried to punish me for it.

"Gimme twenty-five!" he said.

I argued with him, saying that I simply never used those words, that they never even entered my mind. It was true, but he didn't believe me. He also didn't understand why I wouldn't just take my punishment and continue on my way. I could handle the punishment; it was admitting guilt that I couldn't handle, especially when I knew I didn't bear any. That offended me. I was pretty self-righteous.

So, when that Ranger said I'd cursed up on Takur Ghar, he hit a nerve.

Did I cry out the Lord's name in vain? He says I did. He'd told me in a tone of surprise and amusement. All the guys thought the situation was so bad that even Captain Self cursed. I denied it. Told him it was someone else. Laughed it off, knowing I had never—and I mean *never*—done that before. Not the Lord's name. I felt kind of like Peter in the Bible, when he was accused of knowing Christ. "No! No! No!" Emphatic denial.

But why should I feel like Peter? I really hadn't betrayed Jesus Christ. I hadn't said what they accused me of saying. I'd never let it stand before, and I wasn't going to let it stand now. Not after I had been active in the Bible study. Not after I had been trying to be an example, trying to lead spiritually. Not after God had delivered me from that snowy and bloody mountain. It would be almost blasphemous to let the accusation go uncorrected. I told that Ranger he was wrong, and I dismissed it.

But alone, I thought about it. What had actually transpired during those first few seconds of combat?

Snapshots zipped through my mind as I tried to remember it. Sometimes those pictures, if I got them right, would evoke split-second re-creations of the emotions I'd felt in those first few moments. I wanted to find those images in my mind. The right ones, the ones I'd really seen. The fluid gurgling from the bullet holes in the bird. The sparks flaring off the oxygen tank. The pool of blood.

As fast as those pictures and emotions came and went during that first minute, that's how fast they came and went when I tried to capture them now. After replaying those frames in my mind, visualizing the rest of what played out, maybe I remember saying something in those moments.

What if it did happen? What if I used the Lord's name in vain? If it happened, then it must have just come out. It was not something that would have come from habit. It had to have been a subconscious, natural, reflexive cry for help. Something inside me had cried out on its own, with no intervention of the mind.

I hadn't had time to think in that moment. It was a time for action, and my soul had fought back spiritually before I could even begin to fire my weapon—an exclamation of the Holy Spirit that struck fear into the demons who, moments before, had held total dominion over the situation. Just as the demon named Legion in the Bible was terrified by Jesus' name and begged for mercy, the demons on that mountain shrank back in horror upon hearing the name of Jesus invoked.

Was this all just wishful thinking? My self-righteousness rearing its head again and blinding me to my sin? Well, it wouldn't be the first time. Yet I came across a biblical precedent, another such cry for help, in the Psalms:

> FROM THE END OF THE EARTH I WILL CRY TO YOU,
> WHEN MY HEART IS OVERWHELMED;
> LEAD ME TO THE ROCK THAT IS HIGHER THAN I.
> (PSALM 61:2, NKJV)

In the light of Scripture, the scene fell into place. As a believer in the Lord Jesus Christ, as a lover of his precious name, I could not have profaned it even under peril of death. No—as with David in the wilderness, when my own heart was overwhelmed, I shouted the name of the Lord from a mountaintop in southeastern Afghanistan: "JESUS CHRIST!"

I believe the Holy Spirit used me, in spite of myself and my sin. He used me as a spiritual warrior as much as a Ranger warrior. And I didn't even know it. He touched my soul in a fraction of a second and made it react in a powerful way, manifesting in his spoken name the power of the Lord.

Now does it look to be in vain?

Now am I ashamed?

Now do I deny using the name of Christ?

No.

64

Before we knew it, it was time to go home.

Everything was about to change. When we stepped onto the waiting airplane, we would leave behind the war; and when we stepped off in Savannah, we'd be back to our normal lives—or so we hoped.

We were already one week removed from Afghanistan, enjoying some downtime on Masirah Island. For the past several days, we had cleaned and counted weapons, packed equipment, played basketball and spades, and spent time in the sun. I had a blister the size of a quarter on my chest from falling asleep in the East Arabian sun for thirty minutes. Now we were less than an hour from leaving on a flight that would take us to another world.

I saw the chartered aircraft outside the hangar. It had flowers painted on the tail and the words *Hawaiian Airlines* across the fuselage. We joked that the Army had a surprise waiting for us in Hawaii. We filed into the tan metal warehouse next to the tarmac, the same warehouse where we had assembled on New Year's Eve, prior to flying to Bagram.

The building housed several battle-ready desert Humvees, just like the ones we'd had in Bagram, and pallets of ammunition and additional equipment ready to resupply units in Afghanistan.

We squeezed our normal company-size formation in between the metal racks of equipment that reached to the ceiling. The company's first sergeant needed to conduct the final manifest call before we could board the chartered plane back to Savannah.

Our spirits rose as we anticipated going home, and the chatter grew as the first sergeant droned through the names, calling them out in alphabetical order, and we called our responses.

"Brosnan!"

"Andrew P., First Sergeant!"

"Conley!"

"Christopher F., First Sergeant!"

"Crose!"

My face got hot before I even knew why. The first sergeant had just called out Brad Crose's name by mistake. Brad had died on that mountain, yet he was still listed on the company manifest roster.

There was no more chatter in the hangar.

The first sergeant resumed the roll call, speeding through the names. When he finished, he told us we'd be loading the aircraft in ten minutes. We meandered outside into the hot, salty coastal wind.

I sensed an urge to talk to the platoon. I felt as if they were slipping away; that the moment was slipping away. I called the platoon in around me.

"Get in here tight, guys, real tight!"

The wind and the idling jet engines and the active runway made it difficult to hear.

"Get close!"

They knew there was nothing left to plan, nothing to do but ride home, but they looked at me as if they were under fire. They were locked in.

"Listen, guys. Nothing special here. I just want to tell you a couple of things."

I could feel them getting closer.

"First of all, I want you to know that I'm proud of you. You are the best. And you proved that. You proved it every day; you proved it on that mountain; you've proved it since then."

I put my arm on the shoulder of the Ranger next to me.

"You don't have to prove yourselves anymore. Don't feel like you need to prove yourselves to anybody. *Anybody.* Do you understand that? No one else. You've proven yourselves to each other, to yourselves, and to me. That's all that matters.

"We're about to get on that plane, and as soon as we do, everything changes. For the rest of your lives, this all goes away. It becomes a memory, and you can't get it back. Enjoy what you have around you right now. It will all be gone when you get on that plane. And if not then, you'll go to sleep, and when you wake up in Savannah, it'll all be gone."

Some of the guys looked at the ground. Some looked at the plane. Some looked at each other.

"I love you guys, every one of you," I said. "Now make sure that Matt's and Brad's and Marc's sacrifices aren't wasted. Live your lives and remember them. Don't ever forget this."

Moments later, we climbed the stairs to the jet and left it all behind.

65

Home at last. We poured off the chartered aircraft into the muggy Low Country air. We all had long, bushy hair and sideburns from the few months of relaxed grooming standards, and bronze tans from a week in the sun in Oman. Our chartered Hawaiian Airlines jet fooled most of our families into thinking we had stopped in Honolulu for a few days of R & R on the way home.

We marched into the hangar and halted in formation in front of a massive American flag, the size of a basketball court, that hung from the ceiling. After a quick welcoming speech and a prayer, we bolted toward our family members in the audience. They met us halfway across the void.

Julie was there, a tender mother holding Caleb, who was a small-scale version of me. I imagined that he had been her picture of me throughout the deployment, and now we were all together. Julie was more beautiful than ever. She gave me the sweetest kiss. She looked too skinny; she'd no doubt lost some weight while I'd been gone. Caleb was crying before I held him and was even worse after I took him in my arms. He was one handsome little boy.

My parents were there, and I gave them long hugs.

Before we left the hangar, I had the unexpected and difficult task of meeting some of the parents of the men who had died on the mountain. All I could do was hug them. I couldn't find words. After that, I felt guilty holding Caleb.

Julie, my parents, and I went home to our apartment, where I unpacked my bags, watched Caleb eat solid food for the first time, and tried to catch up on the past five months. It was awkward but exciting. They told me everything Caleb was doing now that he was almost six months old. I had missed so much of his life. There was so much I wanted to tell him, but he was still too young for that. He had been with me through it all.

Julie and my parents also told the story of how they had learned of the battle, the deaths, and my wounding. I had been so out of touch with them. This was our first chance to put all the pieces together.

My mother told how, on the morning I was shot down, she had woken up sensing that something was wrong. When she'd arrived for work at the hospital, she had left her office and gone downstairs to find the hospital chaplain.

"I need to pray with you. I'm not sure what has happened, but I feel like Nathan's in danger and we need to pray for him."

My mother knelt in the chaplain's tiny, quiet office and prayed for me. She had no way of knowing what I was enduring at the time, but she knew something was wrong. She felt it all day.

Julie was informed of the battle, vaguely, by way of a cryptic phone call. She tried to call some other people to clarify what was happening, but their answers were also ambiguous. Not knowing what was happening, she panicked, fearing the worst. Finally, she was informed that I had been wounded and some other men had been killed but I was going to be okay. For the first time, the news stories she had been watching in fear had come true.

Julie had gone straight to my parents' house. When my mother opened the door and saw Julie standing there holding little Caleb and crying, she fell to her knees. She said she felt like she was about to vomit. Her intuition had been correct. Her son was dead.

Julie rushed into the house, reached for my mother, and told her I was going to be okay.

My mother said to me, "For a few seconds, I knew what it was like to lose a son."

66

"You ready, man?"

I nodded, but probably not enough for him to notice. I stared across the shaded square to see the battalion of Rangers filing into Savannah's largest Catholic cathedral, which had recently been renovated. Its cream-colored spires towered above the neat rows of green-suited warriors flowing silently through the doors. I would follow the Rangers into the church within a few minutes to honor and say good-bye again to the men who had died on the mountain.

"You're gonna do fine, Nate. You've always been good at this stuff."

Dave Blank, my old roommate, was a faithful encourager. I was happy and grateful that he had driven from Fort Benning to be with me for the memorial service.

Dave had called out of the blue. I hadn't seen him since his wedding. He'd had a Christmas wedding in Columbus, Ohio, and I'd been his best man. I was a new Ranger platoon leader then, and I'd worn my uniform.

Now it had been six weeks since I'd led my platoon into battle; six weeks since I'd lost my boys. I reached to my right leg and circled my index finger around the divot in my thigh. I liked to make it hurt a little. The nickel-size hole just under the black stripe down the leg of my dress green trousers was packed with gauze and still oozing. I had been taught at West Point that the black stripe was one of the signs of an officer. Those signs triggered salutes. But it took a lot more than pants stripes to live up to those salutes.

I had written letters to the families of the men who had lost their lives, and today I would meet most of them for the first time. Their boys—my boys—had been buried at home here in the United States more than a month ago, while the search for al-Qaeda and Usama bin Laden was still underway in Afghanistan. Arin Canon had flown home with the bodies because he knew all the families. After today, I would know them all too.

The boys had been buried exactly six months after 9/11. By the time we left Afghanistan, we still had not found bin Laden, nor had we recovered the aircraft known as Razor 03, the aircraft that had gone down and caused us to scramble and fly through the cold into that stiff, metallic scent of oil and cedar, and carry these men to their fate. In our hearts now, we sensed there was something left undone. Part of that something was a proper memorial for our fallen comrades. But perhaps it was something more. Perhaps it would always be incomplete—at least in some of our minds.

The 1st Ranger Battalion filled the cathedral. The Rangers were quiet, all hurting to some degree. Some had known Brad. Some had known Matt. Some had known Marc. Some were likely struggling with the fact that they'd been here in Savannah while we were contributing to the war, while we were experiencing combat. Maybe some saw *themselves* in our dead comrades—Rangers just like themselves.

Someone told me to go downstairs to the basement of the cathedral before the ceremony began. There they had finger food and tart punch, a small group of high rankers, and too many flower arrangements. This is where I would meet the families that I hadn't already met and become reacquainted with the families I had met at the welcome-home ceremony. In the basement. I remember meeting Brad Crose's mom there. All the mothers were there.

Nothing to say. Just to be there.

I studied Brad's mom. She wore black, unlike the rest. Her hair was long and blond and curly. She wore a heart-shaped pendant.

"That necklace you're wearing sure is beautiful," I said in a soft voice.

"Oh . . . really?" she said. "Here, you can have it if you really like it." She started to put down her punch, which she wasn't drinking anyway.

"No, ma'am. No," I said. "No, you've already given me more than enough."

She tilted her head and struggled to smile.

"Oh," she said quietly, as if she were shucking off a compliment. Her eyes glistened. She put her hand on my cheek, just as a mother would. Just as my mother would.

Brad's mom had lost her son.

67

Julie and I stepped out of the warm, midday sun to the sound of country music and the crunch of peanut shells that littered the concrete floor of Logan's Roadhouse on Abercorn Street. The restaurant was the platoon's spot to hold farewell dinners for departing Rangers. These gatherings were always fun, but saying good-bye to a member of our platoon was always hard. On this occasion, they were saying good-bye to me, as I was leaving Savannah for Fort Benning and yet another Army school.

In many ways, I had already left. I had been replaced as their platoon leader five months earlier, within a couple of weeks of our return from Afghanistan. Eighteen months in the job had been long enough for the Army. It was time for a new lieutenant to take over, and time for me to move on.

I was touched that they had remembered me enough to hold a farewell dinner at Logan's and to staple my green canvas name tape to the barracks hallway wall next to so many others who had been a part of 1st Platoon.

I hadn't seen the men from my platoon much at all since we'd come home, but we were close like brothers. The meal was great, as were the conversations and the reminiscing. Caleb slept in his car seat on the floor throughout the meal. After an hour of hot buttered rolls and steaks, a couple of the NCOs asked for our attention.

"Captain Self, can you come up here?"

I squeezed Julie's hand and stood up. I stepped alongside one of the NCOs. As he addressed the platoon and recounted my progression as their platoon leader—from the stressed-out fast-roper at Hunter to the captain aboard Razor 01—he presented me with a brand new pistol. It was a Colt .45 ACP commemorative World War II edition, parkerized, with plastic grips. I couldn't believe it. I was so shocked by the gift that I didn't hear much of what he said. I refocused just in time to hear his final words to me.

"Captain Self, leaders like you come along once in a lifetime. Rangers lead the way, sir."

I sat down at my table, squeezed Julie's hand again, and took a sip of sweet tea to cover my embarrassment. She looked at me with admiring eyes and patted my leg.

The Rangers told me that they'd bought the gun from Brad Crose's stepdad, who was a gun dealer. They said he'd given them a great deal on it. I spent the next half hour saying good-bye to the men of the platoon and making promises to stay in touch. Julie and I left Logan's feeling great about our time in the Rangers, and that we had made a difference there. But I realized that night that I already missed the men of 1st Platoon more than I had expected. It was time to leave, and I hoped that if things went well later in the Army, maybe they'd invite me back to lead a company of Rangers in a couple of years.

Later that week, I decided to take my new .45 to the pistol range to break it in. I took off early one afternoon, bought a couple boxes of ammunition and an extended magazine, and drove to the range. I lubed up the gun with some oil, practiced some dry-fire "ready-ups," and then started shooting. It felt good to fire a weapon again. I think this was the first time I'd shot since Afghanistan. The pistol felt bigger than the Beretta 9mm I'd carried in the Army. It was maybe a tad big in my hands. My hands are pretty small anyway, but I could hardly reach the slide release with my thumb.

After a few clips, I started finding a rhythm, getting the feel of the trigger weight, pacing the recoil of the gun to double-tap and hammer the targets. The familiar scent of searing gun oil and gunpowder created a subconscious nostalgia in me. My stomach stirred. With each steady roll of the trigger, I could feel the rearward cycle of the slide, the recoil transferring momentum from the weapon to me.

I shot surprisingly well for a while. Then I realized that something was awkwardly missing. I cleared the pistol and examined the top of the barrel. The front sight post was gone. There was an empty notch where it had been. That tiny piece of steel was somewhere at my feet in the grass and sand. I looked but never found it.

I thought later about getting the gun fixed. I knew that Brad's stepdad would be happy to repair it. But I didn't want to bother him over it. Besides, I didn't expect to use the pistol again. It would just be nice to have as a reminder of the great men I had once led. And to know that they loved me.

68

Greg Commons and I talked in his kitchen in Alexandria, Virginia. I noticed how much he resembled my own dad—grayish beard, bald mostly on top with some hair on the sides, glasses, husky. Greg told me what it was like to find out that Matt had been killed. About the notification process. About burying Matt.

"You know, March eleventh means as much to me as March fourth, because they buried Matt on the eleventh."

The kitchen was quaint. I think I remember white tile countertops.

"On March eleventh, I stood in this kitchen and put my palms on the kitchen sink and told God, 'I can't do this today; take this from me.' Linda walked in and asked, 'Greg, are you all right?' I told her, 'Linda, I can't do this today, I can't go; I can't bury my son.' She put her arms around me, gave me the most loving hug, and said, 'I'll be with you. We'll get through this.' I felt God come into my heart to help. It was a great day."

Earlier in the day, Greg and I had visited Matt's grave at Arlington National Cemetery, across from the Pentagon. Matt was buried next to Jason Cunningham, the pararescue jumper who had died on the mountain a few hours after Matt.

Dinner was nice. I don't recall what we ate, but I do remember the clever split-level dining room-to-hallway-to-bedroom area where little Caleb spent most of his time exploring. And that Matt's little brothers, Thomas and Patrick, were there to make sure Caleb didn't fall down the three or four steps between the levels.

Greg asked me to go for a walk. Actually, he had told me as soon as I arrived, and again a couple of times during the evening, that we were going to go for a walk. He slipped a couple of cigars in the pocket of his leather jacket, and we went outside.

Cigar smoke and pipe smoke have always smelled good to me, but I've never had the nerve to try smoking. Greg Commons and I were on our third lap of the block in his tidy little neighborhood in Virginia when he offered me the cigar. There were no leaves on the trees; everything was shaded the soft blue of the street lights. On the next street over, the lights were yellow. It was late. It was cold. Greg offered me the cigar again, and again I declined. The man's son had died under my command, and when he asked me to join him for a single cigar, I told him no.

The image of Matt in his open casket, from the photos Greg had shown me, was hurting my head. I bore down to push it away—just for the night—but there it was again. The image of Matt dead that Greg had shown me looked different from the dead Matt I remembered. The dead Matt I had seen on the helicopter ramp looked alive. It was only the pool of crimson under him that told me otherwise. To die like that is to never know.

Greg and I had completed our third trip around the block when he spoke up again.

"You know, I had a dream on March fourth," Greg said. "I dreamed that Matt died. Within the same few hours of when he died. He and I were on the back of a helicopter together, flying into battle."

Greg had been a Marine in Vietnam.

"We're riding along and we get shot down. And Matt gets shot. And he tells me that he's dying. I see him dying. I see him going up to heaven. And he's looking down at me. And he says to me, 'Dad, I love you, too.'"

Greg stopped walking.

"'I love you, too, Dad,' he said. That was the last thing he told me when we talked on the phone. I said, 'Matt, I want you to know I love you.' And he said, 'Dad, I love you, too.'"

All I could do was grunt.

"Captain Self, I want you to tell me everything. Every detail—everything. I want to know how Matt died."

I told him everything.

After I was done, he stopped walking and faced me. I turned to him. I couldn't feel my ears.

"Well, Captain Self. Thank you. That's all I needed. I just needed to hear it all."

I looked down.

"And you need to know, Captain Self, that you did good. You did your job."

69

A typical platoon leader, the average kind that gives officers a bad name, may not know that one of his soldiers' wives is pregnant. A typical platoon leader might not ask enough questions to know what's going on in the lives of his men. A typical platoon leader might not want his men to see him cry, or even sleep. A typical platoon leader might not see someone's son in every soldier he leads.

I wanted to be more than a typical platoon leader. I led fifty-five Rangers during our combat tour in Afghanistan, and I'd thought I had a good relationship with all the men in my platoon.

What I knew about Marc Anderson was that he was a math wizard who was just looking for someone who outranked him to ask a question so he could display his mental prowess. What I knew about Matt Commons was that he loved J. R. R. Tolkien's works and that he had watched our bootleg copy of *The Fellowship of the Ring* several times in Bagram before his final mission. What I knew about Brad Crose was that he was a deeply faithful man, though he never expressed that directly to me.

But there was so much I didn't know.

What I didn't know about Marc Anderson was that as a child, he was so tender that a stern look from his father would result in tears. That he had given up Division I athletic scholarships to attend school close to home because that's what he thought his parents wanted. That he had left a portion of his life insurance policy to a high school student he'd tutored years before.

What I didn't know about Matt Commons was that he had a

giant tattoo of a cross on his back, complete with the name of Jesus. That he'd talked to his mother a few days before he died and told her to use his checkbook if she needed to make ends meet. That in the Bible Randy Kirby had given him the week before we were shot down Matt had left his bookmark at the passage dealing with loving your enemies.

What I didn't know about Brad Crose was that he and his father had knelt in prayer together in front of a Christmas tree two days before Brad deployed. That he loved to bake and cook for the other Rangers. That he had told his mom that I was a "squared away" platoon leader.

Considering what I've learned about my men since they died, I wonder if I was a good platoon leader to them after all. There was so much I hadn't known. I discovered all these fantastic attributes after Brad and Marc and Matt were dead. I got closer to these men—I got to know them better—after they were gone. Some things you just don't know to ask a person about until he's gone. I still struggle with the emotional economy of it all: If the price of knowing these things was that these men would die under my command, then I'd rather have them be strangers to me—and alive.

Still, I call to check on their families, and I go to memorial dedications, for *them*. For Brad and Marc and Matt. And for their families. And for myself. It hurts, but I do it. It's my duty, but it's much more than that. Those events, those men, that day, are a permanent part of who I am. In the same way that Marc will always be a specialist, Matt a corporal, and Brad a sergeant, I will forever be their platoon leader.

70

The 2003 State of the Union Address. I don't want to be here. They told me I *had* to come, and I guess I should be proud to be here, but I'd rather be sitting at home right now watching it on TV. Or doing something else. I never expected the House Chamber to be this small. Like it's some kind of execution chamber. More like it's some prestigious, closed-door, elite club. People in suits acting like they're at a fancy dinner party.

There's Hillary, there's John Kerry, there's Julie across the room. I'm cramped in this hot balcony. There are the stiff judges. There are the generals. I can't clap unless they do.

This is different from how it looks on TV. The room looks bigger on TV. Usually, the president calls out the military designees like me. Usually he recognizes why each of us is here. I hope he doesn't do that this year.

The president is talking a lot. It's obvious we're going to war somewhere besides Afghanistan. I won't be recognized—his speech is too long. I don't care if I am. I believe what he's saying. I'll go, if it comes to that.

Kevin Vance is next to me. It's not the same as the last time we sat together. We're clean now. We're wearing neckties. No one is shooting at us.

Julie and I and an Army sergeant who had also been invited to attend the Address spent half the day in a light colonel's office, trying to figure out if we were invited to the White House for dinner or if we'd be ordering room service.

"Which one of you is the First Lady's guest?"

I looked at the sergeant. He didn't know either.

"Sir, no one's told us anything."

"Okay, it can be either one. What are *you* here for?"

"Sir, I built some schools and hospitals and did some more CA-type work in Afghanistan," the sergeant said.

"Okay, one of you decide who's going to the White House. It doesn't matter."

He was right. It just didn't matter.

"Okay, Sergeant, it's you. I'll have the staff there get in touch with you."

They took us around to a bevy of congressmen and senators. I'd never heard of most of these people. We sat in their waiting rooms for ten minutes, went into their big offices, chatted for two minutes, and stood for a hug in front of a camera. I never expected to see those pictures. I never did.

A colonel from the Pentagon told me to "always accept the praise of a grateful nation." I think he cared. He was a good guy, but I didn't like the advice.

He gave us a tour of the Pentagon.

"This is the wing where the airplane hit. They just reopened it."

These people in the rings, in the halls, in the corridors—how many went to war because of that plane? I went. And I came back to this.

Julie's wearing a suit she just bought in Pentagon City. We were almost late. I can't see her anymore because she's sitting behind a brass rail. When she stands, she's looking down at the back of the president's head. When she sits, she can't see anything.

I didn't tell anyone at the career course at Fort Benning that I was coming here. All the guys in my class would probably figure it out, but I didn't want to talk about it before I left. I'm sitting here at the State of the Union Address, away from them, physically disconnected, and they don't even know I'm gone.

Didn't matter if I was physically back in class with them or not; I still felt disconnected, at least emotionally. Every day, listening to them talk about their own combat in Afghanistan. I was getting tired of hearing about it. Some of them had been in the valley during Anaconda. I was the only officer there who had been on the mountain. Except for one; he had gone to Takur Ghar a few days after my platoon left. Had to listen to him talk about how they had seized or assaulted or secured the top of that mountain. At the time, I thought he was an idiot, but I realize now it's all relative.

One of the guys from class had worked on a high-level staff in Kuwait and had his combat patch. He'd done his part, what was asked of him. During a cold January run at Benning, he struck up a conversation about the war.

"Man, I don't know what you've got, but I came home with some good stuff from the war. I was on staff. I saw everything. I got a video of when one of them Chinooks got f—— up on that mountain. You seen that?"

"No, man. No, I don't think I've seen that."

"Ah, you gotta see it, man. I'll bring it in."

"Cool, man. That's cool."

The president's speech is very long. A lot about Iraq. The major who had coordinated my visit is back at the DoubleTree with his wife, babysitting Caleb. I met him this morning. He did all the work but wasn't invited to the Address. And he volunteered to watch Caleb. What a nice man. I could tell he was a Christian. I think he told me that.

71

I sometimes come to the roof of this building to look out over the swift Tigris River, just to calm myself. This is my second overseas deployment in as many years, and my seventh month in Iraq. Just across the river lie the ruins of ancient Nineveh, the wicked city to which the prophet Jonah reluctantly delivered a message of repentance. Just outside the old city walls stands the dominating Nabi Younis mosque, under which, according to legend, Jonah's bones are buried. The mosque rises high atop the rubble of an ancient Christian church. After what happened today, I could use a little faith, whatever the flavor.

The command sergeant major on this compound was the highest-ranking enlisted man in the brigade. Today, he's the deadest. I hate him for it. I hate him for getting himself killed.

He pushed it one step too far and paid the price. *This isn't Nashville, man; it's Iraq.* He was being so foolish, driving along like that—in an SUV, a white Nissan Patrol, just like the one I drive around Iraq.

One vehicle by itself. Even after General Petraeus had said "no less than three vehicles" so many times over the radio. It was just him and one other man, his driver, a young specialist named Rel. I'd had a soldier named Rel—Jason Rel, a different guy—in Savannah. The Rel in the Nissan Patrol, the one driving the sergeant major, is also dead today. I don't hate him for it—it wasn't his decision. He was doing what he was told.

For two months, I've been tooling around in my own SUV, just me and one other guy, just like the sergeant major and his driver.

We've been checking on and paying thousands of Iraqi security guards. They know we're coming with lots of cash. Many of them probably want to kill me. Maybe I want to kill some of them. Some of them are only waiting for the next payoff to help them determine their allegiances.

The sergeant major, a grown man, an experienced soldier, chose to disobey. Just like I have. Now one of us is dead. Targeted. Murdered. Left for looters on the side of the road. One vehicle, off by itself. Rifles in the floorboard. Two men, dragged out of their seats and shot in the street. I hate the sergeant major for that. For driving alone with his driver. For getting himself killed. For taking himself away from us.

Was *that* part of God's plan?

Are these just random acts of violence?

It could just as easily have been me.

It should've been me.

Twenty-seven years the sergeant major served in the Army. I'm at five years, working on six. He'd been in combat before. He should have been beyond the threat of dying.

He's a celebrity, a VIP. He's not supposed to die.

Just like the guys on those Blackhawk helicopters a few weeks ago. They weren't supposed to die on the way home to see their families. One flight and forty-eight hours away from browsing through Wal-Mart with their wives or girlfriends, from wearing Dockers and button-down shirts to church on Sunday and rubbing elbows with the guys at the donut table, who would ask if they'd signed up for the golf tournament next weekend—a jarring question for these warriors plucked fresh from the fields of war.

They'll miss the golf tournament for sure now, after the crash, but the guys at church will probably make their foursomes. Might not even notice they're missing.

They're calling it a midair collision. Two helicopters crashing into each other. Two of my friends—my classmates—are out there guarding the wreckage, cutting out bodies, recovering sensitive equipment and personal effects. Two Blackhawks down. Eighteen dead. Some of them on their way home for two weeks of leave. One of the Blackhawks crashed onto the flat roof of a house.

A helicopter crash site on top of a building.

My friends are good combat leaders. I know they're doing well, at least when it comes to leading. They're probably strong and decisive and clearheaded and calm. But I know it's hard for them. I'm not there, but I don't need to be. I know what it's like. I can hear the whole story in the tone of their voices over the radio. I can hear the crushing of metal. I can smell the burnt oil. I can feel the blunt cries of the men. And it's hard for me. To know what it's like but not to be in it.

I'm a staff officer, the kind that sits in front of maps and behind computers all day long, and all night long, supporting the guy I used to be, the guy out in the field. It requires another kind of patience altogether to be a weenie, a puke, a pogue, or any of the other names given to staff officers. The guys who are out patrolling every day look at me as if I'm not a real soldier or something.

I get strange and disdainful looks from officers I don't know when they see my left shoulder without a Ranger tab. Of *course* I have a Ranger tab. I just don't wear it. I wear the minimum here. In fact, I *want* these guys to underestimate me. I want them to turn up their noses, to think they're better. I have nothing to prove. Not to them.

Last time I deployed, we didn't need markings or even name-tags. We were such a tight team. Cloth didn't prove anything. Action proved. Creeds proved. Blood proved.

I've seen their looks here. *Oh, you're a staff weenie, an Infantry officer without a tab. You're a pogue. No wonder you're here at headquarters and not leading troops.*

Same thing with the haircut. I let my hair grow longer, so I'm a bad officer. With sideburns and no tab, I'm a slug. Last time I was at war, the men without uniforms and the ones with the longest hair were the best warriors on the planet. Here, I'm a dirtbag. They don't know me. The guys in Savannah know me. DePouli and Canon know me. Crose and Anderson and Commons knew me too. They liked my sideburns.

I'm here in Mosul, in Nineveh, obeying my orders, but I feel as if I'm running away. From what and to where . . . I don't know. Maybe it's the dreaming about combat, which is an eyes-closed version of what I do every day. Maybe it's the jarring wake-up calls, the massive explosions, the rolling over on my cot, trying to go back to sleep—ignoring what I know will be at least one soldier killed or maimed by a roadside bomb—but only because it's not my shift and I know I'll need to be fresh tonight to handle my own crises.

I'm not afraid to face it. I'm just afraid of what might happen to my family back home. I read somewhere that the opposite of fear is love. I think I read that in *Gates of Fire*, the book that Colonel Tony Thomas told me to read when I first got to the Rangers. I remember it was a riddle, to determine the opposite of fear. The book says that love is the opposite of fear . . . but that's not true. It can't be. So many people are petrified of finding love, of losing love; so how could fear and love be opposites? They coexist and cocreate. I've found the answer to the riddle here in Nineveh. The opposite of fear, I've found, for me . . . is faith.

I didn't read that in a book. Sure didn't read it in my Bible; that book went into the duffel bag weeks ago. This lesson didn't even come from using faith as my starting point, as if my strong faith somehow protected me from fear. Maybe at some other time in life that was true. But not here. Here, by starting with fear, by watching my fear destroy my faith, I've learned that fear and faith are opposites. Intense and palpable fear burns my faith, consuming it.

I found the answer inside myself, in that place where I dread the future. *I need more than God for this.*

What do I fear? Not my own death, or the pain of it. Not facing the enemy on the battlefield. I'm not afraid for myself; I'm afraid for Julie and Caleb and what their lives will be like if I'm gone. Am I being selfish? Shouldn't I think of them—of the ones who are left behind when men like me decide to pursue what for them is the most fulfilling job they could have? My family deserves better than this.

It's not my heart that's the problem; it's my mind. My mind tells me that it's just a matter of probability. I fear the random number. I fear the percentages. I fear the dice inside the tumbler. Simple, hard numbers and statistics. That's it. The more I deploy to combat, the more likely it is I'll get killed. The more likely it is that Julie and Caleb will see my temporary absence become a permanent reality. The fear of that—of gambling with the future—has burned my faith beyond recognition. It's charred to a crisp, like some of the eighteen brave men on those Blackhawks.

I didn't see them with my own eyes. I didn't see the sergeant major when he was run off the road, yanked from his Nissan Patrol, and shot to death. I wasn't there. But I was.

72

I think I remember it as an afternoon. Or maybe it was a morning. The sun was low. A cool autumn day, impossible to sweat. *I don't know how we got here, but here we are.* Julie and I were walking down the street in a low-density urban area, a lull somewhere between the factories and the strip malls and the nicer parts of town, with chain-link fences guarding empty lots. A wide street, but quiet. Perhaps it was meant to be busy, or it was busy at some time other than this. Julie pushed the stroller with Caleb resting inside. We talked about nothing in particular. Just where we would go from here. Not here on this street, but from *here*, our current situation. *Where will we go from here?*

I saw two men on the other side of the street. One leaned on a low retaining wall, against the chain-link fence anchored there. He reminded me of an Egyptian major I'd known at Fort Benning, an exchange officer who never did his homework. The other man stood with his back to us. All I could see of him was an untucked plaid shirt. Maybe it was flannel. I tried not to look again. The seated man glanced at us. The street was empty except for us and them.

I wanted to speed our pace and slow my mind. Julie and I walked on across some railroad tracks set into the asphalt. Where those tracks led, I could never guess. From one empty, fenced lot across the street to another. A few lots had buildings inside, warehouses maybe. But they, too, were empty.

I heard a vehicle approaching from our rear. Lately I'd been a little edgy, but I'd been trying to relax. I wouldn't look to see who it was. I wouldn't check to see whether they'd noticed us walking along the sidewalk or whether they were looking at my wife.

My old '65 Chevy truck coasted alongside us, the baby blue one. My dad was driving. I had no idea how he'd found us. The dents and ripples on the truck's hood and roof were gone. It looked like my dad had been working to restore the truck. I had rolled it on a gravel road the day before Julie and I got married. Just trying to show off to a friend, sliding around the curves of a crushed-limestone country road. I lost control and ran it into a ditch. We rolled over and back onto the wheels. That was five years ago. Daddy knew how much fun that old blue Chevy was for me.

"Hey, do I know you people?" he said. The husky engine rumbled clean and tight under the hood.

"Nice ride, Daddy. I had a feeling you were gonna fix 'er up again one of these days."

"Just a little project, that's all."

He shadowed us for another minute and then said, "Wanna ride?"

"We don't have a car seat for Caleb."

"Nathan, this truck doesn't even have seat belts. You'll be fine without a car seat. Come on, let's go."

"Ah, maybe we'll walk."

Through the cab of the truck—past my dad—I saw the two men again from a couple of blocks ago. They were farther back and across the next lot. They had paralleled our progress along the sidewalk, and now they were looking at me through the chain-link fence.

"You know what? I think I will ride with you," I said. "Julie, Sweetie, just keep walking." I stared hard at her. I needed for her to leave. "Please. I love you."

"What? I'll go with you."

"No. Keep walking. Walk away from here."

She saw how serious I was. "Okay. But where?"

"Away from me."

I slid into the truck, onto the same blue vinyl seat I had polished for an hour before prom, when Julie and I were sixteen and seventeen. I'd washed and waxed and buffed and polished that truck all morning. Julie had slipped off the seat three times on the drive to the dance. She was beautiful that night. She was beautiful every second of her life.

"Daddy, drive."

The two men started walking in our direction.

These men know who I am. They know I've killed some of them. They're after me. I have to lead them away from my family.

"Daddy, drive."

"What?"

"Them."

"Do you know those men?"

"No, but we need to get away from here."

He eased away down the empty street. I had no idea where we were.

"Don't drive too fast. Just drive fast enough where they can't reach us on foot. Just take it easy."

"Nathan, what's going on here?"

"Just keep some distance from them."

I adjusted the side mirror to see them crossing the street after us. Julie and Caleb had turned at the next intersection and were headed to safety. The men started to jog after us.

"Daddy, they're jogging."

"Okay. Here's a T-intersection up here. You want me to just run off and leave them?"

"No, I don't want to let them know that I know."

He didn't stop at the intersection; instead, he took a rolling right turn at a large, gray, rusted warehouse, guarded by a taller chain-link fence.

Why did we even come here? They can follow me out of here, but I don't want them to catch me. Everything has followed me home.

After we made the turn, I couldn't see the men in the mirror. I glanced over my shoulder to check their position. Nothing.

Where did they go? Why aren't they there? Oh, no—Julie and Caleb.

"Daddy, stop. They're not behind us anymore."

"Good."

"No. Julie and Caleb."

"We'll go back."

"No, I have to go."

I threw open the truck door and stumbled over the curb. I jogged back to the T-intersection.

All these fences. I can't get there. Why didn't I keep them with me?

I ran back to where Daddy had first pulled up. There was no one. A couple of cars on the street now. *I have to find where Julie turned.*

I sprinted to another intersection and turned down a new street. My stomach was burning. *This has to be it.*

I ran to the end of the street, where the pavement abruptly stopped at the curb. It was a dead end, nearly a complete change of scenery, like I had stepped into another dimension. A wide, open field. A small pond was there. The pond was a perfect square with tall, wispy grass flowing along the water's edge. There was a crowd gathered there, near the pond. They were anxious and concerned.

Why are they here?

I saw the back of Caleb's blond little head of hair amid the tall grass, down near the water.

He's alive. He's just sitting there alive.

I hurried to him.

"Caleb."

He looked over his shoulder at me. It was definitely him. He turned his head back to the pond. I knelt beside him. He was holding in his lap a huge knife, a serrated, survival-type, Rambo knife.

How dangerous. He doesn't need a knife.

"Caleb, hand Daddy the knife."

He didn't say anything. He acted like I wasn't even there. I eased the knife from his little square hands, from his little square fingers. I held the blade up to my eyes. It was beautiful, etched with circles and designs, like a tattoo. I looked up and down the blade. The etchings seemed to be swirling in front of me, dissolving or redrawing themselves. The blade was melting away. The etchings flowed together like seaweed. Just above the hilt of the knife, the etchings swayed and converged into the most beautiful image I'd ever seen, yet familiar. It looked like a pair of eyes. The eyes were Julie's.

The current of the blade pooled and drifted like a mirage, surging to form shapes I knew. The blade looked like water. I saw Julie's gray blue eyes in the blade, her whole face rippling just under the surface of the metallic water. A cloudy puff of crimson swirled and crept up in front of her face and floated just across her sad, silent eyes.

I heard a stranger's voice, from the crowd.

"She's here! She's in the lake."

The crowd of people surged to the edge of the water. A balding man stepped into the water. He had his clothes on.

That seems all wrong.

"She's here. I've found her."

No. Oh, God, no.

I awoke with a start and rolled over to look at the clock, to get my bearings.

Three o'clock in the morning. Two hours before I go on-shift.

Maybe I should just get up now.

73

Fewer than sixty days after our return from Iraq, my unit was deployed again. This time, instead of being sent into combat, we were assigned to West Point for the summer to train cadets in infantry tactics and live-fire exercises. Now a captain and an infantry company commander, I was returning to the birthplace of my military career. But it seemed as if the granite highlands and massive buildings had lost their mystique. On this side of war, West Point seemed more like a vacation spot than a training ground.

I pushed the screen door open and stepped into the heavy morning air. I had slept late this morning in my secluded, screened-in jungle hut, but I still planned to get in a good run. The mosquitoes were waiting for me as the door banged shut behind me. I sat down on the molded wooden deck and reached for my toes, the dew on the deck soaking my legs and running shorts. I was sore from sprints the day before. With a longer run ahead of me today, I needed to stretch properly.

Should I try Bull Hill again?

No, not today.

Bull Hill was steeper than I remembered. The last one hundred meters in particular seemed to shoot almost straight up. I had tried many times in the past couple of months to run from my hut to the top of Bull Hill without stopping. That route was about three and a half miles. Those last one hundred meters were nearly impossible to run, but I hadn't given up trying. I'd save Bull Hill for another day.

It had been six years since Beast Barracks; six years since I'd first passed through on this trail en route to Bull Hill.

I needed a longer run today to sort out my thoughts. I needed to think about what I was going to tell my boss later today. I had finally decided to leave the Army. This was my fourth time to make that decision. This time, though, I was sure of it. I hadn't told my boss yet, but I'd do that sometime today—or tomorrow.

My boss would be surprised, as most people who knew me would be, but he wouldn't need to argue. I was done. Things were only getting more complicated. I knew that if I stayed in this job, I'd be shipping out again for another year, leaving Julie at home with a three-year-old and a baby due in a few months. And it would be my fourth overseas deployment—totaling more than three years—in only six years of marriage. Who was going to be a husband and father in my place? America may have trained me to lead its sons and daughters, but who would lead mine?

I couldn't leave Julie alone again. The circumstances of war and life had sealed my decision. She had always been very supportive of my service in the Army. She didn't want to sway my career choices. But I knew it was time to protect my family. I had made this decision in Iraq several months before; now it was time to act.

I stood and straightened my reflective belt and started off on the trail. I planned to run for maybe ten or twelve miles. I needed time to think. I set out at a lazy pace, trotting through Camp Buckner, past the yearlings on the beach. I reentered the woods on the far side of Buckner and started a long loop around the glassy, elliptical lake, weaving along the crushed-granite gravel roads, bumping up and down the mountains like I was riding waves.

I knew I would need to tell my lieutenants of my decision. And my first sergeant. How would they take the news of their company commander leaving the Army? What would the Rangers think? Hopefully, they wouldn't even know. I could just slip out of the Army and figure out life on the far side. I could just leave all of this behind.

The stone underfoot made a comforting crunching sound with every stride. Going up the hills, I could feel the balls of my feet flicking rocks rearward in my wake. Coming down the hills, my feet slid a little bit with each heel strike. I normally didn't like running much, but today it felt good.

Normally in tough situations like this one, I'd talk to a few Christian friends, read a little in my Bible, maybe see the chaplain, and pray some. But now I thought I couldn't afford that. I was afraid they'd tell me I was making a mistake. How would I know that they'd give me good advice? *Of course they'll tell me to stay in the Army; that's what they all say. That's what I tell soldiers wanting to leave—that we need them.* And it was true. The Army does need them. But maybe somebody else needs them more. I didn't want to touch my Bible or pray—and hadn't since Nineveh. *I'll think about all that later.*

I powered up a series of small hills, back to back to back. I felt strong. I could gauge by the position of the sun and the shimmers of the lake below on my flank that I had nearly completed the loop. Just about three miles to go. I veered past the turnoff to the last leg of the Bull Hill climb, the steepest part, the last hundred meters. I ignored it. The rest was all downhill, down the front slope of Bull Hill.

I lengthened my stride down the gravel road, my breathing totally under control. The wind in my ears grew louder. If I tripped now, I'd hurt myself. *Pick up your legs.*

A group of three runners appeared at the bend in front of me. They were running uphill. I was looking good. I was going to nod at them or say, "What's up?" or something as we met on the trail.

Before I reached them or they could reach me, they darted off the gravel road into the woods. *That's odd.* They cut across my path fifty meters ahead and took off up through the woods, up Bull Hill. I slowed my pace and then walked down to their departure point to see why they had left the road. I stopped and put my hands on my hips, my breathing pace increasing as I stood there. I looked up at the trio running strong up a faintly defined trail, switching back and forth up the side of Bull Hill.

Then I saw it. Something that looked familiar to me. The boulder.

I remembered our march during Beast, when that old chaplain with the bad singing voice had stood there reciting an old psalm and grating on my nerves. I know I was there, but it seemed like only a dream. Just a dream. Dreams didn't matter anymore.

I turned away and started to jog again, downhill. I needed to finish this run and discover the rest of life. The run had given me just what I needed: enough resolve and clarity to know what to say to my boss, to stand my ground, and to finally go through with leaving the Army.

I sped down the hill as fast as I could. My feet were kicking my rear end behind me as they cycled back into rhythm on the last half mile. I was running. Today it felt good to run. To run to something and somewhere other than this.

74

My last day in the Army was uneventful. There was no ceremony, no soldiers anywhere. I was about a thousand miles away from the company I had commanded just days before, at home in China Spring at my in-laws' house. There was no pronounced or formal end to my service. It seemed like the end of a roll of tape or the last grain of sand in an hourglass. I had come home from war, taken control of my future, and steered into nothing. At least I had my family with me.

My grandfather, the soldier, retreated after his war. He ran away. He beat on my uncle, my aunt, and my grandmother. I love that woman. But he dared not touch my mom, the baby. He was too decent for that, I suppose.

When my uncle Larry came of age, he ran away and joined the Marines and went to 'Nam and became an alcoholic just like his dad. And then my Uncle Larry died when he was forty-five because of his own alcoholism.

The first time I saw my grandfather, he was already gone. He looked nice enough in the casket, but it didn't matter. It was too late.

God gave me a replacement grandfather, a step-grandpa, who was much better than the original, the man I never knew, the man who had fought at Normandy. I'm not sure which man is my real grandfather, or even how to define that.

A poster of my biological grandfather's European campaign hangs on Caleb's wall. For what reason, I don't really know. It's just a war story I've read about. It means nothing to me because I never knew the man who fought for his country. Many times, I've seen him as a coward; yet his blood's in my veins—maybe.

My father's blood is there for sure. Now there's a hero. Calmest, most decent man I know. Daddy wasn't much for advice; he just expected me to follow his example. If I had any questions, all I needed to do was watch him a little more closely. He never had to fight in a place like I did, but he fought through me.

I should take down that poster of my grandfather's that hangs in Caleb's room. I don't want him to get any ideas about joining the military. I got away from the Army early enough that Caleb won't remember it. I don't want him to know anything about my service, about West Point, about war. There are plenty of other things he could do with his life. I just want to be a normal father; a father who protects his family from the world and—hopefully—from himself.

75

I'm picking glass out of the sink. Little triangles and pebbles of glass. I can't see the pebbles very well; the tears fill my eyes from the bottom lid up. I sound like I'm choking on a chunk of meat, but it's just pain. I hate myself.

I haven't shaved in at least a week. I don't know when I'll feel like eating again.

The bathroom door has a small hole in it where the corner of a picture frame hit and punched through the wood like an arrowhead. I won't be able to cover that up when we move out.

I'll be surprised if Julie's still here when I come out. If only I were different. If only I were still the man she married. If she hates me, I don't blame her.

There it is, crumpled and torn, the song from our wedding, the sheet music from the piano. The frame is in three pieces, broken at the joints, where it had probably only been glued. Just one joint held together.

My cousins had said that they didn't want to play and sing in our wedding because every time they did that the couple got divorced. My cousins did the song well, and we framed the sheet music as a reminder of our wedding. It has always hung on our wall. "Jesus in Your Eyes." What a joke. I don't even know who I am anymore.

I'm cleaning up the mess. It'll take a while, and I'm sure to miss some pieces. Maybe it'll only be *my* feet that'll get cut. Might be only *my* bathroom from now on. I can't clean up the mess I've made on the other side of the door.

The song's ruined. It now reads "–sus in Your Eyes." It's torn, punched through by the broken glass and creased beyond repair.

I wonder how long Julie will put up with this.

It might be too late to speculate.

76

I drove along the stately entrance to the VA hospital in Waco. Twenty or more American flags lined the median to the main hospital building, but that's not where I was headed. I curved around the lane past the softball fields.

The field closest to the lane was the same one I remembered as a kid. My daddy played church-league softball there. He would bring me to the games and leave me in the stands by myself. I was maybe five or seven years old, but old enough to handle it. The crazies from the mental ward there in Waco would roll over in their wheelchairs, limp over on crutches, and invade the bleachers around me to watch the games. Mostly, they wandered around the campus and sat on the park benches looking angry. One of them tried to talk to me once and told me he had a pair of shoes to give me. He returned thirty minutes later with an old, worn-out pair of men's waffle soles. Daddy told him to keep his shoes, but he was polite about it. Daddy was always polite.

When Daddy saw that I needed help, he called a friend of the family named Jim, a 'Nam vet who worked for the VA in some capacity. Jim got me in to see the doc, and on the day of my appointment, he waited with me outside the office. While I was waiting, I remembered that my step-grandfather—who was really more of a grandfather to me than my real grandpa—used to bring me there on Sunday mornings before church when I was a kid. We'd stop off at Jack 'N' Jill Donuts and bring in a couple dozen for the guys at the VA, and then we'd take a couple dozen more for PaPa's Sunday school class later. I remember those were early mornings, and boring for me. That hospital in Waco kind of scared me.

I first went to the VA in Waco six months ago.

These days I'm at a different hospital—the VA in Temple, just two miles from my house. The same hospital where my uncle Larry died, an alcoholic like my real grandfather—the grandpa I never met.

I'm in my group session. Only vets from Iraq and Afghanistan. This session is dragging on too long. I stare at the paper in front of me. All I can think about is C-4 explosives. *Heat plus pressure renders an explosion.*

I want to punch the guy next to me. Sure, he's got his own problems. Whining about how hard he had it over there.

"That's right, man, they don't care about you."

"I never met a single officer that cared about anybody but hisself."

"Roger, man. Roger."

Some support group this is. I can't tell if these guys know I was an officer, or just don't care, or if they're just trying to get me going.

I generally enjoy the literature, and maybe the videos sometimes. But listening to deadbeats like me talk about no sleep and no jobs and no future—all it does is make me realize I'm not alone. And then it makes me raging mad. Maybe there's some value in one of those conditions.

I like the doc. I like him better one-on-one, though. Maybe I'm angrier than the others because I refuse to take the pills. Yeah, I'll admit I have a problem, but I ain't taking any pills.

I've never understood why they keep us separated from the 'Nam vets. Maybe the guys from 'Nam have it figured out, and the docs are afraid we'll figure it out too. Maybe the 'Nam vets are too far gone, and the docs are still trying to save us. We're not them—yet. Most of us still have short hair and drive family cars. But our eyes are the same: that combination of fatigue, anger, and disdain.

I take notes on the literature. One session we'll talk about anger management. The next session we'll talk about communication with our spouses. Then we'll talk about how to hold down a job. Seems it's all about anger, though. For me, at least. That and being depressed. And alone. Mostly anger, though.

Every so often, I'll have a contradictory revelation about the literature, which gives me further reason to believe that no one understands me. And then I think about all the military books I've read and the points those great authors made that struck me as profound when I was a soldier but now make no sense on this side of war.

I remember this beautiful existential metaphor in *Gates of Fire*. When the Spartans would prepare for battle, they'd wrap a twig around their wrists, break off the end of the twig, and drop it in a basket. After the battle, they would file past the basket, and each warrior would reclaim his jagged twig and fit it together with its mate on his wrist. Those twigs still remaining in the basket were the "dog tags" of those warriors who did not return from battle—those killed in action. I read about this idea when I got to the Rangers, when I read the books I was assigned. I expected this example from the Spartans to be real and practical for me.

Of course, I didn't have an actual twig. But whatever part of me had been my "twig," it just didn't work for me. When I returned home to reclaim the other half of my twig, the one on my wrist had been mangled by war. It just didn't fit. Nothing seems to fit.

My problem with the VA is simple. Completely removed from and independent of the process, the treatment, and the doctors, here's my dilemma: The same guys in my group session that I want to take outside and beat to a pulp are the same guys I love with all my heart. And I can't express either emotion to them. Every session, I just show up, listen, and walk out quietly. And then I dread going back. I dread going back home, and I dread going back to the VA for my next session. I love and hate those guys all at the same time. Just like I love and hate my sergeant major who got himself killed, and how I love and hate everything in my life. Especially myself.

77

I quit. I quit the Army.

Irony used to be funny to me, but now I see how cruel it can be. I left the Army to better care for my family, and now I'm losing my family in the process.

The rifle company I commanded will deploy again to Iraq in a few months—without me. And I'll be here at home in Texas, toting a sales bag on my shoulder in search of commissions. No more rifle, no more uniforms, no more soldiers. Just a closet full of business suits, an expense account, and a total lack of purpose. I can't live like this any longer.

The person I used to be in the Army no longer exists. He's gone. He's dead.

He was once a father, and a husband. Sitting alone in this filth, staring at his Colt .45 ACP commemorative World War II edition, parkerized, with plastic grips, I think of him. He was many things to many people. A coward, though, he was not. The .45 is proof of it. "Leaders like you come along once in a lifetime," they said when they gave it to him. That was three years ago, when he was still a young man. He died young, along with many others.

Maybe I should follow him now.

78

I want to die. I want to kill the man who has taken my place. But no one will let me. My family sees the brokenness and they've closed in around me, forming a tight perimeter. No one is going to get in.

Or out.

Julie won't leave me. My parents won't abandon me. Still, I'm not sure if God is even here anymore. I've rejected him, walked away, too many times. He has every right to let me burn.

I can't function. My whole family is paralyzed by it. No one sleeps—and on top of that, Noah's still a baby, which makes it harder on Julie.

She knows we need to find help, but she doesn't know who to call. She called Randy Kirby, my Army chaplain friend. He was one of the first friendly faces I saw when I joined the Rangers. He was in Afghanistan. He performed last rites on Matt and Brad and Marc. He told me to get my bloody pants off my cot and wash them the day after the battle. He *knows* me. He's been there with me. He'll be with me this time, too.

But even with Randy's help, I can't go to work. Every second is an uncertainty. I've been away from my job for too long. I have to make a decision. The company wants us to move to Kansas City. I can't think past the next hour, much less take a new position. There's no way I can imagine leaving my family behind to start a new job in Kansas City. Not like this. We'd never survive.

It's time to quit.

With this decision, I was about to enter the ranks of unemployed veterans. I had no choice. I'd have to find something local. It was an easy decision, but one I didn't want to make on my own. I had already been down that road. I knew I needed help.

Julie and I got on our knees. We prayed. For the first time in almost a year, I cracked open the cover of my Bible. Even if God had abandoned me, I would cry out to him. I was broken.

I searched for answers. I retraced my path over the past year, over my time in Iraq. *What had gone wrong?* I had been in Mosul, in Nineveh. It was bad for me there. That's where I got scared. After all I'd been through in Kosovo and Afghanistan, I got scared in Nineveh. I started running away from God in Nineveh.

Just like Jonah.

I opened my Bible to the book of Jonah. I read the story. Jonah had been called to Nineveh, but he'd run the opposite direction, away from God's calling. He was near death, in the depths of the ocean, when he cried out to God.

It was in Nineveh that I had run away from God and his sovereignty, away from future deployments, away from my fear. I had run away from God, and out of the Army. I needed to quit this job. But that would be running away again.

I have to stop running.

I looked at Julie.

"We have to go to Kansas City," I said.

"What? You said we *couldn't* go. How are you going to make it?"

I looked at her tired eyes. I reached for her hands. I held them tight.

"I don't know, Julie," I said. "But I've got to stop running from God. If he's called me there, then I have to go. I'm not running anymore."

I called my boss and told him that we would take the job in Kansas City, but I wasn't sure when we'd be ready to leave. I was making a stand, no matter how feeble.

For the next few days, Julie and I spent hours working through things, praying, and loving each other. She could have left me alone, but she stayed.

We were barely hanging on. But we did, by God's grace. We looked to him in prayer and in the Bible—daily. One night, I came upon a special story in Genesis—the story of a father and son. The father was Abraham and the son was Isaac. God had told Abraham to sacrifice Isaac on a mountaintop altar. This command pierced Abraham to the very core as a father, but he prepared to obey. Abraham could have refused to obey; he could have tried to protect his son from the command.

When I read that story, I realized that, in leaving the Army, I had tried to take control of my own circumstances. I had tried to possess and protect everything I had: my life, my family, my future. I had ignored the very God who had delivered me on that snowy mountain in Afghanistan. I acted in fear rather than in faith. I should have followed Abraham's example and been willing to offer up myself, my future, even my family, if that was where God was leading. When I was struggling the most, the answers to my fears were right there in front of me, in the Bible. The answers had always been there.

I read on. I saw that just when Abraham was raising the knife to kill Isaac—to sacrifice his son in obedience to God's command—God halted the act. God stopped Abraham just in time and showed him a ram stuck in a nearby thicket, a perfect substitute sacrifice for Isaac. God saw Abraham's obedience and honored it. God had never intended for Abraham to kill Isaac. The sacrifice was not part of God's plan because God had something better waiting for Abraham.

I was broken with humility by the possibility that this Bible story applied to us, that God might have something better.

Surely, God, I don't deserve this. Do you have a ram for us?

"Julie, I'm reading this story about Abraham, and I don't know what's going on with this, but I have a strong feeling we're not moving to Kansas City."

"What? I thought you said you were sure?"

"I know what I said . . . and I still think that Kansas City is just like Nineveh, that we need to be ready to go there, but I'm thinking that God is just testing our willingness to go. I really believe that God has something better. He has a ram waiting in the thicket. I'm still willing to go to Kansas City, and I'm gonna prepare to go, but that might not be God's plan."

Three days later, I received a phone call offering me an opportunity to work for the Army as a contractor in a civilian capacity. I could leverage my passion for soldiers and share my extensive experiences in a meaningful way. When they made the offer, they said I could live anywhere I wanted to live and that I could work from home—which was exactly what I needed. The man who called, a former Army acquaintance, had tried to offer me the job six months earlier, but I had never returned his messages.

God provided. I deserved to die. I had wanted to die. But God instead gave me an indication that he wasn't through with me yet—and he waited until my heart was ready. This time, I wasn't about to argue.

79

I told myself I wasn't going to visit Hunter Army Airfield. I was in town to visit Fort Stewart as part of my job, having arrived at the airport at 10:30 p.m., and I had to be at work early the next morning. I wasn't going to visit Hunter. But I felt drawn to it. I went anyway.

I drove onto the base around midnight, passing through the same gate I had passed through when I'd heard about the 9/11 attacks on the radio. I could make it from that gate to my parking spot at the company area with my eyes closed. On this night, I drove straight to our company's barracks and parked in my old spot. I got out of my car and walked to the barracks. When I reached the barracks area, something seemed wrong. I looked around to locate the tall pine tree that had once held a climbing rope just in front of where we held our formations.

There's the tree. The barracks should be here.

I was shocked and confused when I found that the barracks had been replaced with . . . nothing. The building was gone. Torn down. Nothing but a field.

The barracks are gone. I wonder what else has changed.

I drove to the battalion headquarters, where I had last seen Miceli's shot-up SAW and Walker's shot-up helmet in a display case. I parked outside the spooky, fenced-in compound. It was still there. I walked to the high gate, where a surveillance camera was aimed at my face. I pushed the intercom buzzer. A Ranger inside the headquarters called over the intercom.

"Yep."

"Can I come in?" I said.

"Come on."

I tried to pull on the gate. Nothing. *Unlock it, man. It won't open.*

"*Push* it open."

I was a fat civilian trying to visit the Ranger battalion's head-quarters after midnight and looking stupid trying to open the gate. *This is going to be a waste of time.*

I pushed the gate open and went inside the headquarters building, where a young Ranger and a Ranger sergeant sat at the reception desk watching TV.

"Can I help you?"

"Yeah, ah, I just wanted to look around inside here some. . . ."

"No, sir, I'm afraid you can't do that."

"Well, I really need to. I came a long way."

"Sir, this place is off-limits to—"

"Okay." I took a deep breath. "Okay, Sergeant. Please just let me start over. I used to be stationed here. I was in this battalion. I was a platoon leader in Alpha Company—"

"I'm sorry, sir, but we just can't—"

"Where's Miceli's SAW?"

"Who?"

"Miceli. His SAW was in here. And Walker's helmet. They were here. Where are the trophy cases?"

"Sir, I'm not sure what you're after. We're moving out of this building soon. Whatever you're looking for, if it was in here, it's probably packed up in storage now."

"Okay. Let me try one more time. I went to Afghanistan with this battalion right after 9/11. I lost three guys in my platoon over there."

"Wait a minute," the Ranger sergeant said. "You mean Crose?"

"Yes. Brad Crose. He was one of my guys. He *is* one of my guys. I was his platoon leader."

"No s—," he said. "I know Sergeant Crose. I had just come to the battalion when he was killed. I remember going to his funeral in Florida. I remember him. You were his platoon leader?"

"Yes."

I went to the water fountain adjacent to the desk, where I remembered the photos of Ranger ten-miler teams used to be. Randy Kirby used to be in those photos. I walked back to the Ranger sergeant. On the wall, I saw a painting of my downed helicopter, Razor 01, and a depiction of our fighting on Takur Ghar. I moved to the artist's print.

"*There*, Sergeant. That's me. Second from the right. That was the day. That was the day Brad died. There's Brad right there."

My finger tapped over the tan figure that was supposed to be Brad. I slid my finger to where Matt Commons should've been, but he hadn't been painted there. And Marc would've been inside the helicopter, and thus unseen from the artist's vantage point. I hadn't seen him inside the helicopter, either. At least not dead.

"I'm sorry, sir. What can I help you find? Maybe there are other things here."

"No, I don't think there's anything left here."

"I apologize, sir. I didn't know who you were."

"That's fine, Sergeant. Sometimes I don't know who I am either."

He laughed. He didn't realize how truthful I was being.

"Well, like I said, sir, everything's in storage until we get the new headquarters building. You're free to look around here, though."

"No, man, that's okay. It's getting late. I've got an early morning ahead of me."

I walked back to my rental car feeling betrayed. I'd been betrayed by this place. Everyone I knew was gone. Even the buildings had gone away. It wasn't the same place. I shouldn't have come here.

I pulled away in my rental car, a compact, and coasted off the base, careful not to speed. The way I remembered it, the MPs on Hunter were prone to write traffic tickets. Then again, nothing was the way I remembered it.

80

Sometimes when I open this closet to grab a belt or a shirt, I glance at those uniforms and wonder if they mean anything at all. The heavy, long, gray wool overcoat, complete with its huge cape, that I wore home as a plebe on Christmas break. The dress gray jacket, with its rows of knobby brass buttons and huge golden chevrons and split tail. I wore that on graduation day. The Army dress green jacket with a black and red 1st Ranger Battalion scroll on the right sleeve, the 101st Airborne Division "Screaming Eagle" patch on the left sleeve, and nothing else. I like that coat to face to the right so the Ranger scroll faces out. I don't remember when I last wore that one. And the dress blue jacket, with its powder-blue Infantry shoulder boards. That jacket still holds all my awards and decorations. Each forty-five-cent ribbon represents a significant sacrifice in my life. For what, I'm not sure anymore.

That ribbon there was for seven months away from Julie. That one, too. Actually, all three of those are for the same seven months. That one there is for being a captain in Iraq. That's it. Just for being a captain and being there. If I had been a sergeant, I would have gotten a lesser award.

That one is for shooting a perfect score at a gunnery exercise. Truth is, my gunner shot ten of the engagements, and I only shot two, but at least I shot my two.

That one is for giving away a chunk of my right thigh and some blood on a mountain in Afghanistan.

That one is for valor—at least that's what it says on the back.

Not a lot of money in the uniform, but it's all supposed to mean something. To me, it seems like a waste. Here I am—I can't fit into any of these uniforms anymore. Seems appropriate.

I was looking for a belt, I think.

81

I've never met this man before, yet I feel as if I know him. His accent is familiar; I have many friends from the Boston area. But it's more than his dialect—much more. I have a connection with him.

Perhaps it's the worn jungle boots on his feet, the same green canvas, Vietnam-era style boots that are sitting in my closet somewhere. This man—his name is Gary—has tucked his black jeans into his jungle boots, the same way we all did with the legs of our camouflage trousers. Perhaps it's the 101st Airborne lapel pin affixed to Gary's gray fleece pullover—the same unit I served with in Iraq. Perhaps it's the way he wears his camouflage patrol cap, high on his head, parallel to the ground, and rolled around the crown, just like a real soldier would. He *is* a real soldier.

During the first few minutes of our meeting, Gary seemed to be sizing me up, just giving me another evaluation to see if I was worth his time. We sat across a coffee table from each other in the lobby of an upscale hotel a block off Times Square. I listened to him. He was angry. He was frustrated with people. With the people on the street. With the people he met. With the people who just didn't understand. I understood.

The reason I knew Gary, the reason he seemed familiar to me, the reason I had a connection with him, was that he was a soldier, through and through. Perhaps I saw myself in him. He and I had never met before, but that wasn't important. We had a shared bond—a bond of service, a bond from the 101st Airborne and Iraq, and a bond as veterans who were searching for answers. We needed each other. This time together was vital to both of us. With the tourists and the families and the normal folk milling around, Gary and I were locked in, tracking each other, completely in sync.

He and I never would have met if I hadn't come to New York to share my story. In a church. In Times Square.

I had no idea there was a church in Times Square. In the heart of Manhattan, in New York City, in the middle of the multistory TV screens and the pulsing Broadway marquees, there's a church known simply as Times Square Church.

I had been invited to talk about my struggles with war and how I was coping in the aftermath. I was invited there to help the people of the church better understand what veterans are experiencing. Gary had been there that day.

Guys like Gary and me needed each other. I had been afraid to share. I had been afraid to talk about my problems and admit weakness. I didn't want to revisit the pain of the last few years. But sitting with Gary in this hotel lobby made me glad that I'd come to New York. Even if it hurt.

The next morning, Julie and I left our hotel and walked across Times Square. It was the dead of winter. The sun was out overhead, but the city streets were dominated by shadows and a piercing wind. It was bitter cold.

We walked through the doors to Times Square Church and stopped to admire the renovated lobby, with its golden baroque arches and columns and scarlet carpet and draperies. The church had once been a Broadway theater. It was now a place of worship.

We moved through the old theater to the area backstage, where we had been invited to join the church staff for breakfast and greetings before the Sunday morning service.

Carter Conlon, the senior pastor, came by to greet Julie and me. He had been a police officer before becoming a pastor.

"Good morning, sir," I said.

"Good morning," Carter said. "I just want to thank you again for yesterday. That was very powerful. Very powerful."

"Thank you, sir."

I could see real compassion in his face, as if he somehow understood how I felt. I thought briefly about his closing comments from yesterday's session. He had explained how he'd never known why his father was so emotionally withdrawn at times, but after listening to us speak about war, he finally understood. Perhaps he saw the same look in my eyes, or in Gary's, that he'd seen in his father's.

"And you'll be attending the worship service now?" he asked.

"Right now? Oh, yes. We're gonna be here," I said.

"Okay. Good. I've got a word for you, but you'll really need to pay attention and stay with me until the end."

"Thank you, sir. I'll be listening."

What is it that he's going to say to me in the middle of his sermon?

Julie and I walked back into the theater and found our seats in the audience. I reflected on Carter's words, about how he'd never known the source of his father's despair. Now he knew. I remembered how the day before, when I was sharing some of my own struggles, I could see how deeply engaged Julie was in what I was saying. It occurred to me that it was the first time she'd heard me talk about some of these things. I was ashamed that she had to hear it along with an audience I'd never met.

Why is it so hard for me to share these deep struggles with those I love the most?

The music in the worship service stirred something in me. I felt a burning around my neck and head. Maybe it was the events of the weekend catching up with me. Maybe it was the rekindling of emotion in me. After an hour of worship, Carter Conlon took the pulpit.

He began to speak about the state of our world, preaching about how God uses different "pictures" to convey messages to us. At times, these pictures are meant to be warnings to us. *Final warnings come in pictures.*

He spoke of the pictures in the news. He spoke of the horrible pictures of 9/11—of the Pentagon, of Flight 93, of the World Trade Center. As New Yorkers, many people around me in the congregation had been deeply and directly affected by 9/11. Carter said those pictures were warnings to us. They were indications of worse things to come. Of war.

"I want you to know that I have a word for some of you this morning," he said. "Turn to Acts, chapter 27."

This is when he's going to talk to me. He has a word for me.

Carter began to tell the story of how the apostle Paul in the Bible was a prisoner on a ship at sea. The ship came under the peril of a storm, and things started to spiral out of control. The ship's crew began throwing some of the cargo overboard to keep the ship from sinking.

"Picture Paul for a moment," Carter said. "He's below the waterline, in the bowels of the ship; there's an incredible storm going on; people are no doubt violently ill; there's excrement and water sloshing about the bottom of the ship; it's literally falling apart. It's a place of despair; it's a place of hopelessness; it's a place where the enemy would want to take the mind of this man of God and literally shut him down. And that's where many of you are right now."

He was right. He had heard me speak the day before to veterans at the church. He had heard me share about the pain and loss I felt. He could hear me searching for answers.

The picture in Paul's story was not good. Everyone aboard the ship thought they were going to die. From below the waterline, Paul prayed, and God assured him that everyone would survive the storm. The ship would be lost, but everyone would live through it. Paul emerged from the bowels of the ship, from that dark room belowdecks, to tell the ship's crew the good news—that they would all live.

"The Lord is preparing you for a day," Carter continued. "If you are in a dungeon of darkness, in a place of despair, understand that a picture comes from a negative. There's a darkroom first. There's a negative that develops. From the negative comes a picture."

My chest got tight. He was speaking straight to me.

"You are going to come out of hiding. You are going to stand among your peers in your cities and towns. Some will be on stages; some will be on street corners. But God is going to set you as the final picture in this generation.

"You are the last picture. You can't live your whole life trying to escape your situation. You've got to find God in it now. It's for the good of everyone around you. It's for your sons and daughters. God, in his mercy, will always have a vessel in the bowels of that ship."

God, I want to be that vessel. But after all I've said and done, I can't be used now.

"You're going through dungeons and dark places of despair. Your battles are in your mind. You're asking God, 'What is wrong with me?' *Nothing* is wrong with you. You're in the *darkroom.* You're about to be made into a picture. Hallelujah."

The pastor paused for a breath. The congregation was moved to shouting and clapping.

"I want to encourage you with all my heart. Find the Word of God wherever you are, and stand on it."

I knew that I had been living in a darkroom, but I had only begun to see that God could use me as a picture to others. I walked out of that church with a broken heart and into the sea of people flooding Times Square, but believing what Carter Conlon had said.

82

I moved to the ottoman across the room so I could get a better view of Caleb's and Noah's faces. They were done opening their presents, and now they sat playing amid a mountain of wrapping paper, torn and wadded up and piled all around. They wore matching Christmas pajamas, their blond hair shooting in all directions. I adjusted the settings on the video camera so it would stay in focus, because the room was illuminated by a single lamp and the sparkling lights on the tree. It was at times like this that I stood amazed at the beauty of a child. Julie sat beyond the boys on the couch, her adoring eyes fixed on the backs of their heads. I watched her for a moment as I filmed the kids. Her eyes seemed meek, but resilient, and as tender as ever.

She saw me staring at her, reacting as if I were looking at something out of place.

"*What?*" she asked.

"Nothing," I said. "I'm just so thankful for you."

"Me too," she whispered.

We both returned our eyes to the boys, who were unaware of their parents' connection.

"Why don't you come over here?" Julie said. "I have something else for you."

I turned off the camera and laid it on the table, tiptoed over the boys and toys and wrapping paper strewn about, and eased onto the couch alongside my bride. She was as beautiful as I'd ever seen her, the model of love.

"What's this?" I asked as she handed me a flat, rectangular gift.

"Just something."

I tore off the golden paper, looking at Julie with expectant eyes.

I reached inside the plain cardboard box and slid out what I thought was a coffee-table book. Instead, I saw that it was the back of a picture frame. I looked at Julie and smiled as I turned it over.

It was the sheet music to "Jesus in Your Eyes," the song from our wedding.

My face curled and crumbled in a moment of sheer brokenness. I buried my face into Julie's hair, at the base of her neck, and wept silently. She gripped the back of my head and held me close. I could feel her cold wedding band on the back of my neck. She was my hero.

83

Mr. Anderson called again. I really needed to call him back. I used to call all the families every Christmas and every March 4, the day they'd lost their sons. After a couple of years of calling them, I messed that one up, and I'd been too embarrassed to start again—like it would be an acknowledgment that I hadn't been calling them. So I didn't call. I didn't call the guys from the platoon anymore, either. DePouli and Polson had left me messages. Canon left me a message. Escano left messages. Miceli, Gilliam—there were more.

Didn't matter. I was embarrassed to talk with them. I was sixty-two pounds heavier than I was when I first stepped into the platoon. I didn't want them to see me. They were doing great things in the Army. *They don't need me, anyway.*

I no longer knew where my medals were. Whenever someone wanted to interview me, they'd ask to see the medals. I'd say they were in a box somewhere, and they'd say they wanted to see the box, that they'd like to get it on film, as if the statement that I didn't know the location of my medals was a novel fabrication of my story. The truth is, I couldn't find them and didn't know where to look.

I'd kept the .45—we'd been through a lot together—but it was somewhere under the desk or a stack of papers in my home office. Didn't matter. I'd lost the key to the gun lock, anyway.

I needed to call Mr. Anderson back. He gave his son to my command, and his son was killed sitting next to me. I needed to call him back. Mr. Anderson had been a Ranger in Vietnam and an Airborne instructor. He lost another son, Steve, to cancer not long after Marc died in the Chinook. Nobody expected Marc to die before Steve. Now they were both gone.

"Dave? Hi, this is Nate . . . Self."

"Nate! Great to hear from you. How are you?"

"I'm fine. Just had a baby girl a couple of months ago. Our world is upside down right now with another kid, but it's neat to have another girl around the house."

"Yeah, a baby girl. That's great. That's just great. What's her name?"

"Her name is Elliot Joy. And the boys love her too. Caleb and Noah are good big brothers."

"That's great. Listen, Nate, I was calling to find out if you're coming to the Ranger Memorial dedication in Savannah."

"When's that? In October?"

"Yeah, it's October eighteenth, and the Ranger Ball is on the nineteenth."

I was scared to go back to Savannah. And Hunter. And all those people.

"Well, I haven't been invited."

"Yes, you have. *I'm* inviting you."

"Well, I've been traveling quite a bit. I'll need to check my calendar."

You jerk. This is Mr. Anderson.

"You know what?" I said. "No, I don't need to check anything. If it's at all possible, I'll be there."

"You will? That's so great. *He said he will, Judy!* Judy says that's great."

"Yeah, I really appreciate you asking me to go."

"Well, you need to be there."

"Thanks."

"And if you stay for the Ball, we'll play golf on Friday morning."

"That sounds like a plan."

Mr. Anderson and I had made it a habit to play golf whenever we were together. Last time we'd played was at Marc's memorial tournament at MacDill Air Force Base in Tampa.

"Nate, I don't know if you knew this or not, but we tried to get in touch with you over the summer."

"No, I don't remember that."

"Well, I called every number I had for you and left messages. We were in Dallas, and we wanted to come down and see you."

"No," I said. "Oh, no. You were in Dallas?"

"Yeah, I was coming to see you. Judy said you might be mad at me, and I told Judy I didn't care if you were mad at me or whatever, I was just gonna come knock on your door and make you see me."

"Of course I'm not mad at you," I said. "I'm so sorry you were here and I didn't respond."

"Oh, that's okay, Nate. We understand. You just had a baby, and you've got the three kids and all."

"I'm so sorry."

"It's okay. Don't worry about it."

"Well, we'll see each other in Savannah soon."

"Yeah, we'll do that," Mr. Anderson said.

"And I'll bring my clubs."

There was a pause of silence on the phone line.

"Nate," Mr. Anderson said, "I don't think you know how much you mean to me. You're one of the most important people in our lives."

"Thank you."

"You need to be there."

"I will."

I didn't even own a business suit that fit me for the Ranger Ball in Savannah. I was about forty pounds away from buttoning the pants on my suits, which hung somewhere in the hall closet with my old Army uniforms. Five years ago, I had decided to skip the Ranger Ball for the same reason: my Army dress blue uniform didn't fit very well. Julie had urged me to go then, and she was urging me to go now. I did have one suit big enough to wear, from the deceased father of a distant relative's husband, no less. It still needed some altering, because my arms were shorter than his.

I wanted to go to Savannah, and I didn't want to go. The last time I'd been in Savannah, I had told myself I'd never go back. But I couldn't say no to Mr. Anderson. I was going for him and Judy, for Matt's parents, and for Brad's parents. But I was afraid. After all the progress I'd made, I sure didn't need to go to Savannah and suffer a setback.

84

I had breakfast with the Andersons at the Golden Corral on Abercorn Street, just a few blocks from Hunter Army Airfield. We swapped stories about Marc and how he loved life and how he loved being a Ranger, just like his dad.

I thought about how tragic it was that Marc had wanted to be a soldier like his dad, how he had followed in his Ranger foot-steps and gotten himself killed doing it. I wasn't going to let that happen to my sons. That's why I hadn't brought Caleb along on this trip.

After the buffet meal, Mr. Anderson and I decided to visit the battalion area early, a couple of hours before the scheduled recep-tion. We drove to the new complex together, just looking to kill some time.

We parked and walked toward the massive redbrick buildings. The whole complex was brand new. The more compact-looking building with antennas on top was the new headquarters. I was anx-ious. More like afraid. I was afraid of how the day would go. I was afraid of what had happened the last time I visited Hunter, that everything had changed and I wouldn't see anyone I knew. At the same time, I think I was even more afraid that I *would* see the guys that I knew—and loved—or that they'd see me.

We checked in with the secretary to confirm our seating for the ceremony and the next night's Ranger Ball, and then we meandered through the hallways. I studied the paintings and photographs that hung on the walls. One painting was of MC-130s dropping airborne

Rangers over an airfield in Central America. Another painting showed a crashed Blackhawk in Somalia. I recognized a few of the artifacts from the old headquarters. Many of them were new, at least to me. Mr. Anderson and I followed the hallway back toward the entrance. It was time to go.

In the entryway, just before exiting the building, I saw it.

Miceli's SAW.

There it was, displayed in a huge trophy case at the entrance to battalion headquarters.

They haven't forgotten. They had put it away for nearly a year, but they'd remembered it. They could have left it in storage or in a trunk somewhere. No one would have known. But they remembered. There it was, with the bullet holes through it. *No one can kill Miceli but Miceli.* They remembered us.

Seeing Miceli's SAW revealed to me part of what I had feared in coming here: the simple possibility of being forgotten. I had feared that Miceli's SAW, along with all the rest of our equipment, our names, and our actions, would've been left in storage or thrown out to the garbage by new Rangers who just didn't know. But Miceli's SAW was there.

I felt a hand on my shoulder.

"Hey, sir."

It was one of my old Rangers.

"Sir, I can't believe you're here," he said. "I thought I saw you, and I was like, 'Is that who I think it is?' It's great to see you, sir."

He gave me a bear hug. I wanted to cry all over him.

"It's great to see you, too, man," I said. "Did you see this? Miceli's SAW?"

"Yep, that's it, sir."

"Where's Sergeant Walker's helmet?"

"Walker's helmet? Ah, I think I saw it at Regiment awhile

back. And DePouli's back plate. They've got that stuff up there at Regiment."

"I was afraid people around here forgot about it."

"No, sir. Nobody here will forget."

85

Mr. Anderson and I walked outside to the magnificent monuments in the courtyard, the memorial to those 1st Ranger Battalion heroes who had died in training and combat. Some of those heroes were men I'd led.

The memorial below was much grander than I could've imagined, filling the entire space in between the mirrored U-shape red-brick barracks, those barracks now known as Commons Hall and Anderson Hall. A massive block of stainless steel stood at the opening of the monument, with a six-foot dagger-shape hole cut through it. Mr. Anderson told me it was a five-ton chunk of steel.

We mingled for a while, found our seats, and awaited the ceremony. There must have been a few thousand people there. It was a hot day in mid-October, hot even for Savannah. The sky was cornflower blue and devoid of clouds. We sat in white folding chairs in front of the giant stainless-steel dagger, with the entire battalion standing around the memorial in formation in their tan berets. I'd last seen the whole battalion assembled four years ago in the Catholic cathedral. Here, I stared at the four Rangers composing the color guard in front of me. Two muscular Rangers held the battalion colors and the Stars and Stripes, flanked by two Rangers holding rifles. I didn't know these Rangers, but I knew that I loved them.

The speeches wore on, and the sun beat down on us. Ushers offered water and Gatorade. I finished my first bottle of Gatorade and opened another. I noticed one of the riflemen in the color guard looking faint. His body was swaying. He had a worried look on his face, as if he knew what was happening. It was hot. He must've locked his knees. Or perhaps he had worked out extra hard that morning. I worried for him. I didn't want to see him fall down or pass out in front of several thousand people. Not a Ranger. Not today.

From the ranks of the battalion, another strapping young Ranger marched out across the memorial grounds to the color guard. He stepped alongside his wavering comrade, gripped the rifle from his hands, and stepped in to assume his position on the flank of the flags. Two other Rangers jogged over and helped the weary Ranger off to the side. I had to look away and squint hard to hold back my tears.

The ceremony concluded. I walked through the memorial. Twenty-nine freshly planted palm trees towered over the grounds, one for each fallen Ranger from 1st Battalion. I strolled over the wide, interlocking circles of stone pavers underfoot. Many pavers had names engraved on them. I found my guys' names, all near each other. Their stones had stars on them, and with some excess paver sand settled inside, the stars looked like gold. The focal point of the memorial stood in the back, underneath three live oak trees: tall granite tablets bearing the names of the men who had died in 1st Ranger Battalion.

At the bottom of the tablets was a Bible verse I had come to hold dear: "Greater love hath no man than this, that a man lay down his life for his friends" (John 15:13, KJV).

I thought of the fallen Rangers and of the One who gave his life for them—and for me.

I walked through Commons Hall with Matt's parents. We were escorted by Drew Phillips, the Ranger whose broken hand in Afghanistan had promoted Matt Commons to the M203 grenade launcher two weeks before he was killed. Drew was now a squad leader. My mind was drawn to the irony; without Drew's freak accident, I could've been standing in Phillips—not Commons—Hall, with Drew's parents, being escorted by Matt Commons. Or I could've been dead too.

No. I dismissed the notion, the what-ifs, the chances. It wasn't a gamble. I had to trust God with it.

We returned to battalion headquarters for the reception. There was cake and punch. There was an ice sculpture. There were people there that I loved. Eric Stebner was there. Brad's mom was there. Some of my West Point classmates were there. Jason Rel was there. Matt Commons's parents were there. The Andersons were there.

Arin Canon was there. Randy Kirby was there.

I was there.

We laughed together. We ate together. We remembered. I could tell they loved me by the way they looked at me. I had never quite seen it before, but I knew it right away. It was an unconditional love. It was the same way that Julie looked at me. It was the way my kids looked at me. I felt a tug of assurance that it was the way God had always looked at me, even when I'd turned my back on him. I hoped at that moment that my daddy had always seen me looking at him in the same way.

Eric Stebner approached and introduced his fiancée. The older version of Eric Stebner standing in front of me was the same man I remembered—the brave team leader on Takur Ghar who had risked his life several times to drag our wounded to safety—only now he held more rank. He was now a platoon sergeant.

"Sir, would you do me a favor?"

"Sure, Sergeant Stebner. I'll do whatever you need me to."

"It's not a big deal. If you have time, and I know you're probably busy, I'd just like you to come meet my platoon leader."

"No doubt, man. I'd love to," I said. "Any particular reason?"

"No, sir," he said. "I just want him to meet you."

86

I arrived at the Ranger Ball in my borrowed dead man's suit. It didn't fit right, but it didn't matter. I had nothing to hide. After all I'd survived, any falsities I had were far removed. I had been stripped to the core.

The Ranger Ball functions as a formal banquet, a reunion, and an excuse to party, all in one. Since I'd left the battalion, they had moved the ball to the new convention center across the Savannah River, where the main ballroom looked over the water to River Street and up the river to the majestic Talmadge Memorial Bridge, which flaunted nighttime lights along its cabled arches.

I enjoyed the company of fellow Rangers and their families at dinner. There were Rangers in the room from World War II, from Vietnam, from Desert One, from Grenada, from Panama, from Somalia, from Takur Ghar, and from conflicts since. Most of the Rangers in uniform had been to Iraq and Afghanistan together, multiple times. I was seated in the midst of my brothers, my fathers, and my sons. My battalion. I felt like we were a family gathered around an intimate dinner table, sharing a cherished moment together. After the guest speaker concluded his moving address, we stood at attention and recited the Ranger Creed. I was afraid at first that I had forgotten the words, that someone might see my bumbling. I remembered it all.

As the formal portion of the Ranger Ball ended, I received several invitations to head down to River Street with this newer generation of Rangers. I had spent the night before on River Street with the guys from my platoon and with Matt's and Brad's and Marc's parents. We reminisced and encouraged each other at Kevin Barry's, the traditional Ranger hangout spot. On this night, I politely declined the offers to go to River Street. I had a 6:00 a.m. flight home the next morning, and I had one more thing I wanted to do while I was in town.

I slipped out of the convention center and walked alone under the orange streetlights, across the vast parking lot to my rental car. The smell of brackish water filled the air. I took off my suit jacket and threw it in the back seat. Two parking rows away, a drunk, shirtless Ranger, wearing only his dress blue trousers, was arguing with someone on his cell phone about why his date had left him at the ball. His friends urged him to get into their 4x4 pickup, which was shiny new and adorned with Ranger stickers. He was upset, almost crying.

I drove away thinking about how these events for Rangers—for soldiers everywhere, for me—were snapshots in time, images between scenes of war: the war with real bullets and blood and dying, and the one with much worse things than dying. And much greater things too. God had a plan for those greater things. It seemed that he even had a plan to take those worse things and use them to make greater things. On this night, I believed that.

The scenes of these two wars played in my mind as I weaved through the squares in Savannah, around the outskirts of town, past our old church, and past the school where Julie had taught third graders.

Kosovo. Afghanistan. Iraq. America. Me. My own soul.

Savannah held an eternal place in my heart. I felt at home as I traced the familiar streets under the canopy of Spanish moss to the west side of town, to the apartment complex where we used to live. The apartments had a gated entrance. I didn't have a gate code or a gate opener, but I wanted to get inside, just to stare at our old door and balcony. I idled in my rental car near the gate until I saw another car drive up. The gate opened, and I followed close behind the car, turned to the right, and eased along, one stairwell down from the office. There it was, my old parking spot, empty. I slid the rental car into the spot, shut off the engine, and rolled down the window. Our apartment was just above me. Second floor. Apartment 806.

On this night six years ago, in that apartment there, Julie and I had watched on Fox News images of 3rd Ranger Battalion parachuting into Afghanistan. I was jealous of them then, but two days later, I realized that God had kept me back to see Caleb's birth and to hold Julie's hand through it all. She held my hand too, but mostly she held my heart. My whole world had been in that hospital room.

Why didn't I bring Julie with me on this trip? Or Caleb?

Caleb's almost six years old; he would've remembered this forever. He would've loved the Rangers, seeing his birthplace, seeing the artifacts that hinted that his daddy was once a warrior.

I stared back up at the second-floor balcony doors, knowing that just beyond the glass was a space that was sacred to me. Our first child. War. Love.

Six years ago, I was forced to let go of Julie and Caleb, and I left them in that apartment just above. I had held them in my grasp, and then I had released them.

How will Caleb ever truly live if I'm always trying to protect him?

That was the problem for me. I now had the same fears my mother had long ago: that my son would become a soldier.

I backed out of that parking spot and made one slow lap around the collection of buildings, in the same direction Julie and I had walked when she had first gone into labor with Caleb. I drove back to the gate and headed west down Abercorn. I stopped at the Hardee's near my hotel and went back to my room. I had four hours until it was time to head to the airport to go back home to my family.

The next morning, my flight was delayed just enough in Houston to cause me to miss Caleb's soccer game. I had hoped to catch a few minutes of the game, but it just wasn't going to happen. It made more sense to drive straight to the house and meet the family there. I couldn't wait to show Caleb what I had bought him.

It was the day before his sixth birthday. He was waiting outside for me. Julie was also outside, holding four-month-old Elliot and chasing two-year-old Noah around the yard. My parents were there, too, helping Julie with the kids.

I eased into the driveway, under the comforting canopy of the giant live oaks. Julie held Noah back from running to my pickup. Caleb stood in the front yard wearing his soccer uniform, smiling and holding both his hands in front of his mouth. I could tell he was excited to see me home.

"Dod-deee!" Noah said, racing to the truck.

I hopped out and intercepted Noah. I gave Julie a long hug with Noah around my legs and made some baby noises to my daughter until she grinned. Then I hugged my parents. Caleb still stood in the front yard. He looked embarrassed.

I walked to him.

"Hey, Caleb," I said.

"Hey," he said. He still held a sheepish grin.

"What's going on?"

"Good."

"Good?"

"Daddy?"

"Mmm-hmm?"

"Will you play with me?"

"Yes, sir. I sure will."

Caleb and I started kicking the soccer ball back and forth.

"How was your game?"

"Good," he said. "I scored six goals."

"Wow, man. That's awesome." The little kids' soccer league didn't keep score, but Caleb did.

"Daddy?"

"Yes, sir?"

"Tomorrow's my birthday."

"I know, Caleb," I said. "What a great day that is. I brought home some stuff for you."

"Cool," he said. "Is it for my birthday?"

"No, just from Savannah. Just some special stuff."

"Did you go to the hospital where I was born?"

"No, sir, I didn't. But I did see where we all lived when you were a baby."

"Cool. . . . Daddy?"

"Yes, sir?"

"The next time you go to Savannah . . ."

"Yes, sir?"

"Can you take me with you?"

"Of course, son. The next time I go to Savannah, we'll go together."

EPILOGUE

Over the years, I've gotten too busy for my grandparents. It's painful to admit, but the woman who used to scratch my back in church and the man who was the subject of my graduation speech became far too distant parts of my adult life. As a boy, I used to beg to spend my Friday nights with them, to go to our favorite restaurant, to sleep in their back bedroom with the air conditioner blasting my face with cold air, to awake to hot chocolate in my favorite Popeye mug. As a grown man, I've lost too many years with them—too busy with the Army, my own kids, and my work. Now, it seems that every precious visit with them yields a treasure of a memory.

We recently dropped by their house so they could see the kids. As always, we enjoyed our time there, but as always, it seemed too short. The boys were getting rowdy, and Elliot needed to take a nap. I had deadlines to meet. It was time to go.

Just as we were leaving, my grandmother pulled me aside to show me a family treasure: a canvas-covered three-ring binder from her school days. The indigo notebook was faded and decorated with names and doodles and signatures from her classmates. With her frail and bony fingers, she opened the binder to reveal some personal notes written inside. There I saw the inked remnants of the youthful romance between her and my biological grandfather—a love that had not yet been consumed by the effects of war and alcoholism and abuse.

Like so many schoolgirls, she had written her name several times over—each time alongside or above or beneath my grandfather's. It was then that I noticed what was distinctive about my grandfather's name: it was written as "Private Milton Scarborough." When I saw it written the same way in a few other places inside the binder, I put my finger on his name and said, "Hmph."

"That's your grandfather, Nathan," Grandmama said.

"I know," I said. "I know."

I had always known he'd been in the military, but the words *I know* meant something deeper in that moment. I now saw myself in my grandfather. He had become a military man even while his childhood love was still in high school. I now saw a memory of him as a doodle on a teenage girl's notebook—this kid who had joined the Army in service to something greater, the hero of my grandmother's heart.

After we got home and put the kids to bed, I went to my office and searched the shelves for *The Longest Day*, the book my grandmother had given me years before that had stirred me so deeply. At one time, that tattered black book had been the only war story I had ever known. Now I know they're all the same.

My grandfather's name was not in the book, but I finally saw at least a hint of why my grandmother had put the book in my hands. Perhaps it had helped her to understand what Private Milton Scarborough had lived through during the war, or even how she had lost him so long ago. Perhaps it marked the invasion and ultimate destruction of the life she'd always dreamed of. Perhaps it showed the noble side of war that justified the wounds that had torn apart her family. In that book, I saw a message I could not explain but intuitively knew. There are no words to describe it, but it can be found in the heartbeat of every soldier.

My grandfather, the only military man in my bloodline, had served in Normandy after the initial Allied invasion of France. I never met him, but on that day I loved him for the first time.

AN ARMY WIFE'S PERSPECTIVE

by Julie Self

A lot has changed since 1992, since that first time butterflies filled my stomach when Nathan Self invited me over to watch a movie at his house. As a naive fifteen-year-old, I could not have imagined that our innocent puppy love would grow into a deep, abiding faith in each other, a commitment so strong that no amount of loneliness, war, or hurt could ever separate us. Fifteen years after that first date, I see that God has been the key to our life together.

Army marriages are not easy, and ours was no exception. We spent our first married year separated by schooling commitments. Once we were together, I still spent time alone, with his weeks in the field, early mornings and late nights, and three deployments. But despite our personal desire to spend more time together, we loved serving our country. We had fallen in love with the Army and with the American Soldier.

Just more than a month after 9/11, Nathan and I welcomed our first child, Caleb, into the world. I fell in love again with Nathan—this time as my son's father, not just as my husband. I'll never forget seeing Nathan hold Caleb for the first time in the hospital rocking chair and feeling overwhelmed with gratitude.

Nathan deployed to war in Afghanistan two days after we quietly celebrated our first Christmas as parents. I had more worries and fears on this deployment than on the previous one, to Kosovo. It was war, and I had a baby to take care of. During the many late-night hours of nursing a newborn, I prayed for Nathan's safety and well-being. With a new war a few days old, he and I had worried about bringing a child into such an uncertain world when Caleb was born, but now I saw that God had given me an additional gift—a piece of Nathan to hold while he was away. And I learned to hold on to God more and more.

I discovered during our time apart that when I had been fortunate enough to have Nathan with me every day, it was easy to take his presence for granted. I hadn't told him the things I most deeply needed or wanted to tell him. But when Nathan was overseas, we communicated through e-mail, letters, and occasional phone calls, and there was no holding back. We were clear and up-front about our fears in life and our feelings for each other. During these times, I found the same to be true with my relationship with God. I relied on him in all my fears, doubts, loneliness—everything. And every time the Lord brought Nathan home to me, I wanted to continue that feeling of "no holding back," that wonderful, vulnerable dependence we had developed when we were apart.

But the aftermath of war brought challenging and difficult times at home. After Nathan came home for good, he started to really experience the emotional effects of having been in war—something that neither of us saw coming. He never talked with me about his deployed experiences. He withdrew from me and, somehow, from himself. It was heartbreaking. Nathan had always been so strong. To see him at a breaking point—to see anyone I loved in pain—was not easy. Where was the Nathan I had married? I wanted the problems to disappear and be fixed right away. I wanted to fix them myself. But I couldn't.

At times, we were desperate. But in our desperation, we sought the Lord—and he was there. We got on our knees at night and simply laid ourselves and our feelings before God. We asked for his help. We looked for answers in the Bible. We also journaled to each other regularly and worked through our feelings that way. We were vulnerable, and we communicated our hurts and frustrations. We learned to forgive both ourselves and each other. By God's grace and mercy, we were able to heal.

God never promised an easy life free of trials and tribulations. He did, however, say that he would never leave us or forsake us. It is during these difficult times that we can become the people God wants us to be. When faced with such challenging events in this life, we have a choice. We can become bitter, resentful, or angry and eventually give up or run away. Or we can choose to be obedient: to love unconditionally, to forgive, and to heal.

Much has changed for us. We are no longer in the Army, and war has altered us, as it has for so many others, in ways that cannot be ignored. At times, I didn't want to go through any of it; I didn't care whether God had a purpose in all of it; I said, "No, God, this is not what I asked for." There was a time when I rejected the changes, when I just wanted my old life back. But I've seen God bringing about even greater changes in me. I've reached a point where I see that it's possible to be joyful even in the midst of trials, in knowing that God is in control. I've reached a point where I love my soldier without qualification—regardless of his wounds, whether seen or unseen. And I love him, regardless of the ways he may have wounded me. I have felt the joy of knowing that even though circumstances change and people change, God stays the same.

Scripture says that "God causes everything to work together for the good of those who love God and are called according to his purpose for them" (Romans 8:28, NLT). Nathan and I look back now and see that during those dark days, we were being drawn to God. He truly did cause our struggles to work together for our good—for the good of our relationship with him and for the good of our marriage.

God has since blessed us with two more beautiful children. Nathan and I are excited that we can one day share our story with them, in hope that they, too, will choose to follow Jesus even through struggles and pain, for he is the solution to our struggles and the ultimate Healer of our pain.

Nathan, I am blessed to be called your bride. I thank you for the love, devotion, strength, and tenderness you give to our family. I look forward to growing old with you, and . . . you still give me butterflies.

AFTERWORD
by Stu Weber

"To those who have fought for it, freedom has a flavor the protected can never know."

I'm not sure who made that statement, but it rings true. That's the bright side of soldiering, the good news—a quiet gratitude for life, lodged deep within a soldier's soul. Beauty, innocence, peace, family, faith, and the simple joys of life possess an extra measure of fragrance and flavor for those who have risked everything to defend them.

But soldiering has a dark side, too.

The old Negro spiritual says it well: "Nobody knows the trouble I've seen." Many servicemen and women who have logged time in combat would say the same thing. *Nobody knows. Nobody gets it. Nobody has any idea what it's like.*

Nobody, that is, except another soldier.

Where there is a battle, there are wounds, and where there are wounds, there are scars—scars of the body and scars of the soul. In one sense, this is the story of every soldier who has lived through the shock and violence of combat. At some point in the last fifty years or so, the long-term effects of such battles acquired a label. You've probably heard it kicked around at one time or another: Post-Traumatic Stress Disorder, or PTSD.

Anyone who knows me knows I love soldiers. As a former soldier myself, I always have and I always will. And nothing pleases old soldiers like watching the next generation of youngsters step up to the line to defend their country. Today, I see a generation of soldiers, sailors, airmen, and marines as skilled, courageous, and dedicated as any this nation has ever known. And they are literally standing between us and all that would destroy us and our way of life.

They pay a heavy price. Some pay the last full measure and give their lives for us. Others are wounded, some severely so. Still others escape without physical wounds. But not one is untouched. And not one returns from combat the same person who entered it.

Nate Self and his platoon of brothers acquitted themselves with valor, honor, and sacrifice on as harsh a battlefield as you can imagine. But the story is not yet complete. The "journey back" to life and living, after staring death and dying in the face, is a long one. Though he is no longer deployed with the Army, Nate in a very real sense is still making his way home. Home to hope and family, to love and purpose, to trust in others and faith in God.

I have an especially deep regard for Nate Self. I like to think of him in the way he once referred to himself—as my "Texas son."

In the spring of 2002, I began devouring stories coming out of the conflict in Afghanistan. My heart was especially drawn to the superb work of our Special Forces troopers and our Rangers. In particular, a desolate patch of high-altitude real estate called Takur Ghar held my attention. Whisked into a fierce firefight to rescue a Navy SEAL who had fallen out of the back of his helicopter, these men had stared "the elephant" of combat square in the eye.

My heart was with them. I could feel it.

The battle that Nate and his platoon fought may very well have been one of the longest single firefights in our Global War on Terror. And it may hold yet another distinction—as the only infantry battle in our nation's history fought at or above ten thousand feet.

I first met Nate Self in March 2003, about a year after his baptism on that mountaintop of ice and fire. I had taught a seminar and had spoken at a chapel service at Fort Leavenworth, Kansas. After the service, a strapping young captain, the epitome of America's finest and a student in the Army's Combined Arms Staff Services School, approached me. From the moment we began conversing, I sensed a palpable depth in the man. After a few minutes, in almost a whisper, he said, "I was the platoon leader of the QRF on Takur Ghar a year ago."

It took my breath away! I wanted to probe but held myself back. I knew he'd been through the most soul-stretching experience a man can face. So I walked carefully into our conversation, not wanting to hurt or embarrass this American hero in any way. I didn't want to go where he didn't want to go. I felt for him both a sense of awe and an overriding compassion. He had survived the worst that war has to offer—the loss of true friends, fellow soldiers, his brothers.

I went back to Oregon, half a continent away, and Nate deployed to war again, this time to Iraq. Nate and I stayed in touch after the seminar, occasionally talking by phone or e-mailing. Even after he left the Army, we stayed in touch. In one of those conversations, he made an offhand comment that I should have picked up on.

"We're experiencing some family stress because of all this."

Of course, I thought. *He's in the wake of it. The aftermath of an experience like that must be devastating.* It's been a part of every war, this near cousin to shell shock and battle fatigue. It's always the next big conflict that every combat veteran faces after returning home to civilian life.

I let Nate's comment about "family trouble" slip by, not knowing what to do with it. Did he want feedback? Was this a call for help? Should I, as a pastor and friend, have simply waded in? Because I didn't hear a direct invitation to get involved, I held back. I was more worried about wounding this young warrior's pride than responding to a need I understood all too well. Over time, I would learn that pride—the unhealthy kind that turns help away—was not an issue for Nate Self.

Along the way, Nate sent an e-mail that said very simply, with no fanfare, "By the way, Stu, NBC's *Dateline* is doing a special on Takur Ghar on June 11." I marked that date on my calendar and made sure I wouldn't be disturbed on the night it aired.

For me, the program was riveting. It was an account of that brutal, heartbreaking battle on Takur Ghar—but that's not where it stopped. The program went on to probe deeper into the hearts of Nate and Julie Self. Here was a young American soldier and his wife dealing with the burden of a deadly fight that had been won on the other side of the world but had come home to Texas to be fought in a different way.

My heart ached for them. I had to talk to Nate. I wanted to get them away from this broken world—if only for a day or two. I wanted that magnificent woman, Julie, to find her man again. I wanted them to experience some kind of oasis in the emotional desert of these overpowering post-traumatic storms. Just as Nate and his men had refused to leave that SEAL alone to fight his own battle, I could not bear the thought of Nate and Julie having to fight this second war alone.

The soldier's core value of leaving no man behind pulled hard at me. But I was half a continent away, tied up with a million details as pastor of a large church. How could I become meaningfully involved in this couple's life?

Then a thought struck me. It seemed crazy at first, but once it had occurred to me, I couldn't put it out of my mind. My wife, Linda, and I have access to a tiny log cabin in the Wallowa Mountains of northeast Oregon. It was built after World War II by a young veteran who came home from the war and lived there with his wife for half a century. Perhaps it could serve, at least for a few days, as a respite for another battle-weary soldier and his equally weary wife. I thought maybe Linda and I could at least briefly wrap our arms around this young couple who were paying a price for serving our nation and its freedom.

My mind went to Elijah and how God, in a time of trouble, had hidden his prophet away in a secret little ravine in Israel's back country. *Kerith* was the name of the small stream and valley that became a refuge for some of the most prominent men in Scripture, including Jacob, David, and Elijah. God had led his man to a sheltered valley and given him a brief season of quiet, refreshment, provision, and rest after a nearly impossible assignment.

While enemies raged, armies searched, kingdoms rose and fell, and the world turned, the shell-shocked prophet found refuge in a secluded spot. It was just a little wrinkle in the landscape, a tiny corner of the world, tucked away from sight, hidden by the shadow of the Almighty.

Could Nate and his wife benefit from a little time in such a hideaway? There is no brook Kerith in Oregon . . . but maybe the banks of Bear Creek would do.

Well, maybe it was crazy and maybe it wasn't. But this time, I wasn't going to hang back. I picked up the phone and dialed Nate's number.

I called Nate to simply express my love for him and Julie. And I invited them to take a minivacation and visit us in Oregon . . . escaping to our rustic little retreat in the Wallowa Mountains.

And they said yes.

When Nate and Julie flew in to Portland on a Friday evening, Linda and I instantly fell in love with them. We felt as if we were meeting our own adult children for the first time. We took them to our favorite seafood restaurant on the banks of the wide Columbia River and talked nonstop for hours.

On Sunday, we went to church together, and then packed up the Ford pickup and headed out toward the northeast corner of Oregon. Our refuge alongside Bear "Crik" was only a few hours away. After stopping for a bite of dinner in one of the tiny towns along the way, we drove through the river canyon into the glory of the Wallowa Valley in winter, where the little cabin awaited us, huddled against the Hayes Canyon hillside.

After settling in, Nate and I stepped outside in the fading daylight to steal a quick look across the meadow at Bear Creek. Snow had begun to fall, laying a soft blanket of white over the landscape. In that quiet interlude on the cabin porch, we talked of soldiers through the generations . . . of old warriors passing the torch to the younger . . . of the human heart, and of hope.

We recalled that God himself deeply loves soldiers. His own Son, in fact, was the ultimate Warrior—shedding his blood, absorbing the enemy's blows, laying down his life for his friends. *No greater love*. We reflected that this same Jesus—the One of whom it was said "a bruised reed he will not break, a smoldering wick he will not quench"—will be back one day astride a great warhorse, wearing a bloodstained robe, and carrying a sword.

And we reflected on Nate's epiphany in Afghanistan, that he had not only a story to tell but also a message to steward: that a man today, like so many prominent men in the Bible, can be both a physical warrior and a spiritual warrior at the same time. That the two are not exclusive. That neither compromises the other.

We glanced through the cabin window at Julie seated on the couch inside, talking to Linda. It struck me that this wonderful woman would follow her husband through anything.

Nate and I slipped back inside, and the four of us watched the

Dateline special again, from start to finish, interjecting conversation along the way . . . and taking some deep breaths together.

Every combat warrior fights two wars. For the soldier, the sheer shock of combat is traumatic enough, but the anguish of losing his bearings in its wake may prove to be even more troublesome. Eventually, the battlefield falls silent. But its horrible echoes do not. And for the war that follows—the inner war—there is no training. It's like throwing a dime-store compass into a room full of magnets. Where is north? What's up, what's down? It is this loss of direction and basic instincts which most typifies the horror of post-traumatic stress.

Though the post-combat soldier may appear to be fully alive to those around him, something inside of him has died. The life he lived and the man he thought he was seem more like mirages than reality. How does he make decisions or move forward when he can't even grapple with his present location? It's a scary thing to be lost in the woods; it's much more terrifying to be lost inside yourself.

Nothing is normal anymore. And "normal" people who have no experience of similar trauma themselves can only stand back, it seems, and question the soldier's sanity. As the inner disorientation compounds itself, a dizzying downward spiral accelerates. And sometimes it erupts in sudden and irrational anger.

Where did that thought come from? Did I just say that? Why did I just do that? Where is this coming from?

Some have described it as a perpetually shuffling deck of cards. Just when the soldier thinks he's got a hand he can play, something or someone scrambles the deck.

Flashbacks. Confusion. Depression. Anxiety. Anger.

My friend Gary Beikirch, a Green Beret Medal of Honor recipient in Vietnam, says that the memories of the initial war blend into the second war. "Life," he says, "feels like a never-ending game of fifty-two-card pickup."

It's as if every combat soldier lives with a hole in his heart. And though that hole is survivable, it seems to draw the soldier away from others and into a lonely place of isolation. It is this growing sense of aloneness that is most destructive.

Rangers leave no man behind. Winning this second war requires the same commitment as the first war—togetherness. The secret to beating post-traumatic stress is not unlike the basic skills of combat patrolling: go slow, and stick together. Friends are what get you through the dark nights. Talking it out—authentic, interpersonal communion—may be the best medicine.

As King Solomon writes, "A man of many companions may come to ruin, but there is a friend who sticks closer than a brother" (Proverbs 18:24, NIV). Among all our acquaintances and associates, one Friend always gets it. When no one else understands, he does. When no one else can sort through the kaleidoscope of chaotic thoughts, he steps in and brings order. When the path ahead seems to wind into darkness, he takes the point and leads the way.

Jesus Christ, who knows more about war and death than any of us will ever experience, is that ultimate Friend. And he will leave no one with a thirsty heart behind.

GLOSSARY

AC-130 gunship
Heavily armed ground support gunship version of the C-130 Hercules. [ADDR]

Apache
AH-64 helicopter, a rotary-wing, armed attack aircraft. [ADDR]

Army mules
Mascots of the U.S. Military Academy. At the time of this story, they were Ranger, Trooper, Traveler, and Spartacus.

attack heading
The interceptor heading during the attack phase that will achieve the desired track crossing angle. Also, the assigned magnetic compass heading to be flown by aircraft during the delivery phase of an air strike. [JP]

back plate
Plate armor protecting a soldier's back.

Beast Barracks (Beast)
An intensive six-and-a-half week training program for new cadets at the United States Military Academy, West Point, New York.

berm
An artificial ledge or shoulder of ground; built to deflect fire. [ADDR]

Blackhawk
In this case, MH-60 helicopter, a rotary-wing, combat assault transport and electronic warfare and target acquisition aircraft. [ADDR]

BMNT
Before morning nautical twilight, the time before sunrise when the center of the sun is between 6° and 12° below the horizon.

Bradley Fighting Vehicle (BFV)
M2 or M3 tracked infantry fighting vehicle/armored personnel carrier. [ADDR]

Bull Hill
Mountain summit (1,411 feet) in Putnam County, New York, on the U.S. Military Academy reservation.

C-4 explosive
A variety of plastic explosive; common explosive for U.S. forces and the variety used in the bombing of the USS *Cole*.

C-130 Hercules
A fixed-wing, medium-range transport aircraft. [ADDR]

cadet
An officer-in-training. [ADDR]

call sign
An encrypted identification for a given radio-transmitter station. [ADDR]

CamelBak
Brand of portable hydration pack.

Camp Buckner
Eighty-acre site at West Point used for cadet field training. Named after General Simon Bolivar Buckner, the highest-ranking American killed in World War II. General Buckner was killed on the Pacific island of Okinawa while inspecting the fighting there.

Camp Monteith
Base camp established in June 1999 in a former Serbian Army post in Gnjilane, Kosovo, to be used as staging points for the bulk of U.S. forces stationed in the multinational brigade. Named for 1st Lieutenant Jimmie Monteith, posthumously awarded the Medal of Honor for his actions on D-Day, June 6, 1944. [GS]

CAS (close air support)
Air action by fixed- and rotary-wing aircraft against hostile targets that are in close proximity to friendly forces and which require detailed integration of each air mission with the fire and movement of those forces. [JP]

CCT (combat controller)
U.S. Air Force ground combat forces assigned to special tactics joint air and ground forces. The mission of a combat controller is to establish assault zones for aircraft, and provide air traffic control, command and control communications, and terminal attack control. [CCA]

chalk
Designated troops, equipment, and/or cargo that constitute a complete aircraft load. [FM]

chem-light
Chemical light sticks that glow continuously once activated by breaking an internal vial to combine the chemicals.

Chinook
In this case, MH-47 helicopter, a rotary-wing, medium transport aircraft. [ADDR]

Colt .45
Brand of .45 caliber automatic pistol.

Corps of Cadets
More than four thousand men and women who are pursuing an undergraduate education and a commission in the United States Army. At the time of the events of this book, the Corps was organized into thirty-six cadet companies; the companies are grouped into battalions (then, three companies each), regiments (then, three battalions each), and the Corps (four regiments). [USMA]

CP (command post)
The location of a unit's headquarters commander and staff. [ADDR]

CSAR
Combat search and rescue. A mission to locate, communicate with, and recover downed aircrews and isolated personnel. Could also refer to the unit assigned this mission. [FAS]

defilade
Arrangement of fortifications so as to protect the lines from frontal fire or gunfire directed from a flanking position, and the interior from fire from above or behind. [MW]

DZ
Drop zone

exfil (exfiltration)
The surreptitious movement of soldiers out of an enemy-controlled area. [ADDR]

Forward arming and refueling point
A temporary facility to provide fuel and ammunition necessary for the employment of aviation maneuver units in combat, permitting combat aircraft to rapidly refuel and rearm simultaneously. Also called FARP. [JP]

FARP Texaco
Code name of forward arming refueling point (call sign "Texaco") established between Gardez, Afghanistan, and Takur Ghar mountain.

fatwah
A legal opinion or ruling issued by an Islamic scholar.

firebase

A secured site from which small-scale fighting units can stage, support, and sustain their operations.

fire team

The basic infantry fighting unit, consisting of four soldiers with various weapons and support. Two fire teams make up a squad; four squads make up a platoon.

flashbang grenade

A nonlethal, low hazard, non-shrapnel-producing explosive device intended to confuse, disorient, or momentarily distract the enemy. [GS]

flight line

In this case, the line of aircraft parked on the apron of an airfield. In Bagram, the helicopters were parked on an apron constructed of corrugated steel.

forward operating base (FOB)

An airfield used to support tactical operations without establishing full support facilities [DOD]. Also, a secure site within a combat zone that functions as a soldier's "home away from home," giving respite from the rigors of extended deployment.

Garmin GPS

Brand of handheld global-positioning system.

GBU-12 bomb

Guided Bomb Unit, a 500-pound laser-guided general-purpose warhead.

guided-missile destroyer

Multi-mission, fast warships that can operate independently or as part of carrier battle groups. [USN]

guidons

A reference to the military flag, or guidon, carried into battle. Military usage can also refer to the leader of an organization.

H-Hour

The scheduled time for the start of a combat operation.

Hellfire missiles

Air-to-ground tactical guided-missile system, with heavy antiarmor capability. [FAS]

higher headquarters

In this case, a general reference to any unit that has direct operational control over a lower-ranking unit.

HVT (high-value target)

A target the enemy commander requires for the successful completion of the mission. The loss of HVTs would be expected to seriously degrade important enemy functions throughout the friendly commander's area of interest. [JP]

infil (infiltration)

The undetected movement of a small force or of individuals through enemy-held territory. [ADDR]

JDAM

Joint-Direct Attack Munition, a GPS-based guidance kit to provide accurate delivery of general-purpose bombs in adverse weather conditions. [FAS]

JOC

Joint Operations Center, a joint force commander's headquarters that is jointly manned for the planning, monitoring, and execution of the commander's decisions.

JSOC

Joint Special Operations Command, a joint headquarters designed to study Special Operations requirements and techniques; ensure interoperability and equipment standardization; plan and conduct joint Special Operations exercises and training; and develop joint Special Operations tactics. [GS]

Kevlar

Brand of fiber used in lightweight body armor; slang for a military helmet made from Kevlar.

KFOR (Kosovo Force)

NATO-led peacekeeping force in Kosovo.

KIA

Killed in action

Little Bird

Light assault helicopter that provides support to Special Operations forces and can be armed with a combination of guns and folding fin aerial rockets. [FAS] Military nomenclature is AH-6 or MH-6.

LZ

Short for HLZ, or helicopter landing zone, a specified ground area for landing assault helicopters to embark or disembark troops and/or cargo. A landing zone may contain one or more landing sites. [JP]

MAKO

A type of shark; here used as a radio call sign to identify an element of SEAL snipers.

Manifest "Alpha"

One of the many predetermined manifests, or rosters, used by 1st Platoon, 1st Battalion, 75th Ranger Regiment to designate who would be a part of a mission. Used to expedite the planning process.

MBITR

Multi-Band Inter/Intra-Team Radio, a rugged, lightweight, handheld radio that offers enhanced interoperability with existing military and commercial radio systems.

medevac

Acronym for *medical evacuation*, an evacuation of casualties concurrent with medical care.

Mercator projection

A mathematical method of showing a map of the globe on a flat surface.

Mi-8 HIP

Soviet multi-role transport helicopter capable of carrying troops or supplies as well as conducting armed attacks with rockets and guns. [FAS]

MRE

Meals Ready to Eat, a totally self-contained complete meal designed to be consumed without cooking or heating. The standard combat rations for the U.S. armed forces.

mujahideen

Coalition of Muslim insurgents who fought against Afghan Army and Soviet forces during the Afghan War of 1978–1992.

NCO

Noncommissioned officer, a subordinate officer (as a sergeant) appointed from among enlisted personnel. [MW]

Night Stalkers

Nickname for 160th Special Operations Aviation Regiment of the U.S. Army.

night vision goggles

An electro-optical image-intensifying device that detects visible and near-infrared energy, intensifies the energy, and provides a visible image for night viewing. Can be handheld or helmet-mounted. Also called NVGs. [JP]

OP

Observation post, a position from which military observations are made, or fire directed and adjusted, and which possesses appropriate communications. [DOD]

Operation Anaconda

Combat operation that began March 1, 2002, in the mountainous Shah-i-Khot region south of the city of Gardez in eastern Afghanistan. Operation Anaconda was part of an ongoing effort in Afghanistan to root out Taliban and al-Qaeda forces holed up in Paktia Province. [GS]

PJ

Air Force pararescue jumper; specially trained personnel qualified to penetrate to the site of an incident by land or parachute, render medical aid, accomplish survival methods, and rescue survivors. [JP]

Predator

Unmanned Aerial Vehicle used for reconnaissance, surveillance, and target acquisition. The Predator system was designed to provide constant intelligence, surveillance, and reconnaissance to U.S. strategic and tactical forces. It can also perform a search-and-destroy mission using guided Hellfire missiles. [FAS]

PTSD

Post-Traumatic Stress Disorder, an anxiety disorder that can develop after exposure to a terrifying event or ordeal in which grave physical harm occurred or was threatened. [NIMH]

QRF

Quick Reaction Force, a military force poised to respond on very short notice, with a main mission of establishing security or reconnaissance. [GS]

Ranger tab

A black and yellow cloth shoulder insignia to be worn by soldiers who have successfully completed a Ranger training course.

RPG

Rocket-propelled grenade, a handheld, shoulder-launched antitank weapon capable of firing an unguided rocket equipped with an explosive warhead.

SAW (squad automatic weapon)

M-249 lightweight, gas-operated, portable machine gun capable of delivering a large volume of effective fire. [FAS]

SEAL (SEa, Air, Land)

U.S. Navy special forces.

Skedco litter

Brand of stretcher used in aerial rescue missions.

Special Forces

Highly trained military units that conduct specialized operations such as reconnaissance, unconventional warfare, and counterterrorism.

Special Operations
Use of small units in direct or indirect military actions focused on strategic or operational objectives. They require units with combinations of trained specialized personnel, equipment, and tactics that exceed the routine capabilities of conventional military forces. [GSO]

Stinger missile
Short-range surface-to-air missile system designed for air defense against low-altitude airborne targets, to protect combat forces, forward bases, or high-value targets. [FAS]

TF
Task Force, a temporary unit or formation established to work on a single task or activity.

UAV
Unmanned Aerial Vehicle, remotely piloted or self-piloted aircraft that can carry cameras, sensors, communications equipment, or other payloads. [FAS]

WIA
Wounded in action.

Glossary Sources:

[ADDR] *Army Dictionary and Desk Reference* (Stackpole Books, 2004)

[CCA] Combat Controllers Association (www.usafcct.com)

[DOD] U.S. Department of Defense

[FAS] Federation of American Scientists (www.fas.org)

[FM] Field Manual 55-9, Unit Air Movement Planning, Department of the Army, Washington, D.C., April 5, 1993 (from Section II [Definitions]
    of the Glossary)

[GS] Global Security (www.globalsecurity.org)

[GSO] Global Special Operations (www.globalspecialoperations.com)

[JP] Joint Publication 3-09.3, *Joint Tactics, Techniques, and Procedures for Close Air Support,* September 3, 2003, page ix

[MW] *Merriam-Webster Collegiate Dictionary,* eleventh edition

[NIMH] National Institute of Mental Health (www.nimh.nih.gov)

[USMA] United States Military Academy (www.usma.edu)

[USN] U.S. Navy (www.navy.mil)

SELECTED BIBLIOGRAPHY

The following is a list of sources that have been of use in the writing of this book. This selected bibliography by no means represents the full record of the sources I have consulted but indicates the substance and range of reading that has informed my version of the story. It is my hope that this list will be an aid to those who wish to pursue the study of the Army, the Global War on Terror, the Rangers, and the Battle of Takur Ghar.

"Aesop Quotes." http://www.brainyquote.com/quotes/authors/a/aesop.html.

"Ahmed Ajaj." http://en.wikipedia.org/wiki/Ahmed_Ajaj.

Aita, Judy. "Bin Laden Associate First Witness in Embassy Bombing Trial." February 6, 2001. http://usinfo.state.gov/is/Archive_Index/Bin_Laden_Associate_First_Witness_in_Embassy_Bombing_Trial.html.

———. "Embassy Bombing Prosecution Links Defendant to bin Laden." February 14, 2001. http://usinfo.state.gov/is/Archive_Index/Embassy_Bombing_Prosecution_Links_Defendant_to_bin_Laden.html.

———. "Bombing Trial Witness Describes Nairobi Surveillance Mission." February 22, 2001. http://usinfo.state.gov/is/Archive_Index/Bombing_Trial_Witness_Describes_Nairobi_Surveillance_Mission.html.

———. "Amb. Bushnell Testifies on Carnage of Terrorist Bombing in Kenya." March 1, 2001. http://usinfo.state.gov/is/Archive_Index/Amb._Bushnell_Testifies_on_Terrorist_Bombing.html.

———. "FBI Agent Recounts Confession of Bombing Trial Defendant." March 1, 2001. http://usinfo.state.gov/is/Archive_Index/FBI_Agent_Recounts_Confession_of_Bombing_Trial_Defendant.html.

———. "Embassy Bombing Trial Hears of Confession by Accused Terrorist." March 7, 2001. http://usinfo.state.gov/is/Archive_Index/Embassy_Bombing_Trial_Hears_of_Confession_by_Accused_Terrorist.html.

———. "Victims Retell Horrors of Nairobi Embassy Bombing in Court." March 7, 2001. http://usinfo.state.gov/is/Archive_Index/Victims_Retell_Horrors_of_Nairobi_Embassy_Bombing.html.

———. "Victims of Tanzanian Bombing Tell of Tragedy." March 13, 2001. http://usinfo.state.gov/is/Archive_Index/Victims_of_Tanzanian_Bombing_Tell_of_Tragedy.html.

———. "Court Hears of Confession by Tanzanian Charged in Embassy Bombing." March 19, 2001. http://usinfo.state.gov/is/Archive_Index/Court_Hears_of_Confession_by_Tanzanian_Charged.html.

———. "Evidence Piles Up in African Embassy Bombing Trial." March 29, 2001. http://usinfo.state.gov/is/Archive_Index/Evidence_Piles_Up_in_African_Embassy_Bombing_Trial.html.

———. "Confession 'Tap Dances with the Truth,' Prosecutor Says." May 2, 2001. http://usinfo.state.gov/is/Archive_Index/Confession_Tap_Dances_with_the_Truth_Prosecutor_Says.html.

———. "Bombing Trial Death Penalty Defendants Plead Their Case." May 8, 2001. http://usinfo.state.gov/is/Archive_Index/Bombing_Trial_Death_Penalty_Defendants_Plead_Case.html.

———. "Victims Remembered at Bombing Trial Closing." May 9, 2001. http://usinfo.state.gov/is/Archive_Index/Victims_Remembered_at_Bombing_Trial_Closing.html.

———. "Ali Mohamed: The Defendant Who Did Not Go to Trial." May 15, 2001. http://usinfo.state.gov/is/Archive_Index/Ali_Mohamed.html.

"Attack on the USS Cole." *Yemen Gateway*. December 12, 2001. http://www.al-bab.com/yemen/cole4.htm.

"Blaise Pascal Quotes." http://thinkexist.com/quotation/you_always_admire_what_you_really_don-t/200774.html.

Blumenson, Martin. *The Patton Papers*. Vol. I: 1881-1940. Vol. II: 1940-1945. Boston: Houghton Mifflin Co., 1972 and 1974.

"Bombing of Afghanistan and Sudan (August 1998)." http://en.wikipedia.org/wiki/Bombing_of_Afghanistan_and_Sudan_%28August_1998%29.

Bowden, Mark. *Black Hawk Down*. New York: Atlantic Monthly Press, 1999.

Briscoe, Charles H., Richard L. Kiper, James A. Schroder, and Kalev I. Sepp. *Weapon of Choice: U.S. Army Special Operations Forces in Afghanistan*. Fort Leavenworth, KS: Combat Studies Institute Press, 2003.

Burnett, Betty. *The Attack on the USS Cole in Yemen on October 12, 2000 (Terrorist Attacks)*. New York: Rosen Publishing Group, 2003.

Camus, Albert. *Resistance, Rebellion, and Death*. New York: Knopf, 1961.

Castaneda, Carlos. *Tales of Power*. New York: Pocket Books, 1974.

Childers, J. Gilmore; Henry J. DePippo (1998-02-24). "Senate Judiciary Committee Hearings: Foreign Terrorists in America: Five Years After the World Trade Center." (US Senate Judiciary Committee.)

Clausewitz, Carl von. *On War*. Ed. and trans. by Michael Howard and Peter Paret. Princeton, NJ: Princeton University Press, 1976.

"Climbing Related Quotes." http://www.terragalleria.com/mountain/info/quotes.html.

Coll, Steve. *Ghost Wars: The Secret History of the CIA, Afghanistan, and Bin Laden, from the Soviet Invasion to September, 10, 2001* (paperback ed.). New York: Penguin Books, 2005.

"Combatant Status Review Tribunal Hearing for ISN 10024." March 10, 2007. http://www.defenselink.mil/.

Confucius. *Confucian Analects*. New York: Penguin Books, 1979.

Conlon, Carter. "The Final Warning Comes in Pictures." Times Square Church, New York, New York, February 25, 2007. http://media.tscnyc.org/mp3/2070225S1.mp3.

"Context of 'February 26, 1993: WTC Is Bombed but Does Not Collapse as Bombers Had Hoped.'" http://www.cooperativeresearch.org/context.jsp?item=a022693wtc bombing.

"Distances in Afghanistan." http://www.joma.org/images/upload_library/4/vol2/liteapplets/JOMA_article/afghanistan_distances.html.

"Douglas MacArthur Quotes." http://www.brainyquote.com/quotes/authors/d/douglas_macarthur.html.

"Ernest Hemingway Quotes." http://www.rightwords.eu/quotes/quote-details/7670/once-we-have-a-war-there-is-only-one-thing-to—.

Evans, Bob. "'If' You Were Wondering: Rudyard Kipling's poem still teaches a valuable lesson in the 21st Century." December 11, 2000. http://www.informationweek.com/816/16uwbe.htm.

Federer, William J., ed. *America's God and Country*. FAME Publishing, 1996.

"General Douglas MacArthur: Sylvanus Thayer Award Acceptance Address." http://www.americanrhetoric.com/speeches/douglasmacarthurthayeraward.html.

Grau, Lester W., ed. *The Bear Went over the Mountain: Soviet Combat Tactics in Afghanistan*. Washington, D.C.: National Defense University Press, 1996.

Grau, Lester W. and Ali Ahmad Jalali. *The Other Side of the Mountain: Mujahideen Tactics in the Soviet-Afghan War*. Quantico, VA: The United States Marine Corps Studies and Analysis Division DM-980701, 1998.

———. "The Campaign for the Caves: The Battles for Zhawar in the Soviet-Afghan War." *The Journal of Slavic Military Studies*, Volume 14, September 2001, Number 3.

Grau, Lester W. and Mohammad Yahya Nawroz. "The Soviet War in Afghanistan: History and Harbinger of Future War?" *Military Review*, September/October 1995. http://fmso.leavenworth.army.mil/documents/waraf.htm.

Grau, Lester W. and William K. Jorgensen. "Medical Implications of High Altitude Combat," *U.S. Army Medical Journal*, April 2002.

Greeley, Jim. "Desert One: A Mission of Hope Turned Tragic. A Case of What Could've Been." *Airman* magazine, April 2001. http://www.af.mil/news/airman/0401/hostage.html.

Hulse, ed. *Bugle Notes*, 86th Edition. West Point, NY: United States Military Academy, 1994.

"Jason Dean Cunningham: Book details war heroism of airman. Military medic was awarded the Air Force Cross posthumously." October 3, 2005. http://www.arlingtoncemetery.net/jdcunningham.htm.

"John Milton Quotes." http://www.worldofquotes.com/author/John-Milton/2/index.html.

"Joseph Conrad Quotes." http://conrad.thefreelibrary.com/.

"Khalden Training Camp." http://en.wikipedia.org/wiki/Khalden_training_camp.

Kim, Susan. "Earthquake Hits Afghanistan." Disaster News Network. January 3, 2002. http://www.disasternews.net/news/article.php?articleid=1000.

Kirby, Randall. (Personal deployed journal, Afghanistan), 2002.

"Lise Hand Quotes." http://thinkexist.com/quotation/that-s_what_it_takes_to_be_a_hero-a_little_gem_of/179714.html.

MacPherson, Malcolm. *Roberts Ridge*. New York: Bantam Dell, 2005.

Malik, Muhammad Asim. "Mountain Warfare—The Need for Specialized Training." *Military Review*, September–October 2004.

Manning, William A., ed. "The World Trade Center Bombing: Report and Analysis." *Fire Engineering*. USFA-TR-076, February 1993. United States Fire Administration, Department of Homeland Security.

"Marc Anderson, 30, was an outstanding student athlete, a teacher and a brave soldier." *Florida State Times Online*. August 2002. http://www.fsu.edu/~fstime/FS-Times/volume8/aug02web/13aug02.html.

"Matthew Allen Commons: Soldier, Son, Brother Laid to Rest." March 12, 2002. http://www.arlingtoncemetery.net/macommons.htm.

McIntyre, Jamie and Reuters. "U.S. missiles pound targets in Afghanistan, Sudan." August 20, 1998. http://www.cnn.com/US/9808/20/us.strikes.01/.

McRaven, William H. *Spec Ops: Case Studies in Special Operations Warfare: Theory and Practice*. New York: Ballantine Books, 1996.

"Medal of Honor Recipients, World War II (M-S)." http://www.history.army.mil/html/moh/wwII-m-s.html.

Moran, Lord Charles Wilson. *The Anatomy of Courage*. London: Constable and Company, Ltd., 1945.

Morgan, Forrest E. *Living the Martial Way: A Manual for the Way a Modern Warrior Should Think*. Fort Lee, NJ: Barricade Books, 1992.

"Mosques and shrines of Mosul." http://en.wikipedia.org/wiki/Mosques_and_shrines_of_Mosul.

Naylor, Sean. *Not a Good Day to Die*. New York: Berkley Books, 2005.

"Ninevah." http://en.wikipedia.org/wiki/Nineveh.

Nye, Roger H. *The Challenge of Command*. Wayne, NJ: Avery Publishing Group, 1986.

Office of the Press Secretary, The White House. "Address to the Nation by the President." August 20, 1998. http://clinton6.nara.gov/1998/08/1998-08-20-president-address-to-the-nation.html.

"Operation Anaconda: An Air Power Perspective." Washington, DC: U.S. Air Force, 2005.

"Operation Enduring Freedom: The United States Army in Afghanistan." CMH Pub 70-83-1, 2003. http://www.history.army.mil/brochures/Afghanistan/Operation%20Enduring%20Freedom.htm.

"Part 1: Einstein's Unfinished Symphony: The Unpredictable Results of the Theory of Relativity." http://www.bbc.co.uk/sn/tvradio/programmes/horizon/einstein_symphony_prog_summary.shtml.

Patton, George S. Jr. *War As I Knew It.* 1947. Reprint, New York: Bantam Books, 1981.

Philander D. Chase, ed., The Papers of George Washington: Revolutionary War Series volume 9, March—June 1777. Charlottesville and London: University Press of Virginia, 1999.

Phillips, Noelle. "Rangers March On: Parade is bittersweet for those left behind." *Savannah Morning News.* March 17, 2002 http://old.savannahnow.com/stories/031702/LOCpatrangers.shtml.

Pressfield, Steven. *Gates of Fire.* New York: Doubleday, 1998.

"Ranger History." http://www.specialoperations.com/Army/Rangers/History.htm.

"Robert E. Lee Quotes." http://www.brainyquote.com/quotes/quotes/r/robertele153230.html

Ryan, Cornelius. *The Longest Day.* New York: Simon and Schuster, 1959.

Russian General Staff, The (Runov, Colonel Professor Valentin; P.D. Alexseyev; Yu. G. Avdeev; Yu. P. Babich; A.M. Fufaev; B.P. Gruzdev; V.S. Kozlov; V.I. Litvinnenko; N.S. Nakonechnyy; V.K. Puzel'; S.S. Sharov; S.F. Tsybenko; V.M. Varushinin; P.F. Vazhenko; V.F. Yashin; and V.V. Zakharov). *The Soviet-Afghan War: How a Superpower Fought and Lost.* Translated and edited by Lester W. Grau and Michael A. Gress. University Press of Kansas, 2002.

"Saadi Quotes." http://www.quotationspage.com/quote/2842.html.

Seismo-Watch. "An M7.3 earthquake hits Northeast Afghanistan." March 3, 2002. http://www.seismo-watch.com/EQS/AB/2002/020303.Afghan/020303.Afghan.html.

Seven Stars: The Okinawa Battle Diaries of Simon Bolivar Buckner, Jr., and Joseph Stilwell. Nicholas Evans Sarantakes, ed. College Station: Texas A&M University Press, 2004.

Sun Tzu. *The Art of War.* Edited by James Clavell. New York: Dell Publishing, 1983.

Tanner, Stephen. *Afghanistan.* Cambridge, MA: De Capo Press, 2002.

"Ten House." www.fdnytenhouse.com.

"The Day the World Shook." http://www.fdnewyork.com/wtc.asp.

The National Commission on Terrorist Attacks Upon the United States. *The 9/11 Commission Report.* July 22, 2004.

U.S. Army Field Manual (FM) 7-8. "Infantry Rifle Platoon and Squad." Washington, DC: Headquarters, Department of the Army, April 22, 1992.

U.S. Department of Defense, Department of Defense Intelligence Production Program, *KFOR Handbook*, DOD-2630-011-99, July 1999.

U.S. Department of Defense. *Executive Summary of the Battle of Takur Ghar.* May 24, 2002.

Wilkerson, David. "A Target of Satan's Envy. Sermon at Times Square Church, New York, New York, February 4, 2007. http://media.tscnyc.org/mp3/2070204S1.mp3.

"William Butler Yeats Quotes." http://thinkexist.com/quotation/the_innocent_and_the_beautiful_have_no_enemy_but/178843.html.

"Winston Churchill Quotes." http://www.brainyquote.com/quotes/authors/w/winston_churchill.html.

Wright, Lawrence. *Looming Tower.* New York: Knopf, 2006.

ACKNOWLEDGMENTS

Soldiers are special people. They are unique in so many ways, but in many ways, their stories are all the same. I have tried to remain open and humble in the journey of writing my version of the story, understanding that my perspective is limited and that I am just a part of the greater story. My purpose is to honor God first and foremost and to honor those who participated in and were affected by the events reflected in this book.

This has been both a revealing and restoring experience for me. It has been a time of reflection, healing, and appreciation. I have so many people to thank for enabling me first to survive, then to steward the story of the past ten years of my life. Above all, I must thank God, who has rescued me from the pit of death, both physically and spiritually. He's allowed life's trials to "sift" my character, but he's carried me through it all. He is a God of restoration. And I'm amazed at how personal he is.

Julie, my tender bride and my best friend—you are my absolute hero. Without you, this story would have been lost. You did the work of two parents and carried our family as a single parent during my deployments—and again during the writing of this book. My two fondest memories of writing this book are sliding in bed next to you after hours of writing and having you roll over to hold my hand; and of watching you read a chapter. Julie, thank you for choosing me. I adore you.

To my parents and sister, who taught me how to be brave and how to love. To my grandparents, who overcame harder times to pull our family off a path of destruction. To my in-laws for nurturing such a beautiful woman and for loving me the same way. Thank you all for giving Julie and me the support, prayer, and love we've needed to work through life's many challenges.

My beautiful children—Caleb, Noah, and my little princess, Elliot Joy—have kept me laughing when I felt I had no other reason to. Thank you, kids, for letting me hold you while you sleep. God is good. Where would we be without our family?

My utmost admiration goes to the men who fought on Takur Ghar: Chuck Gant, Don Tabron, Greg Calvert, Cory Lamoreaux, Sean Ludwig, Brian Wilson, Dave Dube, Keary Miller, Gabe Brown, Phil Svitak, Marc Anderson, Matt Commons, Brad Crose, Ray DePouli, David Gilliam, Kevin Vance, Anthony Miceli, Aaron Totten-Lancaster, Josh Walker, Jason Cunningham,

Arin Canon, Randy Pazder, Omar Vela, Oscar Escano, Jonas Polson, Chris Cunningham, Harper Wilmoth, Matt LaFrenz, Eric Stebner; Pat George, Neil Roberts, John Chapman, and the remainder of MAKO 30.

I have the greatest respect for the men of 1st Platoon, the men of Alpha Company, the men of 1st Battalion, and the men of the 75th Ranger Regiment: Rangers Lead the Way! And to the awesome soldiers with whom I served in 2-2 Infantry and the 101st Airborne Division. You're the reason I love the Army. To my peers in the Army, to the noncommissioned officers, and to the great men I worked for: Thanks for your leadership; the Army's in good hands.

All of you who are still serving in our military give me a feeling in my chest I can't explain. Our future depends on you.

To the precious veterans of our armed forces who have shouldered more than their share of the burden for our country's freedom: Thank you. I am humbled by your service and proud to be one of you.

I also want to thank the American people, who have been overwhelmingly supportive of us during deployments, and after, by sending letters and e-mails, books and pamphlets, and phone calls offering to help.

To the families of the men who gave their lives fighting on Takur Ghar: Anderson, Chapman, Commons, Crose, Cunningham, Roberts, and Svitak. Thank you for raising up such mighty men. I'm humbled by their sacrifice and by the privilege of having served with them. Thank you for your love, compassion, and resiliency through such a time as this.

I'm thankful to the journalists, authors, news anchors, and scholars who continue to see the power and purity in soldiers' stories and have treated the events surrounding the battle of Takur Ghar with respect and honor as they interviewed those of us involved. Thanks to Bradley Graham, Michael Hirsch, Malcolm MacPherson, Sean Naylor, Tony Koren, Stone Phillips, Tim Gorin, John Lu, Greg Jaffe, John Partin, Richard Stewart, Dave Crist, Les Grau, and Pete Kilner.

The many Christian brothers who have been "paralytic's friends" to me, willing to carry me up and lower me through the hole in the roof: Nate Allen, Tony Burgess, Chris Miller, Justin Johnson, Pete Marques, Dave Blank, Will Alley, Matt Benigni, Neal Mayo, Jan Beer, Daddy, and Jeff Talbert. As iron sharpens iron, so one man sharpens another.

The pastors and Army chaplains who have spoken the Word into my life when I've needed it the most and loved me through the valley. They are true shepherds: Randy Kirby, Sonny Moore, Arden Taylor, Brad Davis, Dave Howard, Carter Conlon, Stu Weber, John Cook, and Andy Davis.

Close friends and first line editors Luke Gilliam and Brett Martin, who beat the rust and cobwebs off of me as a writer, and then still had their work cut out for them in early drafts and content development. It's amazing that God has blessed me with world-class writers as friends.

I must convey my heartfelt gratitude to the leadership at Tyndale House Publishers, especially Ron Beers and Mark Taylor, who took on this project despite its challenging content and made it a reality in such a professional and God-honoring way. Thank you for not being afraid of this message.

The team at Tyndale has been fantastic. To Cara Peterson and Dave Lindstedt, my editors, I'm amazed by your detail, insights, and creativity. Thanks for handling the manuscript and me with such love and patience, and for correcting my multitude of military-related ambiguities and grammatical incapacities. Thanks to Jon Farrar for taking this project from proposal to completion in such a supportive way, and to Ron Kaufmann for passionately designing this story as if it were his own. Thanks also to Maria Eriksen for her leadership in determining the audiences and knowing the messages in this book. The Tyndale team has been an absolute joy to work with, and I'm grateful for the respect and autonomy they gave me in sharing this story.

The team at Phenix & Phenix, especially Rusty Shelton and Tolly Moseley, for their enthusiastic and professional presentation of this story to our great nation.

The team at Alive Communications, first with my agent, Beth Jusino, who handled all of us with grace and skill, and Jackie Johnson, who saw the unsolicited proposal come in via e-mail and, having recognized the story from *Dateline*, rushed it into Beth's office for review. I also need to thank Barret Neville for sparking this project as a reality in my mind.

I'm humbled by the many churches who have prayed for my soldiers and me while I served—and after: Park Lake Drive Baptist Church, The Church under the Cross, Wynnbrook Baptist Church, Oak Grove Baptist Church, First Baptist Belton, First United Methodist Church, Good Shepherd Community Church, and many others.

Ultimately, I have Jesus Christ to thank for life, for living, and for his example as a warrior to all of us in need of rescue. He'll never leave you.

ABOUT THE AUTHOR

NATE SELF graduated from West Point in 1998 as an Infantry officer and led soldiers in Kosovo before being selected to serve in the Army's elite 75th Ranger Regiment.

As a platoon leader in the Rangers, he deployed to Afghanistan shortly after 9/11 as part of a Special Operations task force with the mission to kill or capture Taliban and al-Qaeda's top leaders. Once there, he led his Ranger platoon into the teeth of an al-Qaeda strongpoint to rescue a missing and captured Navy SEAL on top of Takur Ghar mountain, where he earned the Silver Star, Bronze Star, and Purple Heart. His soldier's story has been highlighted recently in the media, and as a result of his actions in Afghanistan, he attended the 2003 State of the Union address.

Following a tour in Iraq with the 101st Airborne Division, where he wrote and directed daily operations and trained Iraqi Security Forces, Nate commanded a rifle company before leaving the Army in 2004 in order to better care for his family. He continues to work with young officers in the Army, focusing on professional development through personal interaction and facilitation of learning via the Army's CompanyCommand and PlatoonLeader online professional forums, where he is able to share his experiences and lessons learned in a public venue. He also spends time speaking to business and churches and interacting with veterans dealing with Post-Traumatic Stress Disorder.

Nate lives in Texas with his wife, Julie, and their three children, Caleb, Noah, and Elliot.

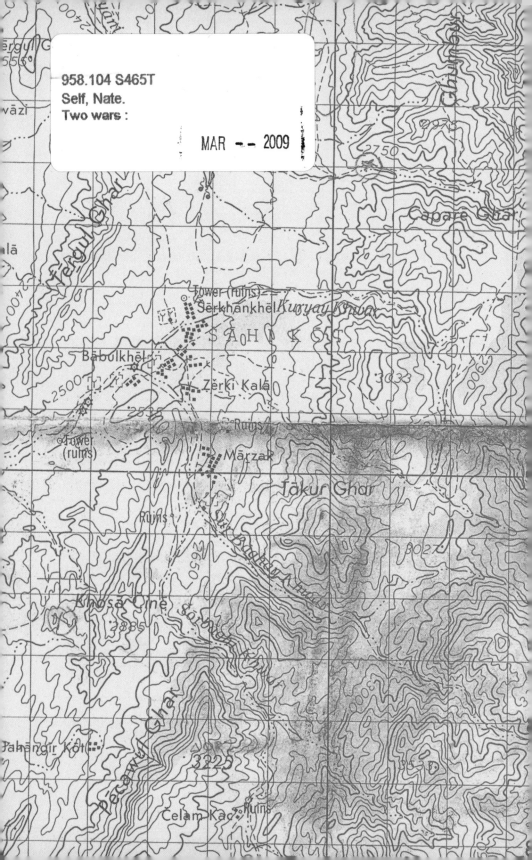